I. M. DESTLER

Making Foreign Economic Policy

THE BROOKINGS INSTITUTION
Washington, D.C.

Copyright © 1980 by
THE BROOKINGS INSTITUTION
1775 Massachusetts Avenue, N.W., Washington, D.C. 20036

Library of Congress Cataloging in Publication Data:

Destler, I   M
  Making foreign economic policy.
  Includes index.
    1. United States—Foreign economic relations.
  2. United States—Commercial policy.   3. Food
  supply—United States.   I. Brookings Institution,
  Washington, D.C.   II. Title.
  HF1455.D47   382.1'0973   79-5119
  ISBN 0-8157-1822-5
  ISBN 0-8157-1821-7 pbk.

1 2 3 4 5 6 7 8 9

THE BROOKINGS INSTITUTION is an independent organization devoted to nonpartisan research, education, and publication in economics, government, foreign policy, and the social sciences generally. Its principal purposes are to aid in the development of sound public policies and to promote public understanding of issues of national importance.

The Institution was founded on December 8, 1927, to merge the activities of the Institute for Government Research, founded in 1916, the Institute of Economics, founded in 1922, and the Robert Brookings Graduate School of Economics and Government, founded in 1924.

The Board of Trustees is responsible for the general administration of the Institution, while the immediate direction of the policies, program, and staff is vested in the President, assisted by an advisory committee of the officers and staff. The by-laws of the Institution state: "It is the function of the Trustees to make possible the conduct of scientific research, and publication, under the most favorable conditions, and to safeguard the independence of the research staff in the pursuit of their studies and in the publication of the results of such studies. It is not a part of their function to determine, control, or influence the conduct of particular investigations or the conclusions reached."

The President bears final responsibility for the decision to publish a manuscript as a Brookings book. In reaching his judgment on the competence, accuracy, and objectivity of each study, the President is advised by the director of the appropriate research program and weighs the views of a panel of expert outside readers who report to him in confidence on the quality of the work. Publication of a work signifies that it is deemed a competent treatment worthy of public consideration but does not imply endorsement of conclusions or recommendations.

The Institution maintains its position of neutrality on issues of public policy in order to safeguard the intellectual freedom of the staff. Hence interpretations or conclusions in Brookings publications should be understood to be solely those of the authors and should not be attributed to the Institution, to its trustees, officers, or other staff members, or to the organizations that support its research.

To
HARRIETT
with love

Foreword

IN AN IDEAL WORLD, U.S. policies would be derived from explicit domestic and international goals; specific government actions would be calculated steps to advance these goals. But in reality officials find themselves coping with situations as they arise, choosing as choices present themselves. Hence policy often turns out to be little more than an accumulation of ad hoc decisions. Is there a better way?

This book explores the process by which U.S. foreign economic policy choices are made. It begins by asking broad questions about the nature of foreign economic issues and how they should be managed. It then analyzes the making of recent U.S. food and trade policy, concentrating on such episodes as the grain sales to Russia during the 1970s, the soybean embargo of 1973, and passage of the Trade Act of 1974. Drawing on his analyses, the author then offers prescriptions for managing the food and trade issues—and for improving the focus and coherence of foreign economic policy generally.

I. M. Destler is a senior associate at the Carnegie Endowment for International Peace in Washington, D.C. He completed most of the research for and writing of this book as a member of the Brookings Foreign Policy Studies staff. He is coauthor (with Priscilla Clapp, Hideo Sato, and Haruhiro Fukui) of *Managing an Alliance: The Politics of U.S.-Japanese Relations* (Brookings, 1976).

The author thanks Henry Owen, director of the Brookings Foreign Policy Studies program until 1978, for his support and encouragement throughout the project, and John D. Steinbruner, Owen's successor, for his help in the final stages. He is grateful to Edward K. Hamilton, William R. Pearce, Philip H. Trezise, and Hugh Heclo, each of whom read the manuscript and offered many helpful suggestions. Others who provided valuable advice on the design of the research project and reactions to preliminary drafts include C. Fred Bergsten, Lawrence B. Krause, Edward L. Morse, Robert L. Paarlberg, Graham T. Allison, Edward R. Fried, Lincoln Gordon, Raymond Hopkins, Henry Nau, Joseph S. Nye, Jr., Robert A. Pastor, Paula Stern, Peter L. Szanton, Gregory F. Treverton, and several official participants in the events the book deals with. He also thanks Ralph L. Boyce for research assistance, Sharon Machida and David Morse for secretarial support, Diane Hammond for editing the manuscript, Penelope S. Harpold for verifying its factual content, and Kathryn M. Tidyman for preparing the index.

Abbreviated versions of Destler's analyses of food and trade issues have appeared as "United States Food Policy 1972–1976: Reconciling Domestic and International Objectives," *International Organization*, vol. 32 (Summer 1978); and "United States Trade Policymaking During the Tokyo Round," in Michael Blaker, ed., *The Politics of Trade: U.S. and Japanese Policymaking for the GATT Negotiations* (Columbia University, East Asian Institute Project on Japan and the United States in Multilateral Diplomacy, 1978).

This study was financed in part by the Department of State and the Rockefeller Foundation. The author's analyses and conclusions are his alone and should not be ascribed to the Department of State, the Rockefeller Foundation, or to the trustees, officers, or other staff members of the Brookings Institution.

BRUCE K. MACLAURY
President

October 1979
Washington, D.C.

Contents

CHAPTER ONE

The Problem

THE CORE OF THE PROBLEM of foreign economic policy is the need to balance domestic and international concerns. Particular decisions inevitably affect both. But policymakers do not always address these concerns in a balanced way.

Domestic–International Trade-offs

In June 1963, a democratic reformist government came to power in Peru, espousing many of the goals of President John F. Kennedy's Alliance for Progress. But it was "greeted by the U.S. with a partial embargo . . . on new AID loans,"[1] to induce it to settle its dispute with the International Petroleum Company, a subsidiary of Standard Oil of New Jersey. The Kennedy administration initiated this embargo in response to strong congressional concern about possible expropriation of American investments; when no settlement followed, the embargo was maintained for three years. The embattled Peruvian government was replaced in 1968 by a military regime far less responsive to either Alliance for Progress goals or other U.S. economic and political interests.[2]

On January 21, 1969, Richard M. Nixon's administration embarked on a frustrating three-year effort to negotiate limits on exports of synthetic

1. Gregory F. Treverton, "United States Policy-Making Toward Peru: The IPC Affair," in Abraham F. Lowenthal and others, "The Making of U.S. Policies Toward Latin America: The Conduct of 'Routine' Relations," *Commission on the Organization of the Government for the Conduct of Foreign Policy, June 1975: Appendices*, vol. 3, app. I (Government Printing Office, 1976), p. 205. The full report and its appendixes are referred to hereafter as *Murphy Commission Report*.
2. For further detail see ibid. and Jessica Pernitz Einhorn, *Expropriation Politics* (Lexington Books, 1974), chap. 2.

1

and wool textiles from Japan to the United States. This drive was under-taken not for general trade or foreign policy reasons but to deliver on a presidential campaign promise to the U.S. textile industry. That goal was ultimately achieved after the administration threatened to impose import quotas under the Trading with the Enemy Act. But the whole effort seriously impaired overall U.S. trade policy and U.S. relations with Japan.[3]

In June 1973, the United States imposed temporary export controls on soybeans as part of an effort to dampen sharp rises in the prices of domestic feed and meat. But the main effect was to provoke widespread European and Japanese concern about America's reliability as a supplier of agricultural commodities, thus undercutting the long-standing U.S. effort to increase overseas markets for these products.[4]

On March 12, 1975, assistant to the president Donald Rumsfeld reported to President Gerald Ford: "On that business, yesterday, of the countervailing duties on European cheese and so on [Secretary of the Treasury William] Simon went ahead on the basis of domestic pressures—no contact with State, which has to deal with the repercussions in the European Economic Community. Something to think about."[5]

These four episodes in U.S. foreign economic policy differ in specifics. But each involved U.S. actions taken for domestic reasons, economic and political, which had significant international economic and political consequences. Each involved *trade-offs* between domestic and foreign policy interests in which the latter were given short shrift. In one case, the problem was apparently an overly restricted conceptual or policy framework: the soybean controls in 1973 seem to have been decided upon by officials who thought overridingly about domestic economic stabilization. In another, the problem was that actions were

3. For a full analysis of this episode, see I. M. Destler, Haruhiro Fukui, and Hideo Sato, *The Textile Wrangle: Conflict in Japanese–American Relations, 1969–71* (Cornell University Press, 1979).

4. This decision is analyzed in detail in chapter 4.

5. Quoted in John Hersey, "The President," *New York Times Magazine,* April 20, 1975, p. 50. The decision to which Rumsfeld alluded was apparently not final, because on April 24 the Treasury Department waived imposition of countervailing duties in return for European removal of export subsidies on those cheeses most directly competitive with U.S. production. *New York Times,* April 25, 1975; and Richard S. Frank, "Regulatory Report 10/New Trade Talks May Reduce Government Role," *National Journal,* May 10, 1975, p. 700.

tailored to accommodate a narrow domestic interest, the textile industry, at the cost of the broader welfare, domestic as well as international.

In two instances—aid to Peru and textiles from Japan—the domestic–international trade-off involved a question of tactics: how much the United States would employ coercive instruments, which might weaken long-term international ties, to win concessions to domestic interests. In all of the cases the United States gave too little weight to the legitimate economic interests and the domestic politics of other countries. And in all of them the United States responded to current domestic interests, either industry-specific or economy-wide, at some cost to the maintenance and strengthening of institutions for international cooperation from which Americans derive considerable long-range benefits.

These cases reflect broader trends. The growing intractability of the U.S. economy, with the combination of inflation and unemployment at levels without postwar precedent, increases pressure on presidents and congressmen to enhance welfare at home notwithstanding the international costs. The decline in U.S. grain stocks in 1972–75 exposed American consumers more directly to fluctuations in international grain prices and simultaneously made such fluctuations more acute. The growing American dependence on oil imports subjects foreign economic policy to other powerful domestic pressures. The decline in international competitiveness of some U.S. labor-intensive industries brings an additional source of political pressure, reflected in organized labor's altered trade policy stance and its denunciation of the "export of jobs" by multinational corporations.

And not only do such domestic economic factors and pressures seem to be gaining force; the standard postwar counterargument and source for counterpressure—that domestic economic interests be subordinated to the exigencies of the cold war and the maintenance of the free world alliances—carries far less weight. The postwar presumption of the "priority of foreign policy," in George F. Kennan's phrase, survives in highly diluted form if at all.[6] Similarly diluted is the unusual postwar preeminence of the U.S. economy, which helped Americans bear any apparent sacrifices of immediate economic interests.

Thus there is evidence to support a conclusion that there is a per-

6. 1963 memorandum published in *Administration of National Security*, Hearings before the Subcommittee on National Security Staffing and Operations of the Senate Committee on Government Operations, 88 Cong. 1 sess. (GPO, 1965), p. 363.

sistent bias in U.S. foreign economic policymaking, as Graham Allison
and Peter Szanton put it, "in favor of immediate domestic concerns over
broader foreign policy objectives."[7] Yet there are also recent episodes
that point in the opposite direction:

*In July 1972, six weeks after the Moscow summit conference, President
Nixon announced a three-year agreement providing credit to sell $750
million in grain to the Soviet Union. And even as that agreement was
being completed, the Russians were making record grain purchases in
the U.S. market. Here the prime impetus was international—a strengthening of détente on the political side, a major sale on the economic. And
the prime cost was domestic. Because they depleted American grain
stocks, the sales contracted that summer were an important contributor
to the food price inflation of 1973 and 1974. And this inflation was exacerbated when the Department of Agriculture failed to relax acreage
restrictions until January 1973, several months after the winter wheat
crop was planted.[8]*

*When he came to office in January 1977, President Jimmy Carter was
determined to reduce U.S. dependence on foreign oil. He ordered his
chief energy official, James Schlesinger, to prepare a comprehensive
program for submission to Congress within ninety days of the inauguration. Schlesinger met the deadline by excluding other senior advisers
from the process as long as possible. Though his program proposed tax
and price changes with substantial overall economic impact, senior economic officials did not weigh in until late in the process, and only when
they finally insisted. Thus the program was poorly coordinated with the
administration's macroeconomic policy proposals. (Since the program
was not adopted as proposed, this process failure had little practical
impact.)*

In these two cases, like those cited earlier, the trade-offs between
U.S. domestic and foreign policy interests were anything but simple. A
major economic interest at home, grain producers, stood to gain from
the Russian sale. And among the domestic interests affected by the
Carter energy program, some saw themselves as gaining and some as
losing. But in both cases, domestic economic stabilization was neglected
—disastrously in the first case, potentially in the second. In light of these
cases, the problem for foreign economic policymaking is to assure not

7. Graham Allison and Peter Szanton, *Remaking Foreign Policy: The Organizational Connection* (Basic Books, 1976), p. 151.
8. This decision is analyzed in detail in chapter 3.

just international consequences a full hearing but domestic consequences as well.

And yet, the picture is still more complicated, as two other major episodes show:

On August 15, 1971, President Nixon announced a number of unilateral steps to buttress the domestic economy and strengthen its international payments position; these steps included a suspension of the dollar's convertibility into gold and a temporary surcharge on imports. In the months that followed, the secretary of the treasury led an aggressive, high-pressure drive to win very large economic concessions from our European and Japanese allies. This push was popular at home, as were the immediate economic benefits from the program—higher employment and temporarily lower inflation. But it shook relations with Europe and Japan and undermined confidence in the international economic order which U.S. statecraft had nurtured since World War II.

In the short run, international values were sacrificed to domestic gains. But in the years that followed, the policy had international benefits. The realignment of currency values led to improvement of the U.S. trade balance in 1973, which facilitated the enactment of new trade legislation calling for comprehensive negotiations with our major trading partners. The subsequent move to flexible exchange rates put the world economy in a better position to absorb the shock of the 1973 increase in the price of oil by the Organization of Petroleum Exporting Countries (OPEC). And to further complicate the story, the implementation of Nixon's new economic policy also had important domestic (and international) costs, for the expansionary U.S. monetary and fiscal policies of 1972 helped fuel the worldwide inflation that followed.

When the Carter administration came to office in 1977, it adopted a stimulative national economic policy and encouraged the other major allied governments with strong economies, Germany and Japan, to do likewise. The aim was to strengthen national—and world—economic recovery from the recession which began in 1974. And as a consequence of this policy, U.S. leaders were willing to accept, in the short term, a moderate U.S. trade deficit and some downward floating of the dollar.

This policy was a sophisticated effort to maximize both domestic and international welfare and thereby to buttress political ties as well. And U.S. growth performance was in fact strong in 1977. But consumer demand in Germany and Japan grew less rapidly, in part because their governments pursued more conservative economic policies. When this growth imbalance plus higher U.S. oil imports led to a *massive* American trade deficit, several times the previous record, the dollar fell sharply in value—and continued to fall. Europeans and Japanese grew increasingly alarmed about this fall and about the will and capacity of the United States to call a halt. A rise in our inflation rate compounded this concern. By November 1978, U.S. policy had generated a crisis of international confidence, which forced the president to take strong action to support the dollar in international markets. But this action was bound to dampen American (and world) economic growth and increase the prospect of recession in 1979 and 1980.

In neither of these two cases did policymaking favor either international or domestic considerations in any simple sense. In the Carter administration case, moreover, domestic and international economic officials were initially in basic accord and felt that policy would serve the goals of both. But foreign nations saw things differently. And when their economies did not play the roles the United States had cast for them, the scenario written in Washington became economically unrealistic and politically counterproductive.

Domestic–International Coordination

Substantive complexity brings with it organizational complexity. Tensions among domestic and international objectives are hardly new to U.S. experience, but their apparent increase both offers evidence that domestic–international interdependence may be growing and illuminates the problem in American policy management that results.[9]

9. Analysts of interdependence and transnational relations emphasize that the contemporary combination of (1) high domestic demands on governments to maintain general economic welfare and (2) the impact of international transactions on their ability to meet these domestic demands is what makes international economic relations so important (and frequently so intractable) for these governments. As Richard Rosecrance and Arthur Stein put it, the "horizontal interaction of transnational processes is higher than at any point since World War I" at the same time that "vertical" (domestic) pressure for policies enhancing national economic welfare has "moved to a new peak." "Interdependence: Myth or Reality?" *World Politics*, vol. 26 (October 1973), p. 21. See also Robert O. Keohane and Joseph S. Nye, Jr., eds., *Transnational Relations and World Politics* (Harvard University Press, 1971); and Edward L. Morse, "The Transformation of Foreign Policies: Modernization, Interdependence, and Externalization," *World Politics*, vol. 22 (April 1970), pp. 371–92.

The increased importance of economic issues in foreign relations widens official participation in foreign policymaking. Such central foreign policy institutions as the State Department must share responsibility with institutions traditionally labeled domestic. A similar broadening of responsibility takes place among congressional committees. The central foreign policy institutions must increase their sensitivity to domestic policy problems and interests if they are to represent foreign policy considerations effectively in internal government debates. The converse is also true—domestic actors must become more sensitive to international concerns. But what specific prescriptions for U.S. foreign economic policymaking can serve these goals? How can government act more carefully, more wisely, in addressing the complex trade-offs which today's foreign economic issues inevitably bring?

Defining the Terms

What is foreign economic policy? The simple answer is that it encompasses government decisions and actions that affect both foreign and economic concerns. But then we must ask whether the term excludes any actions, since in this age of interdependence it is hard to find policy actions without some impact beyond U.S. borders and even harder to find actions without significant economic content. One must retreat to the unsatisfying ground of relativity: *foreign economic policy, for purposes here, includes government actions with important impact on U.S. relations with other governments and on the production and distribution of goods and services at home and abroad.*

Many matters covered by this definition fall into one of three functional policy areas: trade, monetary, and aid. But to treat foreign economic policy simply as the sum of the actions within these "tracks"[10] risks inadequate treatment of issues like food, energy, and domestic economic stabilization. Decisions on acreage restriction programs or taxes, for example, affect international economic relations but may not technically fall within these tracks.

The difficulty of drawing precise boundaries raises a broader question: whether foreign economic policy should be treated as a distinct,

10. Richard N. Cooper, "Trade Policy is Foreign Policy," *Foreign Policy*, no. 9 (Winter 1972–73), pp. 18–36; and *U.S. Foreign Economic Policy: Implications for the Organization of the Executive Branch*, Hearings before the Subcommittee on Foreign Economic Policy of the House Committee on Foreign Affairs, 92 Cong. 2 sess. (GPO, 1972), pp. 121–23.

separable sphere of government activity for either analytic or organizational purposes. Analyses and prescriptions generally assume that it should but usually do not face the matter explicitly.[11] But are its components necessarily linked more closely to one another than to policy concerns outside the international economic area? Is international energy policy, for example, more closely related to international trade negotiations than to U.S. tax and economic stabilization policies or to Middle East diplomacy? Responding to this overall question requires careful examination of specific foreign economic policymaking experience.

The broad range of official foreign economic policy actions requires coordination. As the term is employed here, coordination involves above all (1) *the management of policy decision processes* so that trade-offs among policy interests and goals are recognized, analyzed, and presented to the president and other senior executives before they make a decision; and (2) *the oversight of official actions,* especially those that follow major high-level decisions, so that these actions reflect the balance among policy goals that the president and his responsible officials have decided upon.

In practice, these two tasks are closely related. It is often in reaction to an action that appears unbalanced that officials charged with coordination are able to bring a broader policy choice to the attention of senior officials. And both tasks require interagency communication—facilitated by committees, working groups, and so on—and analyses of the effects of alternative policy courses. Moreover, as the opening examples illustrate, coordination requires the consideration of nonforeign or non-

11. President Nixon's Commission on International Trade and Investment Policy used the following words to praise the establishment of the Council on International Economic Policy (CIEP) in the Executive Office of the President (EOP) in 1971: "This is the first time that a central coordinating body has been created to deal with all aspects of international economic policy"; thus it was "a significant step in providing a unified perspective." *United States International Economic Policy in an Interdependent World,* Report to the President submitted by the Commission on International Trade and Investment Policy, July 1971 (GPO, 1971), p. 277, hereafter cited as the *Williams Commission Report.* See also Harald B. Malmgren, "Managing Foreign Economic Policy," *Foreign Policy,* no. 6 (Spring 1972), pp. 42–63. Stephen D. Cohen does face the issue explicitly: he argues that, for organizational purposes, "international economic policy must be viewed as being a separate phenomenon," though he recognizes its critical connections to national security and domestic economic concerns. *The Making of United States International Economic Policy: Principles, Problems, and Proposals for Reform* (Praeger, 1977), p. xxii.

economic interests and goals (the soybean embargo, for example, affected domestic inflation and U.S.-Japanese relations).

Reviewing the Past

Successive administrations have made explicit provision, formal or informal, for coordinating the international economic policy activity of the many government agencies (over sixty by one count)[12] involved in foreign economic policymaking. In examining their experiences, one must distinguish between organizational form and policymaking reality.

Under President Dwight D. Eisenhower formal responsibility for policy coordination was vested in the cabinet-level Council on Foreign Economic Policy located in the Executive Office of the President (EOP). But the council seldom met and its staff, headed by a senior presidential assistant, was never effective in forcing a resolution of issues, though it was involved in many.[13] Instead, the Treasury Department dominated international monetary issues (as it generally does); leadership in other foreign economic areas, particularly trade and aid, was increasingly exercised by Under Secretary of State Douglas Dillon.[14]

President Kennedy decentralized foreign economic policymaking both in form and in practice. He abolished the Council on Foreign Economic Policy, formally transferring its functions to the State Department. But in fact he reduced State influence over aid and trade issues by creating the semiautonomous Agency for International Development (AID) in 1961 and in 1963—at congressional insistence—the special representative for trade negotiations (STR) within the executive office. Under both Kennedy and Lyndon B. Johnson, however, an important staff-coordinating role was played by the deputy special assistant to the president for national security affairs, first Carl Kaysen and later Francis M. Bator, who specialized in economic issues and U.S.-European relations. This deputy had intermittent direct access to the president and was able to communicate with the president through the special assistant

12. *Williams Commission Report,* p. 275.

13. A 1961 Bureau of the Budget report concluded that this council never became "the principal interagency forum for any [policy] area." Quoted in *The Coordination of United States International Economic Policy,* a report prepared for the House Committee on International Relations by the Congressional Research Service, 95 Cong. 1 sess. (GPO, 1977), p. 15.

14. For Dillon's description of how this worked, see *U.S. Foreign Economic Policy,* Hearings, pp. 92–107.

for national security affairs.[15] Primary responsibility for particular economic issues remained in the cabinet departments and STR, but the deputy assistant served the president by monitoring the issues, and intervening selectively, to link foreign economic actions to one another, to foreign political concerns, and to presidential priorities.

In the first two years of the Nixon administration, there was no effective focal point for international economic policy coordination at all. Henry A. Kissinger, President Nixon's national security affairs assistant, did not designate an economic deputy and was both uninterested in economic matters and disinclined to delegate to his chief economic staff aide. Secretary of the Treasury David Kennedy played only a limited role, the State Department boasted no strong, economically oriented official above the assistant secretary level, and Secretary of Commerce Maurice H. Stans achieved temporary, de facto control of STR. This institutional gap, widely recognized, led to a rather ambitious "solution": creation of the Council on International Economic Policy (CIEP) in January 1971. The council was chaired by the president and staffed by an assistant to the president for international economic affairs and about twenty professionals under him. It was thus an organizational analogue to the National Security Council. But though the first occupant of this position, Peter G. Peterson, was labeled "the economic Kissinger"—and did in fact succeed in dramatizing certain important international issues—neither he nor his successors ever developed comparable leverage. The council itself virtually never met, and after three years of ad hoc involvement in particular issues, the CIEP staff lapsed into obscurity. The Carter administration allowed the council to expire in September 1977.

What emerged in its stead in the early seventies was increased foreign economic policy leadership and coordination by senior economic officials, above all the secretary of the treasury. John B. Connally quickly became dominant after his December 1970 appointment to this position, and both the domestic and international elements of Nixon's "new economic policy" of August 15, 1971, bore his personal mark. Connally's successor, George P. Shultz, also became Nixon's economic czar, through a combination of presidential confidence, the trust of other

15. For Bator's description of this system, see ibid., pp. 107–20. For another analysis advocating return to this approach, see Edward K. Hamilton, "Summary Report: Principal Lessons of the Past Decade and Thoughts on the Next," in Griffenhagen-Kroeger, "Cases on a Decade of U.S. Foreign Economic Policy: 1965–74," *Murphy Commission Report*, vol. 3, app. H, pp. 11–13.

senior officials, and some modest institutional reforms. Shultz assumed the Treasury Department position in May 1972 and in December became also assistant to the president for economic policy and chairman of a new, cabinet-level group, the Council on Economic Policy (CEP). However, his primary procedural vehicle for coordination was informal daily meetings at 8:00 A.M., which included senior Treasury Department and executive office economic officials; a council staff of two professionals managed the process.[16]

Less than two months after Gerald R. Ford assumed the presidency, he created the Economic Policy Board (EPB) to "oversee the formulation, coordination, and implementation of all economic policy," both "national and international."[17] Secretary of the Treasury William Simon was named chairman; L. William Seidman, assistant to the president for economic affairs, served as the board's executive director, with an EPB staff which eventually totaled four professionals. By early 1976, the board was appropriately labeled "perhaps the most important coordinating body in the Ford Administration,"[18] though its greatest weakness was dealing with international economic issues in which Henry Kissinger, now secretary of state, took strong interest. The board met daily at the cabinet level, and President Ford attended once a week.

The Carter administration also sought, in its early months, to coordinate foreign economic issues through an institution, the Economic Policy Group (EPG), built around senior economic policy advisers. Like the EPB, it covered domestic and international issues and met regularly at the cabinet level. Unlike the EPB, neither the EPG forum nor the EPG staff was able to establish close enough links to the president to become a prime policy coordination vehicle.

Framing the Questions

As this brief recounting of recent experience suggests, the way a coordination system actually operates depends not only—not even mainly—on its formal structure and procedures but also on the roles, informal

16. In October 1973 Shultz replaced the president as the formal chairman of CIEP as well. For a retrospective description of the Shultz system, see George P. Shultz and Kenneth W. Dam, *Economic Policy Beyond the Headlines* (Stanford University Alumni Association, 1977; W. W. Norton, 1978), p. 176.

17. Executive Order 11808, September 30, 1974, 3 C.F.R., 1971–75 compilation, p. 902.

18. Daniel J. Balz, "Juice and Coffee and the GNP—The Men Who Meet in the Morning," *National Journal*, April 3, 1976, p. 426.

styles, and working relations of the president and his senior officials. This includes particularly the major administration barons affecting foreign economic policy—the secretaries of treasury and state—but also the secretaries of commerce, agriculture, and labor, and the special trade representative. Moreover, while it is possible, up to a point, to make specific organizational decisions for foreign economic policy, any administration's system for foreign economic policymaking will, in practice, be strongly influenced by organization in other policy areas, particularly domestic economics and national security.

Recent experience also suggests that the most important choices for coordinating foreign economic policy lie in two areas: (1) degree of centralization and (2) the policy orientation of the coordinating institution.

Should leadership (and perhaps also day-to-day management) of all foreign economic issues be concentrated in one organizational entity? Or should it be dispersed among a number of agencies? Maximum centralization would involve, by one formulation, "creation of a new Cabinet-level department with exclusive formulative and management responsibilities for the totality of foreign economic policies."[19] This goal could also be approached by consolidating as much responsibility as possible in an existing department, State or Treasury, or in an office of foreign economic policy within the executive office, as proposed by The President's Advisory Council on Executive Organization (the Ash council).

A decentralized approach, by contrast, would distribute leadership responsibility among existing institutions according to subject matter: for example, the STR for trade, the Treasury Department for monetary matters, the State Department for commodity issues involving strong political interest in developing countries, the Department of Agriculture for food aid, the Department of Energy for issues in its sphere, and so on. But such leadership designations will not, of course, go uncontested; there would be fear that State, for example, would sacrifice U.S. economic interests to win favor with foreign governments.

Linked to the degree of centralization is the size of the coordinating institution. The largest, presumably, would be a new department. The smallest are Shultz's staff of two (CEP) and the three-person office of the 1960s, headed by a deputy national security assistant. In the middle is the CIEP with its staff of twenty professionals. Large coordinating

19. Presented as an option in *The Coordination of United States International Economic Policy*, p. 28.

institutions can handle issues more thoroughly and comprehensively than small staffs, but they can weaken the roles of cabinet departments and agencies and thus the links between foreign economic policy and other major domestic and foreign policy concerns, like farm policy or Middle East diplomacy.

The policy orientation of the central coordinating institution is a separate choice, whatever its size. Should it be connected to a *foreign* policy institution, like the National Security Council or the State Department? To an *economic* policy institution, like the Treasury Department, the Economic Policy Board, or the Economic Policy Group? Or to an institution that tries to *bridge foreign and economic perspectives,* like the Council on International Economic Policy or a new cabinet department for foreign economic policy?

Other questions about policy coordination also need to be addressed. How much reliance should be placed on collegial, cabinet-level forums which actually handle serious policy business (EPB) and how much on staffs and interagency groups operating at well below cabinet level? How useful are highly structured, formal procedures for management of specific issues, as opposed to informal interagency communication networks and ad hoc groups? Different administrations have resolved all of these questions in different ways; this study concludes with its own specific prescriptions.

This Study

Until recently, there was remarkably little in print about U.S. foreign economic policymaking, particularly that within the executive branch. The comprehensive and insightful book by Bauer, Pool, and Dexter analyzed trade policymaking but concentrated on congressional decisionmaking and business–congressional relations.[20] There were also a number of other case studies or analyses of selected issue areas. But in contrast with the wealth of studies of defense decisionmaking and the growing literature on foreign policymaking and bureaucratic politics in

20. Raymond A. Bauer, Ithiel de Sola Pool, and Lewis Anthony Dexter, *American Business and Public Policy: The Politics of Foreign Trade,* 2d. ed. (Aldine-Atherton, 1972). Not the least of its virtues was that it inspired a provocative review by Theodore J. Lowi, suggesting the existence of three major types of policymaking issues—distributive, regulatory, and redistributive. See "American Business, Public Policy, Case-Studies, and Political Theory," *World Politics,* vol. 16 (July 1964), pp. 677–715.

the political–strategic field,[21] U.S. government experience in foreign economic policymaking went largely unexplored.

Since 1971, however, there has been increased attention paid, a product in part of the increased prominence of international economic issues. In 1972, the Culver subcommittee of the House Foreign Affairs Committee elicited insightful general statements from former foreign economic policy officials such as Francis M. Bator, Richard N. Cooper, Douglas Dillon, and Robert V. Roosa.[22] Two years later, the Commission on the Organization of the Government for the Conduct of Foreign Policy (Murphy commission) commissioned three studies focused on international economic issues and gave these issues prominence in its own final report.[23] And the past few years have brought considerable new analyses of particular cases, outside as well as within the Murphy commission enterprise.[24]

21. For bibliographies of this literature, see Graham T. Allison, *Essence of Decision: Explaining the Cuban Missile Crisis* (Little, Brown, 1971), pp. 312–16; I. M. Destler, *Presidents, Bureaucrats, and Foreign Policy: The Politics of Organizational Reform,* rev. ed. (Princeton University Press, 1974), pp. 323–42; and Morton H. Halperin with Priscilla Clapp and Arnold Kanter, *Bureaucratic Politics and Foreign Policy* (Brookings Institution, 1974), pp. 322–30.

22. Subcommittee on Foreign Economic Policy, chaired by John C. Culver. See *U.S. Foreign Economic Policy,* Hearings.

23. Griffenhagen-Kroeger, "Cases on a Decade of U.S. Foreign Economic Policy: 1965–74," pp. 5–195, combines eleven specific cases and an insightful summary report by former NSC senior staff official Edward K. Hamilton. Robert O. Keohane and Joseph S. Nye, Jr., "The Management of Global Issues," *Murphy Commission Report,* vol. 1, app. B, pp. 43–255, similarly includes a summary report by the project directors and twelve case analyses stressing economic and science/technology issues. Lowenthal and others, "The Making of U.S. Policies Toward Latin America: The Conduct of 'Routine' Relations," pp. 203–95, covers seven cases, largely economic. The commission's own recommendations for international economic policy are incorporated in *Murphy Commission Report,* chap. 5.

24. See, for example, David Howard Davis, *How the Bureaucracy Makes Foreign Policy: An Exchange Analysis* (Lexington Books, 1972); Destler, Fukui, and Sato, *The Textile Wrangle;* Einhorn, *Expropriation Politics;* Ann L. Hollick, "Seabeds Make Strange Politics," *Foreign Policy,* no. 9 (Winter 1972–73), pp. 148–70; Stephen D. Krasner, *Defending the National Interest: Raw Materials Investments and U.S. Foreign Policy* (Princeton University Press, 1978); John S. Odell, "U.S. Foreign Monetary Policy, 1962–1973: Policy-Making Structure and Process," paper delivered to the 1976 annual meeting of the American Political Science Association; Robert A. Pastor, "Legislative–Executive Relations and the Politics of United States Foreign Economic Policy 1929–1976" (Ph.D. dissertation, Harvard University, 1977); Paula Stern, *Water's Edge: Domestic Politics and the Making of American Foreign Policy* (Greenwood Press, 1979); and Gregory F. Treverton, *The Dollar Drain and American Forces in Germany: Managing the Political Economics of Alliance* (Ohio University Press, 1978).

These studies have vastly increased the information about U.S. foreign economic policymaking available in print. They have also contributed to an enlarged, more realistic conception of its scope: the Murphy commission study directed by Edward K. Hamilton, for example, includes four cases with predominantly domestic roots: soybean export controls, suspension of oil import quotas, the wage-price freeze of 1971, and the decision not to raise taxes in 1966. And in broadening the information available, these studies provide a new empirical base for general prescriptive efforts.[25] That they have not generated a new consensus about the "best" way of organizing for foreign economic policy is not surprising: the choices are difficult. Nor have they resolved the dilemmas which beset all such studies (including this one): how to combine objectivity with sensitivity to the real world of decisionmaking;[26] how to join sufficient detail about specific policy experience with an information base sufficiently representative to provide a solid foundation for conclusions about foreign economic policymaking as a whole.

This study approaches these dilemmas differently. Like several of the Murphy studies, it joins exploration of specific government experience to general analysis of policymaking choices. Unlike those studies (typically team efforts working under very tight deadlines), here the

25. In fact, the *Murphy Commission Report* has led to two such efforts. One is Allison and Szanton, *Remaking Foreign Policy*, which bases its central prescriptions on "the intertwining of foreign and domestic issues" (p. 76). Szanton was the commission's research director; Allison directed one of its major studies. A second is Cohen, *The Making of United States International Economic Policy;* Cohen was the commission's staff associate for international economic policy organization.

26. For example, Francis M. Bator's testimony before the Culver subcommittee is unrivalled in conveying the flavor of actual government foreign economic policymaking and the links between substance and process. His prescription is that foreign economic policy be coordinated by a small group within the White House national security staff and headed by a deputy "known to carry the President's flag." This is essentially the system he ran in the mid-sixties. Similarly, Edward K. Hamilton (who worked with Bator) urges coordination by "a single senior appointee of the President" with "a title equivalent to principal Deputy to the Assistant to the President for National Security Affairs," Douglas Dillon calls for centering authority in a high State Department official, and Robert V. Roosa (former under secretary of the treasury for monetary affairs) argues that "Treasury should have a function comparable in economic affairs to the virtually coordinate responsibility that Defense has with State in national security affairs." For remarks by Bator, Dillon, and Roosa, see *U.S. Foreign Economic Policy*, Hearings, pp. 113, 95–96, 151; Hamilton's opinion appears in his "Summary Report," pp. 12–13.

same analyst has undertaken both and has sought to apply a common framework to both analysis and prescription.

This framework begins with the problem of trade-offs between domestic and international concerns. It recognizes that in a government where the domestic–international dichotomy still prevails organizationally, "foreign economic policy . . . must bridge foreign and domestic policy."[27] But while dividing U.S. policy concerns into these two categories offers a useful introduction to the foreign economic policy problem, it proves on further examination both oversimple and misleading. Both "foreign policy" and "domestic policy" are umbrella terms covering a range of varying, oft-competing values and objectives. Domestic concerns may conflict with one another: farm policy officials may want grain prices up while inflation-fighters want them down. Domestically oriented officials may find themselves aligned with officials with international concerns in seeking to stimulate domestic energy production, for example. Nor are the requirements of domestic economic policy necessarily in conflict with those of international economic relations; sometimes the opposite is the case. Opening up wheat acreage for the 1973 harvest would have served U.S. international as well as domestic interests; and America's post-1975 recovery from economic recession has been a boon to countries exporting to our market and has contributed to progress in the Tokyo Round of trade negotiations at Geneva.

Thus foreign economic issues typically involve interplay among a number of policy concerns; in Hamilton's words, "it is critical to sensible policy that national purpose be conceived as a plural construct."[28] And pluralism applies not just to interests outside government that seek to influence policy but to the legitimate, competing objectives that the government itself pursues and must pursue. Moreover, there are usually no established priorities to govern trade-offs among these objectives; for such priorities are hard to establish both analytically and politically.

Assuming pluralism in U.S. foreign economic concerns, this study sets out first to determine the *form* pluralism takes in particular issue areas. What are the predominant concerns; which officials, departments, and agencies represent them; how do the trade-offs among these concerns present themselves to officials; and how are these trade-offs, in practice, made? Second, what is the effect of the coordinating institutions on the *resolution* of pluralism: are they relatively neutral and objective

27. *Murphy Commission Report*, p. 57.
28. Hamilton, "Summary Report," p. 7.

vis-à-vis competing concerns or do they raise certain ones to prominence and neglect others?

To address such questions, this book explores U.S. government experience in two broad, overlapping areas of foreign economic policy, food and trade, over roughly the same period, 1972 through 1976. One of these, food, is among those interdependence issues for which the boundaries between domestic policy and foreign policy are difficult to establish; the second, trade, is one of the standard functional tracks. On trade policy a major decision arena was the Congress, as for twenty-one months it deliberated over the Nixon administration's 1973 trade reform proposal. Food policy issues in this period, by contrast, were resolved primarily in the executive branch, though congressional intervention was frequent and sometimes effective.[29]

The immediate and obvious question is whether food and trade, taken together, are completely representative of foreign economic issues. They are not. The study was nonetheless undertaken on the premise that detailed investigation of these issue areas would shed light on the problems that foreign economic policy officials face and on the effectiveness of particular procedural and institutional arrangements for addressing these problems. Both the food and trade investigations treat a sequence of decisions and actions, extending over several years. The study thus pursues a course more general than case investigations, which do not readily support broad conclusions, and more detailed than general analyses, which are not usually founded on detailed comparative investigation of recent government experience. And though the experiences analyzed most intensively took place entirely within the Nixon and Ford administrations, they cover a period of substantial change, both in world and national policy environments and in policy institutions and the officials who ran them. This enhances their usefulness as a basis for analyzing the effectiveness of coordinating institutions.

The food and trade investigations were pursued through examination of publicly available materials and interviews with thirty officials during, or subsequent to, their involvement.[30] Broad explanatory ques-

29. The 1973 amendments to the Agricultural Act of 1970 proved to have only limited impact on U.S. crop production, prices, and exports, because the support and target price levels it established were well below market prices in 1973–76; a bill raising them was vetoed by President Ford in May of 1975.

30. Interviews were also conducted with a number of close observers of policymaking during this period. A list of those interviewed is the appendix to this study.

tions are posed. The section on food policy asks, for example, why the government allowed grain sales contracted in 1972 to empty its grain bins and then, the following summer, imposed an embargo on soybean exports. And it asks why policy choices of equal and perhaps greater difficulty received better-balanced handling in 1974 and 1975. The trade policy analysis raises similar questions. Why, in a period when protectionist pressure was apparently mounting, was it possible for the administration to propose, and the Congress to enact, a bill giving the president broad new authority to reduce trade barriers? How much, if at all, did the organization of the executive branch contribute to this outcome? And how has that experience, plus the Trade Act of 1974's specific provisions, changed the role and the orientation of particular trade policy institutions, above all the Office of the Special Representative for Trade Negotiations?

These issue analyses are perhaps useful as history, and can be read for their own sake. But throughout, attention returns to the question of what policy concerns, represented by whom, were competing for influence. It is not assumed that organizational factors were the sole or even the predominant influence on the substance of policy. Judgment of the extent and nature of their impact, however, must await the specific issue chapters that follow. The concluding chapter will then treat, among other issues, the question of what contribution organizational changes might make to improved government performance. In so doing, it will draw also on sources beyond the issue chapters: the general and case literature already cited; the author's own previously published research;[31] and interviews with officials about recent policy coordinating institutions, particularly the Council on International Economic Policy, the Economic Policy Board, and the Economic Policy Group.[32]

31. On general U.S. foreign policy organization, *Presidents, Bureaucrats, and Foreign Policy;* and "National Security Advice to U.S. Presidents: Some Lessons from Thirty Years," *World Politics,* vol. 27 (January 1977), pp. 143–76 (Brookings Reprint 323). On U.S.-Japan economic relations, with coauthors Fukui and Sato, *The Textile Wrangle;* "Country Expertise and U.S. Foreign Policymaking: The Case of Japan," *Pacific Community,* vol. 5 (July 1974), pp. 546–64 (Brookings Reprint 298); and with coauthors Hideo Sato, Priscilla Clapp, and Haruhiro Fukui, *Managing an Alliance: The Politics of U.S.-Japanese Relations* (Brookings Institution, 1976).

32. The author's insight into these was increased by his service, in the spring of 1977, as consultant to the Carter administration, working on reorganization of the Executive Office of the President, with particular responsibility for economic policy advisory institutions.

CHAPTER TWO

Food Policy

BETWEEN 1972 AND 1975, food issues moved front and center on the international economic stage. Production shortfalls in major agricultural countries brought world grain stocks to postwar lows. The value of U.S. farm exports tripled, as did grain prices within the United States. Secretary of Agriculture Earl Butz hailed the new "policy of plenty"—the end of acreage controls for grains; record farm income and exports. Critics emphasized the negative—fierce inflation at home and a diminished ability to respond to food emergencies abroad.

Critics also scored the recurrent vacillations and contradictions that marked U.S. food policymaking during this period:

In 1972, even while pursuing a comprehensive anti-inflation program, the Nixon administration fueled price rises through its agricultural policy actions—spurring and subsidizing very large grain sales to Russia, yet continuing to limit U.S. wheat acreage well after these sales had made earlier supply projections obsolete.

In 1973, as that same administration was giving continued emphasis to expanding farm exports and liberalizing world trade, it clamped down a sudden and total (if temporary) embargo on exports of soybeans, the primary U.S. export crop measured in dollar sales.

In 1974, as the United States led in planning a world food conference under United Nations auspices, it was squeezing food aid to the lowest amounts since 1955 and allocating more to political clients than to peoples with the most urgent food needs.

In 1975, caught between farmers dependent on sales to Russia and unions threatening not to load the ships, the Ford administration sought a compromise resolution—a temporary suspension of sales, which was lifted with the signing of a bilateral agreement to regularize Soviet buy-

19

ing on world grain markets. But if this resolution looked sensible to many in Washington, it outraged the grain farmers. To them, an administration that had summoned them to record production to meet unprecedented world demand was now standing between them and a major export market. Their ire only increased as U.S. grain prices fell and the Russians took some of their business elsewhere.

How does one explain this seemingly sorry performance? As noted in chapter 1, the Nixon and Ford administrations devoted considerable energy to building effective policy coordinating institutions. But what made the management problem particularly difficult was the plural purposes of international food policy. Food policy inevitably involves conflicts among entirely legitimate U.S. government policy objectives, as well as among interested parties inside and outside government seeking to advance one or more of these objectives. Food issues frequently cannot be resolved without some damage to important policy values.

Four Competing Concerns

At the center of U.S. international food policy is *farm policy:* what the government does to influence the production and marketing of agricultural commodities. But the supply–demand balance for major U.S. farm commodities is an important influence on the broader U.S. economy, especially when tight markets drive prices upward; hence, food policy is *domestic economic policy* as well. Food policy is also, frequently, part of *general foreign policy;* access to U.S. food supplies, on favorable terms, is sought by many other governments and thus can be used as leverage over these governments. Finally, food policy is *global welfare and development policy;* subsidized food sales and donations abroad can improve nutrition and save lives; capital and technical assistance can help developing nations expand their own production.

Each of these concerns is represented by individuals and institutions inside and outside the government who give it priority. The group of individuals emphasizing a particular concern can be called, with some oversimplification, a community—the farm policy community, for example. And members of one policy community frequently combat members of another, because their goals compete: higher farm prices

help producers but hurt consumers; food aid for humanitarian purposes serves welfare goals abroad, but in times of scarcity it either contributes to inflation at home or reduces the amount of food for general foreign policy purposes.

This does not mean, of course, that those who give priority to the same area of concern necessarily agree with one another on what specific actions government should take. The American Farm Bureau Federation and the National Farmers' Union, the two most important general farm organizations, differ markedly on how much they want government to manage the agricultural marketplace. Economic policy advisers differ on how much government can and should seek to stabilize grain and food prices and on how it should go about trying. Foreign policy officials differ on the efficacy and morality of using food for diplomatic leverage, as well as on which countries should be the targets. Those concerned with development disagree on how much food aid the United States should provide and on how damaging it is to recipient countries' efforts to expand their own food output. Moreover, there is overlap among communities: agricultural economists frequently focus on both farm and domestic economic issues and policy goals; some foreign policy officials are development-oriented as well. And individuals vary widely in the breadth of their perspectives, their capacity to understand and accommodate other concerns.

But most actors on international food issues can be placed within one of these communities. And though they may differ about the answers, members of each tend to ask the same questions and watch the same variables. It is important, therefore, to assess each community in some detail. What are the major *goals* of its members? What *questions* do they ask about government policy; above all, what *variables* do they watch? What official U.S. policy *instruments* are responsive to their influence and relevant to their purposes? What *officials and institutions* within the U.S. government typically house this concern? What *private groups* share it and seek to affect government actions?

Farm Policy

The American agricultural policy community has generally given priority to three related *goals*. The first and oldest is improving productivity through education and technological advance. The second is protecting the farmer against depressed prices caused by gluts in the commodity markets. The third is maximizing farm income.[1] All involve allocation of public funds, hence all are subject to overall federal budget constraints. Programs supporting productivity are long-term and are relatively autonomous in day-to-day operations. They relate only indirectly to immediate foreign economic decisions. Protecting and maximizing farm income, however, require short-term responsiveness to market developments and trade-offs with other foreign economic goals.

Those concerned with farm income watch *variables* affecting that income: agricultural production; farm prices and their relation to prices farmers pay for inputs; the value and volume of agricultural exports; existing and projected grain stocks. And the key farm policy *questions* center upon the impact of government actions on that income. Some involve basic farm policy issues. Should the government guarantee farmers' prices or income? If so, at what levels? Should the government adopt a comprehensive supply management approach, seeking to adjust annual grain production to overall needs and employing reserve stocks to cope with shortfalls and surpluses? Or should government intervention be minimal, with domestic and international markets carrying the main burden of adjustment through trade and price fluctuations? How should farm exports be promoted? Other questions involve broader-purpose policies. How can trade negotiations serve to reduce overseas barriers to American agricultural products? How can government-subsidized food aid sales under Public Law 480 be expanded so that they can strengthen farm income when commercial demand is soft? How can they be allocated to promote long-term development of dollar markets?

A primary farm policy *instrument* since the Great Depression has been the commodity program, which aims to increase the income of producers by, usually, limiting the supply of the commodity by reducing acreage that is planted. Other policy instruments for increasing farm income aim at expanding international demand—Commodity Credit Corporation financing for commercial exports; food aid for countries and people unable to pay the market price in dollars. A recurrent theme of farm policy discussion is how much U.S. production world demand

1. See, for example, Don F. Hadwiger, "The Old, the New, and the Emerging United States Department of Agriculture," *Public Administration Review*, vol. 36 (March/April 1976), pp. 155–65. A related goal, particularly important in rhetoric, has been to facilitate the continued existence of small and middle-scale producers: "preserving the family farm."

can absorb: the more it absorbs, the less acreage cutbacks and government subsidies are necessary. This theme was evoked vividly in 1934, a time of depressed U.S. farm exports, by Secretary of Agriculture Henry A. Wallace in his best-selling pamphlet, *America Must Choose*. The choice, he argued, was between permanently retiring 40 to 100 million acres of cropland and lowering tariffs enough to increase imports by $1 billion, so that other countries could finance an extra billion dollars worth of U.S. farm products.[2]

The central farm policy *institutions* are, of course, the Department of Agriculture (USDA) and the Senate and House agriculture committees. The Office of Management and Budget (Bureau of the Budget until 1970) exercises oversight of farm commodity and export subsidy programs. The major *private groups* are the general farm organizations and those with interest in particular commodities.

Domestic Economic Policy

The primary *goals* of U.S. economic policy are full employment and price stability; other goals of frequent but varying importance include an adequate balance of international payments, economic growth, resource mobility, and moderate income redistribution.[3] The economic policy community has also shown particular interest in the cost-effectiveness of federal expenditures.

Hence the food policy *variables* economic policy advisers watch include the dollar return on farm exports, the distribution of farm program benefits, and the efficiency of farm subsidy programs—whether they bring gains to intended beneficiaries commensurate with costs to the treasury and to consumers.[4] The variable of greatest concern to the economic community, however, has been farm prices, since these can trigger (and recently have triggered) broader inflation. Rises in farm prices

2. Henry A. Wallace, *America Must Choose: The Advantages and Disadvantages of Nationalism, of World Trade, and of a Planned Middle Course*, World Affairs Pamphlet no. 3 (New York: Foreign Policy Association, 1934), pp. 10–11, 27.

3. This section draws upon E. S. Kirschen and others, *Economic Policy in Our Time*, vol. 1 (New York: Rand McNally, 1964; Amsterdam: North-Holland, 1964), pp. 5–6.

4. For critical views on this subject, see Kermit Gordon, "How Much Should Government Do?" *Saturday Review*, January 9, 1965, pp. 25–27 ff.; Charles L. Schultze, *The Distribution of Farm Subsidies: Who Gets the Benefits?* (Brookings Institution, 1971); and D. Gale Johnson, *Farm Commodity Programs: An Opportunity for Change* (American Enterprise Institute for Public Policy Research, 1973).

normally bring rises in consumer prices. And inflation in food prices, being most visible to consumers, is most likely to stimulate union demands for increased wages, which fuel the wage-price cycle.

So the most urgent food *questions* the economic community asks are about prices. How will prices be affected by farm production? By farm exports? By food aid shipments? By reserve stocks? However, economic officials are inclined to place considerable value on markets and to urge the reduction of government intervention in markets when they feel it impedes adjustment to changing economic circumstances. For example, they frequently criticized the farm commodity programs of the fifties and sixties for slowing the flow of resources out of agriculture and thus encouraging overinvestment and continued surplus production.

There are many policy *instruments* to combat inflation, but most tend to dampen output and increase unemployment and few are dramatically effective in the short term. An exception is the adjustment of commodity programs to increase output, which can lead to greater supplies within a year after the adjustment is made. But this policy tool is only available when acreage is being cut back. Other anti-inflation policy instruments include price and export controls, but most economists regard these as last resorts, at best, since they distort the flow of resources.

The major *institutions* that help frame domestic economic policy are the Treasury Department, the Federal Reserve Board, the Office of Management and Budget, and the Council of Economic Advisers. Their senior officials (except for the Council of Economic Advisers) come more often from business and financial circles than from the economics profession. In Congress, the key institutions are the tax-writing committees (the Senate Finance Committee and the House Ways and Means Committee), the appropriations committees, and the new budget committees. The Joint Economic Committee has no legislative role but seeks to influence policy through hearings and reports. The primary *private groups* concerned with economic policy are labor and business organizations and consumer groups.

General Foreign Policy

Foreign policy, of course, is concerned with how foreign governments behave. Its *goal* is to influence this behavior, and it is also concerned with influencing international transactions between private parties. It may seek direct impact, trying to affect a specific foreign action or set of related actions. Or it may seek indirect impact through institution-building, establishing or amending the rules and arrangements under which international transactions take place.

The *questions* foreign policy officials tend to ask reflect two foreign policy orientations: (a) "food power," or using food supply to influence the behavior of foreign governments in areas not related to food;[5] and (b) longer-term institution-building efforts. For the first, the question is, how can any country's need for American food be turned to diplomatic advantage in particular situations—for example, in moderating Soviet geopolitical behavior? The second orientation generates such questions as, how can Soviet grain purchases be stabilized to limit disruption of world grain markets? How can an international system be constructed under which major exporters and importers share responsibility for maintaining and managing stocks to minimize such disruption? How can American-induced disruption—like export controls—be avoided or minimized?

The major government *instruments* relevant to foreign policy are Public Law 480 (food aid) and export credit programs, formal export controls or informal export restraints, and the negotiation of international trade agreements. These instruments can be used for food power: for example, easing Soviet access to U.S. food to strengthen détente, and food aid to South Vietnam in the late sixties and seventies to support the regime in power. Or access can be made more difficult, as with the special requirements (in effect until 1971) limiting grain sales to the Communist world, or the restrictions on food aid to countries that trade with Cuba. Over the long term, trade negotiations seek a more liberal commercial regime in agriculture, and the foreign policy community has generally worked for an international system of food reserves.

Institutions most likely to reflect a food power orientation are portions of the State Department and the National Security Council staff, the latter often reflecting presidential interest in this source of leverage. Economic specialists within these institutions, however, are more likely

5. For arguments stressing the potential of food power, see Lester R. Brown, *The Politics and Responsibility of the North American Breadbasket,* Worldwatch Paper 2 (Washington, D.C.: Worldwatch Institute, October 1975), pp. 36–43; U.S. Central Intelligence Agency, Office of Political Research, *Potential Implications of Trends in World Population, Food Production, and Climate* (Washington, D.C.: CIA, August 1974). For more skeptical conclusions, see Emma Rothschild, "Food Politics," *Foreign Affairs,* vol. 54 (January 1976), pp. 285–307; and Robert L. Paarlberg, "Food, Oil, and Coercive Resource Power," *International Security,* vol. 3 (Fall 1978), pp. 3–19.

to concern themselves with international institution-building and seek
to limit use of the above instruments for short-term political goals. And
they find frequent support from other parts of the government—the Department of Agriculture, with its interest in long-term market development; the office of the special trade representative, which leads in multilateral trade negotiations. *Private groups* looking at food policy from
similar perspectives include commentators and critics from academic
and research institutions and the press; the trade policy community
(with links to business and transnational contacts); and businesses and
business organizations with stakes in international food trade, particularly the grain companies.

Global Welfare and Development Policy

Food policy affects whether food is available to countries with severe
food shortages and malnutrition. It also influences the policies of developing countries, particularly their programs to grow more food for themselves. The development policy community views food issues in terms
of the sometimes-competing *goals* of making food available in times of
need to persons in need, and encouraging greater food production in
developing countries in the years ahead. It asks its own *questions*. Will
a particular food aid agreement assist the recipient country's development, on balance, by stabilizing domestic prices and reducing the drain
on foreign exchange? Or will it undercut development by (a) depress-
ing prices received by local farmers, reducing their incentive to adopt
new technology and (b) lowering the recipient government's priority
to expand domestic food production? More generally, this community
asks whether the volume of U.S. production and concessional sales is
adequate to meet needs and keep world food prices from skyrocketing.

Major *instruments* for pursuing development and welfare goals are
Public Law 480 and general development assistance programs. The
latter include capital and technical assistance and both bilateral and
multilateral programs. Domestic farm programs are related to Public
Law 480, since that law restricts the commodities in the food aid program to those the secretary of agriculture declares "available" after
domestic and international commercial needs are met.

The primary *institution* for development and welfare goals within
the government has been the Agency for International Development
(AID), which administers bilateral aid and shares responsibility for
Public Law 480 with the Department of Agriculture. But AID also administers nondevelopment aid; and since the mid-sixties its influence

has declined progressively as the bilateral development assistance program has declined. The Treasury Department, which instructs U.S. representatives to international development banks, has played an increasing role in development policy as these banks have absorbed the major share of U.S. development finance. Treasury's other roles—protector of the balance of payments, watchdog against domestic inflation, minimizer of drains on the treasury—tend to outweigh its development concerns when hard trade-offs must be made. (In 1979, the Carter administration established an umbrella agency, the International Development Coordination Agency, to oversee U.S. development programs.)

The weakness of the development community within the U.S. government is partially offset by persistent and articulate *private groups*, particularly national and international organizations dedicated to fighting world hunger. These are allied frequently with influential liberal and/or farm state members of Congress. These groups have a strong impact on food issues, since world hunger can be dramatized as more complex development problems cannot.

Food Policy until 1972: Farm Policy Primacy

To delineate these four perspectives is not to argue that they have been of equal importance in food policymaking. In fact, farm policy concerns had primacy until 1972. Food policymaking was centered in the Department of Agriculture; its impacts on other policy concerns were largely byproducts of actions taken to strengthen farm income and bring the domestic "farm problem" under control. This primacy was politically predictable—the farm community was most directly and deeply affected by food policy decisions; its lobbyists weighed in to affect these decisions; farm voters watched farm conditions and (to some degree) voted accordingly. But its weight rested easily on the other policy actors because, under market conditions existing until 1972, the policies that resulted also contributed to their goals.

The farm problem was chronic surpluses and low prices. A remarkable technological revolution had generated dramatic productivity increases. An acre in Iowa yielded 50 percent more corn in 1960 than in 1950; nationwide farm output per man-hour doubled over the same ten years.[6] This leap in production depressed prices because it exceeded the

6. Don F. Hadwiger and Ross B. Talbot, *Pressures and Protests: The Kennedy Farm Program and the Wheat Referendum of 1963* (San Francisco: Chandler, 1965), pp. 8, 11.

growth of commercial demand, both domestic and worldwide; and it depressed them severely because of the price inelasticity of both demand and supply.

The government's response to the farm problem was a set of extremely complex programs to influence production and price levels for particular commodities. Initiated in the New Deal and periodically reshaped thereafter, they provided income support for farmers through some combination of government-guaranteed minimum prices (price supports) and direct subsidy payments. These in turn were usually conditioned on restrictions on acreage planted, in order to limit total production and thus limit the amounts that flowed into government warehouses when prices fell to support levels. When price support programs kept domestic prices above world market prices, export subsidies were provided to enable American sellers to compete internationally.

By 1960, a combination of price supports well above market-clearing levels, dramatic increases in crop yields, and the ineffectiveness or obsolescence of acreage limitations had generated record grain stockpiles, predominantly under government ownership. Wheat stocks controlled by the Commodity Credit Corporation (CCC) equaled annual U.S. production; feed grain stocks were nearly half of annual production.[7] The cost to the government just to store these and other commodities was about $1 billion in fiscal year 1961.[8]

The Kennedy and Johnson administrations sought to get better control of the farm problem—and of farm program costs—by imposing much stricter acreage limitations as part of a broad supply-management approach. After failing to get wheat farmers to agree to mandatory acreage restrictions,[9] the Department of Agriculture under Orville Free-

7. From 1959 through 1962, wheat production ranged from 1.1 billion to 1.35 billion bushels; CCC-controlled stocks ranged from 1.2 billion to 1.4 billion bushels. Privately held stocks were small, ranging from 26 million to 130 million bushels. U.S. Department of Agriculture, *Agricultural Statistics, 1970* (Government Printing Office, 1970), p. 10; see also Dale E. Hathaway, "Food Prices and Inflation," *Brookings Papers on Economic Activity, 1:1974,* table 6. Corn production in 1960 was 3.9 billion bushels, and corn in CCC storage (as of December 31) totaled 1.5 billion bushels; sorghum production was 620 million bushels and CCC stocks totaled 557 million bushels. USDA, *Agricultural Statistics, 1970,* pp. 33, 52, 524; see also Hathaway, "Food Prices and Inflation," table 7.

8. Hadwiger and Talbot, *Pressures and Protests,* p. 12.

9. The law provided that two-thirds of wheat farmers would have to approve the mandatory program. The Farm Bureau strongly opposed it, and in a referendum held on May 21, 1963, only 48 percent of wheat growers voted in favor. For the full story, see ibid.

man won congressional enactment in 1964 and 1965 of voluntary programs under which price supports would be set lower—at or near world
market levels—and farmers would receive income support through
direct payments. Such payments were conditioned on participation in
commodity programs, which meant accepting the planting restrictions
established by the secretary of agriculture in the program regulations
for the current year. The secretary could adjust these restrictions according to whether more or less production was desired, based on the level
of existing stocks, projected demand, and projected production during
the coming crop year under various program and price assumptions.
Before the secretary issued the program regulations, the Executive
Office of the President, particularly the Bureau of the Budget (which
became the Office of Management and Budget in 1970) reviewed them,
primarily to control costs.

For the farm community, these programs were a middle ground between two politically unworkable alternatives, a thoroughgoing regime
of production controls and a complete dismantling of commodity programs. It was, in the words of one advocate of stronger government regulation, a "leaky and inefficient means of controlling production," but,
he added, "most farmers want it that way."[10] And commodity programs
did transfer resources from the nonfarm to the farm sector and made
farmers' incomes more stable than they would have been without such
programs. They also reduced government stocks substantially.

Farm policies brought important benefits to the goals of foreign, welfare, and domestic economic policy, as well. Food was available through
Public Law 480 to buttress the autonomy of certain states (Yugoslavia),
to sustain the economies of clients (Vietnam), and to purchase concessions on other issues (Korea).[11] The United States could respond
quickly and generously to food emergencies overseas: under Public
Law 480, it shipped unprecedented tonnages of wheat to India in 1965–
67, when that country experienced its worst drought in decades.[12] And

10. Willard W. Cochrane, *The City Man's Guide to the Farm Problem* (University of Minnesota Press, 1965), p. 147.

11. On October 16, 1971, the United States agreed to increase food aid to Korea
by $275 million over the next several years in order to win Korean agreement to limit
exports to the United States of man-made fiber and wool textiles. See General Accounting Office, *Economic and Foreign Policy Effects of Voluntary Restraint Agreements on Textiles and Steel* (GAO, March 21, 1974), p. 29.

12. This is not to say that welfare was the only U.S. motive. President Lyndon B.
Johnson insisted on personally approving all commitments and held up shipments
repeatedly to (1) get India to commit more resources to agricultural development;

supplies could be managed through commodity programs tailored to meet demand; thus wheat acreage was increased in 1967 to accommodate the needs of the Indian subcontinent and rice acreage was increased in 1968 to supply Vietnam and Indonesia. A major by-product of overcapacity and surpluses was stability in the food price index, at least in relative terms.[13] Moreover, stability was more or less automatic; general economic policy officials were not required to play an active, day-to-day, role, so they generally did not. As Dale E. Hathaway noted about this period, "The Council of Economic Advisers . . . injected itself into the agricultural policy process only sporadically, primarily on issues relating to subsidy costs, and with limited success."[14]

However, there was continuing tension on food aid between the farm policy and the development policy communities. The former wanted to expand food aid ("move wheat") when domestic prices were down and stocks were ample. But since the United States played, reluctantly, the role of reserve-holder and grain-supplier for the world, times of easy availability in America tended to coincide with times of least need in developing countries. Expanding food aid under such circumstances tended to depress prices in recipient countries, reducing incentives for their farmers. Conversely, since food aid was restricted to what was available after regular commercial demand had been satisfied, times of shortage brought cutbacks in food aid, as in 1966, when wheat available for food aid was reduced even as India was experiencing its second successive bad harvest. To development advocates, this meant that food aid tended to have what one analyst called a procyclical impact on devel-

---

(2) press India to promise to purchase a certain amount of commercial grain from the United States; (3) get other developed countries to increase their food aid to India; and (4) express displeasure at Prime Minister Indira Gandhi's public statements about Vietnam, particularly her birthday greetings to Ho Chi Minh. For accounts from divergent American perspectives, see Chester Bowles, *Promises to Keep: My Years in Public Life 1941–1969* (Harper and Row, 1971), pp. 523–36, and Lyndon Baines Johnson, *The Vantage Point: Perspectives of the Presidency, 1963–1969* (Holt, Rinehart, and Winston, 1971), pp. 222–31.

13. Using 1967 = 1.00 as a base, the ratio between the consumer price index for food and the CPI for all other items was between 1.01 and 1.04 during 1955–58; it was 1.00 or lower in every year from then until 1973 except for 1966, when it was 1.02. The ratio jumped to 1.15 in early 1974. See Hathaway, "Food Prices and Inflation," table 1. In absolute terms, the food CPI rose slowly during this period: 81.6 in 1955, 88.0 in 1960, 94.4 in 1965, 114.9 in 1970, and 123.5 in 1972. It had shot up to 175.4 by 1975. See *Economic Report of the President, January 1976*, table B-42.

14. Hathaway, "Food Prices and Inflation," p. 64.

oping economies.[15] Grain producers, in turn, found that projected food aid markets often did not materialize.

In 1968, after the secretary of agriculture increased the national rice acreage allotment to a record 2.4 million primarily to meet the needs of Vietnam, those concerned with Vietnamese agricultural development sought to limit the rice shipped there to assure that Vietnamese farmers received high enough prices to encourage their adoption of modern rice varieties and crop practices. Similarly, the Public Law 480 "wheat market" in India was shrinking even as the record U.S. wheat crop of 1967, induced by supply management of the wheat program, was coming to harvest. Hence the grain producer got squeezed: carryover stocks rose and prices fell.[16] But notwithstanding such continuing tensions over how much and when food aid should be provided, both the farm and development communities found the supply-management/moderate-stocks regime of the sixties preferable to the huge surpluses of the fifties. To the farm community the surpluses meant depressed prices; to the development community they meant the too-easy availability of food for food aid and strong domestic pressure to move it notwithstanding its dampening effect on recipient countries' development programs.

Though commercial agricultural interests were paramount in U.S. food policy before 1973, agriculture's political base was both weakening and changing. Most important was the rapid decline in the farm population, from 25 percent of the total population in the early thirties, when farm commodity programs were inaugurated, to 15 percent in 1950, 9 percent in 1960, and below 5 percent in the seventies. Fewer farmers, plus congressional redistricting, meant reduced congressional support for farm commodity programs, particularly in the House of Representatives. "Rural districts comprised 83 percent of an absolute majority in the House in 1966; the percentage dropped to 71 by 1969, and to 60 by 1973."[17] Congressmen began to debate not simply the form and level of farm subsidies but their very existence. It was hard to defend farm pro-

15. Raymond F. Hopkins, "Global Food Management: U.S. Policymaking in an Interdependent World," in Robert O. Keohane and Joseph S. Nye, Jr., "The Management of Global Issues," *Murphy Commission Report*, vol. 1, app. B, p. 146. See chapter 1, note 1, for full reference.

16. The average per bushel wheat price received by farmers was $1.35 in 1965, $1.63 in 1966, and $1.39 in 1967. USDA, *Agricultural Statistics, 1975*, p. 1.

17. Weldon V. Barton, "Coalition-Building in the United States House of Representatives: Agricultural Legislation in 1973," in James E. Anderson, ed., *Cases in Public Policy-Making* (Praeger, 1976), p. 144.

grams on income redistribution grounds, as the bulk of the benefits went to the most prosperous producers. Particularly vulnerable were large direct payments to big commercial farm operators for their participation in supply adjustment programs for feed grains, wheat, and, above all, cotton, in which large production units were concentrated. As a result, a $55,000 ceiling on payments to an individual farmer from each commodity program was incorporated in the Agricultural Act of 1970. The ceiling was lowered to $20,000 in 1973.

As the overall political power of farm interests declined, divisions within the farm community increased. Willard W. Cochrane wrote in 1965:

> In the 1920s, the 1930s, and during part of the 1940s a recognizable farm bloc worked together reasonably well in the interests of *commercial* farmers in general. But this bloc no longer exists. . . . In fact, the antagonism among farm groups runs high in the 1960s; what we have now in the farm sector is not a bloc—it is more like a jungle.[18]

The American Farm Bureau Federation favored maximum movement toward a free market; the National Farmers Union supported strong government intervention and supply management. Farm commodity groups varied even more, ranging from tobacco and rice producers, who embraced rigid production controls, to cattlemen, who vehemently opposed controls (though they favored controls on imports). In between were growers of feed grains, cotton, and wheat—long the three leading U.S. field crops in value of product marketed.[19] These growers were the beneficiaries of the three principal commodity programs, and coalitions of congressmen from regions where these crops predominate provided the core of support for farm legislation.

While divisions were growing within the farm community during the postwar period, links were forming between farmers and the nonagricultural economy. "Once a distinct economic sector and a unique way of life, agriculture in the United States has become increasingly integrated into the industrial and service economies," a recent report concluded.[20] Farmers had become "vastly more dependent on industrial

18. Cochrane, *City Man's Guide*, pp. 140–41.

19. In the mid-sixties soybeans replaced cotton as one of the top three U.S. field crops in value of production. By 1974 the value of soybeans produced in the United States was nearly four times that of cotton. In fact, cotton acreage has declined precipitously since its peak in 1926, recently stabilizing at only a bit over one-fourth the acreage of that year. USDA, *Agricultural Statistics*, selected years.

20. Committee for Economic Development, Research and Policy Committee, "A New U.S. Farm Policy for Changing World Food Needs" (Washington, D.C.: CED, October 1974), p. 29.

products such as power equipment and agricultural chemicals than they were a few years ago"; and production had become "concentrated on fewer farms. . . . Large operations, run primarily by individuals whose principal occupation is farming, constitute less than 25 percent of all farms in the United States, but they regularly account for some 80 percent of all farm marketings."[21] And small farmers were increasingly earning their income elsewhere: "By 1971 almost two out of three farm families received more than half of their income from off-farm sources," and the lowest ranking 1.5 million farm families earned an average of $1,304 on the farm—and $7,723 off![22]

But the decline in the strength, unity, and separateness of the farm community did not cause federal commodity programs to be abandoned or to be reshaped to accommodate the demands of other societal groups. Farm bills remained farm bills, though the 1973 legislation was labeled the Agriculture and Consumer Protection Act. These bills were enacted by coalitions of farm congressmen and urban representatives responsive to organized labor; the votes of the latter were won in exchange for farm bloc support for bills labor favored—repealing states' right to enact "right to work" laws in 1965; expanding the food stamp program in the sixties and early seventies; increasing minimum wage levels in 1973.[23] These urban congressmen knew, presumably, that farm programs resulted in higher prices to urban consumers. But as long as food prices remained relatively stable, their constituents were not concerned. And the pre-1972 U.S. food policy regime did keep food prices stable, as already noted. The continued dominance of commercial agricultural interests meant, moreover, that it was difficult for a secretary of agriculture to broaden his role and the constituency of his department; nonfarm interests were not sufficiently active on food issues to provide a counterweight. Thus Orville Freeman was frustrated in several such efforts during his tenure (1961–69), including one to change the name of his domain to the Department of Food and Agriculture.[24]

Though ideologically much more sympathetic to a free market and minimum government management, the Nixon administration made only limited adjustments in farm and food policies during its first term.

21. Ibid., p. 30.
22. Johnson, *Farm Commodity Programs*, p. 15.
23. See Barton, "Coalition-Building"; and Weldon V. Barton, "Food, Agriculture, and Administrative Adaptation to Political Change," *Public Administration Review*, vol. 36 (March/April 1976), pp. 149–50. The analysis in this chapter draws upon Barton's studies at other points as well.
24. Barton, "Food, Agriculture, and Administrative Adaptation," p. 150.

The domestic food stamp program was expanded greatly, and the Agricultural Act of 1970 gave farmers more flexibility to shift from one crop to another; but the commodity programs and supply adjustment were maintained. And to most farm policymakers it appeared that the tendencies toward overproduction and surplus stocks were reasserting themselves strongly in the years after the world food crisis of 1965–67. The Green Revolution was increasing output of wheat and rice in Asia, and by some projections, developing countries with food deficits were expected to produce enough for export in the not-too-distant future. Wheat and corn prices remained low through 1971. And when shortages threatened, supply adjustment was effective in averting them—too effective, perhaps. In response to the corn blight of 1970, which had reduced expected production by 500 million bushels, the acreage diverted from feed grain crop production in 1971 was the lowest since 1960. The result was a corn crop 780 million bushels above previous records, dropping the average price from $1.33 to $1.08 a bushel—the lowest since 1967.[25]

In retrospect, it is clear that food supplies in early 1972 were not as ample as they seemed. The package of policies so acceptable to the four major communities concerned with international food policy had one glaring limitation: stock reduction in the United States was paralleled by similar policies in other major grain exporting countries, weakening American and world insurance against a major shift in the balance between food supply and food demand. Wheat stocks held by the United States and Canada had been 100 percent of average annual domestic and export demand in 1963, before the food crisis of 1965–67; in 1972 they stood at 70 percent.[26] In absolute numbers, however—and this was how officials tended to look at them—U.S. stocks seemed high. The carryover of wheat, 863 million bushels, had not been significantly higher since 1964.[27] The carryover of feed grains was 43.9 million metric tons, close to their highest since 1965 and well above the 1971 carryover of 30 million tons.[28] And another good crop was on the way.

25. USDA, *Agricultural Statistics, 1975*, pp. 30, 518; USDA, Statistical Reporting Service, Crop Reporting Board, *Agricultural Prices: Annual Summary, 1974* (USDA, June 1975), p. 12.

26. Fred H. Sanderson, "The Great Food Fumble," *Science* (May 9, 1975), pp. 505–06 (Brookings Reprint 303). See also Philip H. Trezise, *Rebuilding Grain Reserves: Toward an International System* (Brookings Institution, 1976), p. 1.

27. USDA, *Agricultural Statistics, 1975*, p. 4.

28. Hathaway, "Food Prices and Inflation," table 7.

These conditions of relative plenty existed despite a record 56.7 million acres diverted from grain crops.[29] Moreover, 1972 was an election year, and the Nixon administration was not the first to see the best route to the farmer's vote was through his pocketbook. So it is hardly surprising that farm policy officials pushed with particular force for the continuance of policies—export promotion and maximum acreage diversion—aimed at raising farm income. Moreover, in their promotion of exports they were fully in step with U.S. foreign policy. For President Nixon and his national security assistant, Henry Kissinger, were moving to use food sales to Russia as an instrument in the policy which was to be labeled détente.

29. USDA, *Agricultural Statistics, 1975,* p. 518.

CHAPTER THREE

The Russian Wheat Purchases, 1972

In the 1970s, U.S. food policymakers moved into a situation dramatically different from any they had experienced. Between June 1972 and October 1974, the average price farmers received for corn tripled and for wheat nearly quadrupled. Agricultural exports rose from a then-record $8 billion in fiscal year 1972 to over $20 billion in fiscal year 1974, and remained at this high level in 1975 and 1976. Net farm income, which had fluctuated between $10 billion and $14 billion since the late forties, jumped to $19 billion in calendar year 1972 and $33 billion in 1973, dropping back then to $27 billion in 1974 and $26 billion in 1975. Programs to divert grain acreage were suspended; farmers were planting from fence to fence and realizing record income and exports in the process.

The prime goals of the farm policy community were being met, more fully than its members believed possible when 1972 began. But the fulfillment of these goals inevitably involved damage to other goals—price stability at home and the ability to respond to food emergencies abroad. And as food became, suddenly, a scarce resource, American policymakers had to cope with particularly difficult trade-offs among farm, economic, foreign, and development policy values.

Four issues punctuated food policy decisionmaking in the 1972–75 period: (1) sales of wheat to Russia in 1972, 1974, and 1975; (2) export controls (imposed dramatically on soybeans in June 1973); (3) food aid amounts and allocations, which came to a head in 1974; and (4) international food reserves. Each arose in unfamiliar economic and political form, and on each the U.S. government performed at less than its best. And by 1976 the extremely tight market conditions which made them so difficult had receded. Nonetheless, analysis of how they were handled offers information relevant to management of future food issues. This chapter treats the Russian grain sales of 1972; the chapters that follow address the subsequent issues.[1]

Background

In the summer of 1972, the Nixon administration pursued food policies that seem almost calculated to fuel the price inflation that followed. Massive wheat sales were encouraged both through direct intergovernmental negotiations and through export subsidies. And even after the magnitude of the Russian purchases was known, the administration persevered with a wheat program aimed at reducing production in 1973, a program developed before it was known that Russia would buy one-fourth of the 1972 crop.

In the preceding thirteen months the Nixon administration took a series of actions to facilitate trade with the Soviet Union. On June 10, 1971, the White House announced that the president had "decided to terminate the need to obtain Department of Commerce permission for the export of wheat, flour and other grains, to China, Eastern Europe, and the Soviet Union,"[2] and to suspend the requirement that 50 percent of grain sold to these countries be carried in U.S. ships. Thus grain companies were free to deal directly with Soviet trade representatives, without specific government sanction, and in the fall of 1971 they contracted substantial feed grain sales, the first to Russia since 1963.[3] In the first six

1. This chapter draws upon a wide range of public sources, particularly Dale E. Hathaway, "Food Prices and Inflation," *Brookings Papers on Economic Activity*, 1:1974, pp. 63–116 (hereafter *BPEA*); John A. Schnittker, "The 1972–73 Food Price Spiral," *BPEA*, 2:1973, pp. 498–507; James Trager, *The Great Grain Robbery*, Ballantine Books, 1975; General Accounting Office, *Russian Wheat Sales and Weaknesses in Agriculture's Management of Wheat Export Subsidy Program*, Report to the Congress (Government Printing Office, 1973); *Sale of Wheat to Russia*, Hearings before the Subcommittee on Livestock and Grains of the House Committee on Agriculture, 92 Cong. 2 sess. (GPO, 1972); *Russian Grain Transactions*, Hearings before the Permanent Subcommittee on Investigations of the Senate Committee on Governmental Operations, 93 Cong. 1 sess. (GPO, 1973); and *Russian Grain Transactions*, S. Rept. 93-1033, 93 Cong. 2 sess. (GPO, 1974). These and other sources are specifically cited in the text where appropriate.

2. "Trade with the People's Republic of China," June 10, 1971, *Weekly Compilation of Presidential Documents*, vol. 7 (June 14, 1971), p. 891.

3. Feed grains include corn, sorghum, barley, and oats. They exclude, of course, grains like wheat and rice that are primarily for human consumption.

months of 1972, the administration encouraged further sales by negotiating a Commodity Credit Corporation (CCC) financing agreement.
On July 8, 1972, President Nixon announced the result: the CCC would
supply credit and the Soviet Union would purchase a minimum of $750
million in grain over the next three years.

Agriculture Department officials—including Secretary Earl L. Butz—
were convinced the Russians' main interest was corn for livestock. So it
was hardly inconsistent that, one week after completing the credit agreement, USDA announced a program to reduce wheat production for
the coming year (by setting aside 25 million acres, compared to 20 million in 1972).[4] In fact, however, on July 5, 1972, three days before the
credit announcement, Soviet buyers had quietly contracted with the
Continental Grain Company to supply them 4 million tons (147 million
bushels) of wheat as well as 4.5 million tons (177 million bushels) of
corn.[5] And they made this purchase not on credit but for cash. Over the
next month, as information about this sale leaked out, the Soviets purchased an additional 7.8 million tons (286 million bushels) of U.S.
wheat from Continental and five other grain companies. They also purchased about 2 million additional tons of feed grains and 1 million tons
of soybeans.[6]

The total amounts of these sales were several times what anyone had
expected. The 433 million bushels of wheat, for example, equaled about
half of U.S. carryover stocks on July 1, 1972, and a bit over a quarter of
1972 production. The bulk of wheat sold was to be shipped before the
1973 crop was in. The Soviets also made substantial wheat purchases
from Canada, and poor crops in other major exporting countries meant
that little additional wheat was available there. By sometime in August
1972 the evidence was overwhelming that the world wheat market had
become, at least temporarily, a seller's market. But U.S. policies did not
adjust. Officials were apparently slow in learning of the size of the sales
and slower in grasping their market significance. Even after it became
evident that the sales were driving up the world price, U.S. export subsidies were maintained. And most important, U.S. officials failed to take
the obvious step, with which everyone seemingly should have agreed—
encouraging maximum production of wheat (and feed grains) in 1973.

4. Schnittker, "The 1972–73 Food Price Spiral," p. 503.
5. *Russian Grain Transactions*, S. Rept. 93-1033, p. 67.
6. Ibid.

The Failure to Know

Secretary of Agriculture Earl L. Butz later wrote to Senator Henry Jackson that he and his assistant secretary, Carroll G. Brunthaver, did not know until September 19 the "dimensions of the July 5, 1972, sale" by Continental Grain Company.[7] It seems likely that they knew at least the general magnitude of the Russian purchases somewhat earlier; contemporary public sources support John Schnittker's assertion that "it was clear by August," or at least the end of August, "that wheat exports would exceed 1,100 million bushels," compared to the 650 million projected in July 1972.[8] Nevertheless, it is surprising that a department which had devoted so much energy to export promotion in general, and sales to Russia in particular, a department with perhaps the world's best system for monitoring grain production and trade, had not taken steps to ensure that it immediately learn of exports that vast. In subsequent years, it did take such steps. But in 1972, it did not see a need for close monitoring of commercial export contracts, and no system was in place to accomplish it.

The principal reason, perhaps, was that there had never before been any single commercial wheat export sale—or group of related sales—large enough to disrupt the domestic market. Commercial wheat exports had been stagnant for many years and had never exceeded 401 million bushels worldwide. And should the department become concerned about wheat stock levels—as it did in 1966 and 1967—it had a ready vehicle for adjustment: it could tighten Public Law 480 exports, which had exceeded commercial wheat sales almost every year since the program began.[9]

If past American export experience offered no precedent for July

7. Letter of October 2, 1973, cited in ibid., p. 40. The GAO reports that "officials told us in September 1972 they were still unaware of the magnitude of sales made by the trade." GAO, *Russian Wheat Sales*, p. 25.

8. Schnittker, "The 1972–73 Food Price Spiral," p. 503; GAO, *Russian Wheat Sales*, p. 3.

9. As Deputy Assistant Secretary of Agriculture Richard E. Bell told a Senate subcommittee a year later, "We have not had a system of keeping track of weekly sales of exports, basically, because we were the granary of the world and we always had large carryovers and large supplies available for export." *Export Control Policy,* Hearings before the Subcommittee on Foreign Agricultural Policy of the Senate Committee on Agriculture and Forestry, 93 Cong. 1 sess. (GPO, 1973), p. 49.

1972, neither did Soviet import experience. Department of Agriculture officials knew that Russia had a short crop, perhaps a very short one.[10] But this had happened before, without generating large-scale purchases. As Lyle P. Schertz notes:

Traditionally, when the Soviets came up short on production, they steeled themselves to wait out the shortage, sometimes to the point of accepting large-scale livestock slaughter. But not in 1972. . . . Instead of tightening their belts, they made massive grain purchases on the world market. With the aid of these imports, the pace of their livestock development effort continued unabated.[11]

And U.S. grain companies were apparently also caught by surprise, for there was no prior buildup of their grain holdings, and five out of the six had a short position in futures markets in the June–September 1972 period.[12]

Past experience, therefore, suggested no urgent government "need to know" about specific wheat export sales; and the lifting of the requirement for prior clearance by the Commerce Department on sales to Communist countries (a clearance imposed for foreign, not food, policy reasons) removed one procedure through which the government would have learned of the contracts as they were signed, beginning in early July. Thus these most unusual sales proceeded by business-as-usual methods: grain companies kept their dealings secret, particularly from one another, as they competed for Soviet business and moved to acquire in the marketplace sufficient grain to cover their Soviet commitments.

There was one way the Department of Agriculture might have learned about the sales—through the wheat export subsidy program. Although grain companies could delay registering until after contracts were firm,[13] and did so with the Soviet sales, they could hardly commit themselves to massive sales at the current world price until they were confident the wheat subsidy would be maintained at a rate sufficient to

10. See GAO, *Russian Wheat Sales*, pp. 19–20 and *Russian Grain Transactions*, Hearings.

11. "World Food: Prices and the Poor," *Foreign Affairs*, vol. 52 (April 1974), p. 514.

12. GAO, *Russian Wheat Sales*, p. 14; *Russian Grain Transactions*, S. Rept. 93-1033, p. 43.

13. Actual payment of the subsidy awaited evidence that the requisite amount of wheat had actually been exported. But the subsidy paid was based on the rate on the day of registration, not on the actual export sale price or the domestic price when the sale was made.

protect them when they bought the wheat to meet the commitments. For once they began to buy, the price would rise. And USDA had the administrative authority to change the subsidy rate.

Thus on July 3, 1972, Bernard Steinweg, senior vice president of the Continental Grain Co., asked Assistant Secretary Brunthaver if the subsidy would be maintained and apparently indicated that he was inquiring because of prospective sales to the Soviet Union. Brunthaver, who had only been in office for about a week, did not ask about the magnitude of the sales, and whatever specific information he did receive he neither passed on nor assimilated in terms of its policy implications.[14] He did, however, assure Steinweg that the subsidy definitely would be maintained.

The Continuation of the Subsidy

Why were these wheat exports subsidized after they began to drive up the domestic and world prices of wheat? And why did the U.S. government subsidize sales that stabilized the Russian food economy and destabilized its own?

After the farm program reforms of the 1960s brought the support price for wheat to a level near the world price, an export subsidy program was devised to bridge any remaining gap. In the spring of 1972, this subsidy ranged between 1 cent and 16 cents a bushel. On July 3, 1972, the subsidy for hard red winter wheat was 5 cents a bushel. The Department of Agriculture calculated it by subtracting an administratively determined export target price ($1.6325) from the domestic price ($1.6825).[15] In theory, the target price is based on the world price (the target price cited above was "based on the price of competing Canadian

14. The *Russian Grain Transactions* hearings, chaired by Henry Jackson, featured an unresolved conflict in testimony about this meeting—Steinweg said he told Brunthaver the specific, very large amounts the Russians were interested in buying. Brunthaver did not recall being told specific tonnages but that from the general information he was given he "equated" the sales "to be somewheres near the $200 million that was the minimum spelled out in the [July 8 credit] agreement that we were in the process of negotiating and I didn't think anything further of it." *Russian Grain Transactions*, Hearings, p. 100; see also *Russian Grain Transactions*, S. Rept. 93-1033, pp. 33 ff.

15. GAO, *Russian Wheat Sales*, pp. 22, 15–17.

wheat adjusted for quality and freight differentials").[16] But since U.S. exports were a substantial portion of world wheat trade, once the subsidy rate was set, it also influenced the world price in a downward direction.

In mid-1972, USDA officials realized that the world wheat market was growing tight. But they wanted to keep prices down; years of stagnant wheat markets had convinced them that higher world prices could not be sustained, that they eventually would "bring about increased world wheat production, with a resultant glut and future lower prices."[17] Thus USDA held to a target price of around $1.63, even as world demand—specifically, the purchases by the grain companies to meet their Soviet commitments—drove the domestic price up and therefore increased the per-bushel subsidy to 38 cents by late August.

Based on an administratively determined world price with no longer any market basis, the subsidy became totally perverse, limiting U.S. returns from the sales and costing the U.S. treasury over $300 million in wheat subsidies in fiscal 1973 (compared to the $67 million budgeted).[18] And to the degree that the low target price increased the volume of Russian purchases, the subsidy increased inflation in the United States.

When the costs of the subsidy program became evident, the Office of Management and Budget called a series of meetings beginning August 9 with representatives of the Department of Agriculture, the Council of Economic Advisers, and the Council on International Economic Policy. On August 25 a decision was reached to begin immediate reduction of the subsidy, phasing it out over the next month. But the grain companies were given a week's grace period to register under the old rules for whatever subsidies they still required to meet their export contracts. During that August week, the subsidy reached 47 cents a bushel. By September 25, the delivered price of wheat to U.S. ports rose to $2.40.[19]

The subsidy engaged OMB in its area of prime responsibility, budget costs. It posed a clear and immediate problem—a large, rapid, unex-

16. Ibid., p. 17.
17. Ibid., p. 23.
18. Ibid., pp. 14–15.
19. *Russian Grain Transactions*, S. Rept. 93-1033, pp. 31–32; GAO, *Russian Wheat Sales*, pp. 16, 26.

pected outflow of funds, which had to be stanched. Reasonably quick action resulted once the issue was raised. The action the U.S. government did not take, however, was probably far more important: it failed to lift acreage restrictions for the 1973 winter wheat crop.

The Failure to Expand Acreage

In the years after 1972, Secretary of Agriculture Earl Butz would take credit for agricultural abundance that came during his tenure. After years of being "afraid to live with plenty," he said, the United States had moved to "full production" under his regime.[20] In fact, Secretary Butz had to be pushed into the lifting of acreage controls that he later embraced and applauded. In the wheat commodity program his department had a tool for expanding production in 1973 to offset the drains on stocks brought about by the Russian sales of 1972. And the lifting of acreage restraints would have been a step in the free market direction, to which Butz—and other administration officials—were committed. But USDA did not expand wheat acreage that fall, and as late as December Butz was announcing a restrictive feed-grains program. Only in 1973 did he reverse himself—and only when ordered by the White House.[21]

In supply management terms, the 1973 wheat program announced on July 17, 1972, was sensible enough based on information then available. Stocks were high; prices at the farm level were low by recent standards and not discernibly rising. Projected exports of 650 million bushels, while above the average of recent years, were insufficient to cause any fundamental changes. It was consistent with the logic of supply management to increase acreage diversion a bit, and the goal was raised from 20 million to 25 million acres. Increased diversion was also consistent with the election-year goal of getting farm prices up, something that Butz almost certainly saw as his overriding presidential man-

20. The quotations are from his article, "An Emerging, Market-Oriented Food and Agricultural Policy," *Public Administration Review,* vol. 36 (March/April 1976), p. 138.

21. As Treasury Secretary George Shultz described it later, the Cost of Living Council argued strongly in 1972 "that we should expand the supplies of our agricultural products. . . . The Secretary of Agriculture *came to accept that point of view,* and became an advocate of it." Interview in *Washington Post,* April 14, 1974. Emphasis added.

date. But barely had the program been issued than the Russian sales rendered its assumptions obsolete.

Department of Agriculture officials regularly reported the new export developments. As early as July 31, 1972, the quarterly report, *Wheat Situation,* concluded that exports "could rise around a fourth from the 632 million bushels in 1971/72 in light of Soviet purchases" and other developments, "resulting in a moderate reduction in carryover at the end of the 1972/73 season."[22] On September 14, Secretary Butz told the House Agriculture Committee that 1972–73 wheat exports would "equal or exceed a billion bushels—by far the largest total in our history."[23] In November *Wheat Situation* was predicting that by June 1973 carryover stocks would be "the least since 1967," a remarkable turnaround from the July 1972 depiction of "abundant supplies of all major wheat classes."[24]

But insofar as action was concerned, caution was the byword. On August 14, 1972, department officials were quoted as planning "no immediate modification" of wheat acreage goals despite "trade reports" of 400 million bushels in sales to Russia.[25] In a speech ten days later, Brunthaver warned, "We must be careful that we do not overreact to the sudden spurt in overseas demand, as I suspect we did overreact in 1966–67."[26] On September 14, Butz told the House Agriculture Committee the Soviet purchases "will mean less onerous planting restrictions on our farmers as they produce for an expanded market."[27] But he used the future tense.

Why this reluctance to move immediately toward the desired free market? Officials could not have foreseen the dimensions of the 1972–75 market transformation, but they didn't need to; they only needed to know that 1972–73 stock drawdowns would be several hundred million bushels greater than they had projected when they had increased wheat acreage diversion. Reviewing government performance a year later, John A. Schnittker, under secretary of agriculture in the Johnson administration, could find "no economic basis . . . for the failure to change the

22. U.S. Department of Agriculture, *Wheat Situation: August 1972* (USDA, 1972), p. 3.

23. *Sale of Wheat to Russia,* Hearings, p. 9.

24. USDA *Wheat Situation: November 1972,* p. 3; *Wheat Situation: August 1972,* p. 3.

25. *New York Times,* August 14, 1972.

26. Reprinted in *Sale of Wheat to Russia,* Hearings, p. 71.

27. Ibid., p. 10.

wheat program by September 1."[28] This would have been in time for winter wheat plantings in most of the major producing areas.[29]

One contributing factor to the failure to change policy was that the Butz regime was less inclined toward aggressive short-term adjustment of farm programs for supply management purposes than the Orville Freeman–John Schnittker department had been. Another explanation for the failure is that it is more difficult to revise a program after it is announced than when it is still on the drawing board. There are equity reasons for sticking to declared guidelines. Farmers make their planting calculations on the basis of these guidelines, and the purchases and investments they need to implement them. Changing a program in midstream puts them at a disadvantage, particularly those with relatively early planting dates. There are also bureaucratic obstacles to reversing a decision. Until a program is put into final form and announced it is current business and subject to argument and evidence from those with access to the process—economic as well as Agriculture officials in this case. But to change the wheat program after July 17, 1972, required reopening the matter, reestablishing it on the decisionmaking agenda, a considerably more difficult task. The implementing agency is in a strong position to resist such a reopening, especially when it generates the data upon which the decision to reopen depends.

Why didn't the Department of Agriculture reopen the issue itself? Beyond reasons of equity and distaste for aggressive supply management, was USDA's goal of increasing farm prices. (Secretary Butz was particularly vocal and single-minded on this objective, but his predecessors also saw commercial agriculture as their primary constituency and its interests as their primary concern.) The farm community would suffer far more from a glut than a shortage—indeed, it would profit from a shortage. And Butz gave priority to higher farm prices, not implementing his free market convictions through acreage expansion (which would sabotage the first goal if the 1972–73 season for wheat turned out like 1970–71 had for corn). If he had any doubts, commodity interests, burned by the acreage expansions of 1967 and 1971, were more than

28. Schnittker, "1972–73 Food Price Spiral," p. 503.

29. Winter wheat planting in Washington, the third largest producing state, begins as early as August 15 (though it continues to November 20). But in Kansas (by far the largest producer) and Oklahoma (the second largest), winter wheat seeding does not begin until September. USDA, Statistical Reporting Service, Crop Reporting Board, Usual Planting and Harvesting Dates, rev. ed., Agriculture Handbook no. 283 (GPO, 1972).

ready to warn him against "overreaction." Thus when the Price Commission, established by President Nixon to administer phase 2 of his
anti-inflation program, pressed for acreage increases, it found itself re-
buffed. In the words of three of its members, the commission "tried hard
from February through the early summer of 1972 to impress on Agriculture the importance of reevaluating agricultural policy, especially
the acreage set-aside program. It received in return the impression that
departmental policy was directed instead toward raising farm income
and that, if higher food prices were the result, this was the commission's
problem."[30]

An Agriculture Department leader sensitive to food as well as farm
policy concerns, or more committed to supply adjustment, might have
reacted differently in August or September 1972; but given the Butz
regime, pressure to change the wheat program would have to have come
from elsewhere. The development community was one possible source
of such pressure, since developing countries would suffer if shortages
drove world prices up and the amount of food available for food aid
down—which in fact they were to do. But this group was seldom able to
affect acreage decisions, even at a time like the 1965–67 period, when a
major cause of stock drawdowns was expanded food aid to India.

One might have expected effective advocacy for a change in farm
policy from the economic policy officials. They had an established role
in grain acreage decisions. They had major stakes in holding prices
down. And the administration was in fact pursuing a major anti-inflation
program. The Price Commission was a very weak policy actor, whose
admonitions on food prices sometimes embarrassed the White House
by dramatizing the problem in an election year.[31] As a result, "the commission in effect was instructed to take no further action on food."[32] But
there were senior economic policy officials who were much stronger.
Had Treasury Secretary George P. Shultz, CEA Chairman Herbert
Stein, or Cost of Living Council Director Donald Rumsfeld[33] pressed the
issue, a reversal might have been possible. The reversal would have had

30. Robert F. Lanzillotti, Mary T. Hamilton, and R. Blaine Roberts, *Phase II in
Review: The Price Commission Experience* (Brookings Institution, 1975), p. 65.
31. Although grain prices were relatively flat until August 1972, livestock prices
rose rather sharply in 1971 and early 1972, and the Price Commission saw increased
feed grain production as one means of countering this.
32. Lanzillotti and others, *Phase II in Review*, p. 63.
33. Rumsfeld was apparently the individual responsible for squelching the
Price Commission.

the very anti-inflation result—an increase in supplies—that economists, liberal and conservative alike, applaud.

But though some effort was apparently made,[34] there is no evidence that any of these economic officials pushed the matter with real force when it could have affected winter wheat plantings. Apparently they were neither sufficiently sensitive to the problem nor very informed on its specifics.[35] After neglecting agricultural issues for years the economic policy community simply was not alert to its stakes in the maintenance of reasonable grain stocks as a foundation for stable food prices. And unlike the subsidy costs, which were skyrocketing dramatically, the failure to encourage maximum planting of wheat in 1973 was not generating an immediate policy crisis susceptible to immediate government action. The main costs were in the future and were therefore subject to dispute. Moreover, the two issues overlapped in time; some of the officials who should have been pushing for higher wheat acreage in August were scrapping over the subsidy instead.

Finally, an all-out effort by economic officials to overturn Butz's wheat program would have meant bringing the issue to the president in the middle of the election campaign. There is no reason to doubt that, for Richard Nixon that summer, farm policy was important mainly for its connection to farm votes. And that meant higher farm prices. Lifting wheat acreage restrictions would have dampened prices before the election, but the inflationary effects of not lifting them would not be felt until well after November 7.

It was when the economy was burned—and the economists felt the heat—that USDA policies were finally changed. In early January 1973, just as the president was preparing to jettison his phase 2 price control program and replace it with a far looser monitoring regime, the news

34. According to one published report, "The Cost of Living Council staff, and later its chairman, George Shultz, tried in September to get Butz to open up the 1973 wheat acreage because of the Russian grain deal. Butz, still confident the supplies would last, refused and made it stick." Joseph Albright, "Some Deal," *New York Times Magazine*, November 25, 1973, p. 98. See also Shultz's interview, *Washington Post*, April 14, 1974.

35. Personnel shifts may have contributed to this, just as the June change in assistant secretaries of agriculture was a factor in how USDA dealt (or misdealt) with the grain companies. As the issue was breaking, the CEA's staff agricultural economist was new to his job and to government; his predecessor (future CEA member Gary Seevers) was on leave when the wheat program was made final, then returned to a job (assistant to Chairman Stein) which took him largely out of agricultural issues for the next six months.

came that the wholesale price index for food had jumped 6 percent in the preceding month.[36] The causes, of course, went beyond the scarcity of grain, but the need to do something about grain supply was clear. In a matter of hours the Council of Economic Advisers produced a memo listing steps to ease the food price situation; these were discussed and agreed upon in a meeting the president held with his senior economic advisers but without the secretary of agriculture.

These steps included easing of acreage restrictions on grain. Secretary Butz, thus presented with a fait accompli, went along with the decisions, with minor reservations. On January 10, 1973, one day before President Nixon announced the abandonment of phase 2, the Department of Agriculture announced a number of production-expanding steps, including bringing back into production nearly 15 million wheat acres. It was too late to expand the winter wheat crop, but the shift was made in time to affect spring wheat plantings. Later that month the restrictive feed-grains program, announced in December 1972, was amended to expand acreage.[37]

The virulent food price inflation should not, of course, be blamed solely on the Soviet wheat purchases. Grain production in 1972 declined worldwide by 35 million tons, compared to an average annual *increase* of 36 million tons between 1961 and 1973. Moreover, despite an increase of 89 million tons in the 1973 world grain crop, the tight market continued, because world demand also rose rapidly, particularly in the developing countries and the People's Republic of China.[38]

Still, the Soviet purchases appear to have been the major destabilizing influence in the world grain trade during 1972–73.[39] And even if other causes deserve more prominence than they have been given here, the point remains that the U.S. government had in the wheat program an important, obvious, available policy tool for muting the sales' inflationary impact. It failed to use this tool.

How much difference would it have made if wheat acreage limitations had been eliminated by September 1, 1972? Interestingly, no post mortem research either inside or outside Agriculture addresses this

36. *Economic Report of the President, January 1973*, p. 248.

37. Interviews; *New York Times*, January 11, 1973; Schnittker, "The 1972–73 Food Price Spiral," p. 503.

38. USDA, Economic Research Service, *The World Food Situation and Prospects to 1985*, Foreign Agriculture Economic Report 98 (USDA, 1974), pp. 2–3.

39. Fred H. Sanderson, "The Great Food Fumble," *Science* (May 9, 1975), p. 504 (Brookings Reprint 303). For an interpretation giving greater emphasis to other factors, see Hathaway, "Food Prices and Inflation."

issue, although studies on the wheat sales themselves and the export subsidy program are legion. By the crudest calculation—multiplying the 7.4 million acres actually set aside in the 1973 program by the average 1973 yield of 31.7 bushels an acre—the additional wheat would have been about 230 million bushels. But diverted acres were, on the average, less productive than those already in use, and not all of them would have been brought into production.[40] Moreover, farmers respond to more than just wheat program guidelines in determining how much wheat to plant and how much to harvest; despite the increased diversion goal, the acres of winter wheat harvested rose from 34.8 million in 1972 to 38.5 million in 1973, presumably responding to the rise in wheat prices.[41] But in 1974, the first year with no acreage controls, 47.1 million winter wheat acres were harvested. Certainly even had the controls come off a year earlier, less than this would have been harvested in 1973: prices were not nearly so high at planting time as they were in 1974, and farmers in any event cannot bring all the acreage they want into production immediately because additional acreage requires, usually, additional investments. But if, to take a middle estimate, 5 million extra acres of winter wheat had been harvested, with an average yield of 25 bushels an acre, the 125 million additional bushels of wheat would have reduced that summer's sharp price rise.[42]

40. The 1975 Annual Report of the Council of Economic Advisers points to an "illusory land reserve," noting that "crop acreage rose by only 37 million acres between 1972 and 1974, even though about 60 million acres were released from acreage controls." *Economic Report of the President, February 1975*, p. 169.

41. Winter wheat plantings the previous fall rose also, but much less—from 42.1 million to 43.2 million acres.

42. The January 1973 program change may have generated an increase in planted *spring* wheat acreage of about 1.1 million. USDA reported planting intentions of 14.6 million acres as of January 1. *Wheat Situation: February 1973*, p. 7. Ultimately 15.7 million acres were planted. USDA, *Agricultural Statistics, 1975* (GPO, 1975), p. 2.

In one of the most careful and conservative efforts to estimate the relationship between diversion programs and actual planted acreage, D. Gale Johnson concludes that "in the period from 1966 through 1970, an increase in diversion in the wheat and feed grain programs was associated with a change of about half to three fourths as large in the seeded area." Farm program changes "that became effective in 1971 may have reduced the effectiveness of diversion in influencing the area devoted to the major grains." But, he adds, "these were changes at the margin, which tell us little or nothing about the effect of the first 20 million acres of diversion upon planted area." *Farm Commodity Programs: An Opportunity for Change* (American Enterprise Institute for Public Policy Research, 1973), p. 35. Still, the rough estimate of five million added harvested acres suggested here is within the range that his analysis suggests.

CHAPTER FOUR

The Soybean Embargo, 1973

THE MISTAKES OF 1972 contributed to the most dramatic food policy decision of 1973—the temporary embargo placed on soybean exports in June.[1] Like the grain sales decisions of 1972, this decision also involved conflicts among policy objectives, but the reason they were resolved as they were is more complicated. An administration that had stressed farm and foreign policy in 1972 now took an action very damaging to both—and so contrary to its free-market economic principles that George P. Shultz, the president's economic czar, felt moved to offer to resign.

Background

The food price inflation that had exploded in December 1972 continued through most of 1973. The wholesale price index for farm products shot up from 132.6 in December 1972 to 184.5 the following August, before settling back to 168.0 in December 1973. The consumer price rise was only slightly less spectacular: food jumped from 126.0 at the close of 1972 to 149.4 in August and 151.3 in December 1973.[2] And the export demand largely responsible for this inflation was to rise further in 1973–74, with increased purchases by China, Japan, Western Europe,

1. This chapter draws particularly on contemporary accounts and interviews, and on two secondary sources: Edward F. Graziano, "Commodity Export Controls: The Soybean Case, 1973," in Griffenhagen-Kroeger, "Cases on a Decade of U.S. Foreign Economic Policy: 1965–74," *Murphy Commission Report*, vol. 3, app. H (Government Printing Office, 1976), pp. 18–32 (see chap. 1, note 1, for full reference); and General Accounting Office, "U.S. Action Needed to Cope with Commodity Shortages," report to the Congress (GAO, April 1974).

2. *Economic Report of the President, February 1974*, pp. 305, 300.

and the developing countries more than offsetting an 18-million-ton decline in total imports by the Soviet Union and Eastern Europe.[3]

Particularly tight was the market for oilseeds and protein meals, caused by a combination of increased world demand and reduced supply from other countries.[4] Foreign buyers had turned to soybeans to make up for deficits in other foods. And because the United States dominated the world soybean market—producing over 70 percent of the total world crop and supplying the bulk of world exports[5]—some countries' dependence on the United States was almost total. Japan relied on imports for 97 percent of its considerable use of soybeans for food and feed; 92 percent of these imports came from the United States.[6]

Soybeans had become the postwar miracle crop for U.S. farmers, who had responded to the steady increase in domestic and world demand by increasing soybean output from 299 million bushels in 1950 to 555 million in 1960 and a record 1,271 million in 1972. But soybean carryover stocks had always been low compared to those for wheat, and they had been declining—in September 1972 they were just 72 million bushels. As exports moved toward a record 479 million bushels (the previous high was 434 million in 1970),[7] U.S. livestock producers felt increasing cost pressure. For as the price received by American soybean farmers rose— from $3.32 a bushel in June 1972 to $3.95 in December and $10.00 in June 1973—so did the cost of soybean meal—from $6.23 per 100 pounds to $8.67 to $18.70.[8] So meat prices were high and rising, and housewives

3. Fred H. Sanderson, "The Great Food Fumble," *Science* (May 9, 1975), p. 504 (Brookings Reprint 303); U.S. Department of Agriculture, Economic Research Service, *The World Food Situation and Prospects to 1985,* Foreign Agriculture Economic Report 98 (USDA, 1974), pp. 3–4.

4. As Secretary of Agriculture Earl L. Butz told the General Accounting Office, "Exports of Peruvian fishmeal and Indian and Senegalese peanut meal declined by the equivalent of 145 million bushels of soybeans, only 25 million bushels of which was offset by an increase in Brazilian soybean export availabilities. World import demand increased by the equivalent of 105 million bushels, made up of 40 million bushels in the Soviet Union and 65 million bushels among traditional suppliers." GAO, "U.S. Action Needed to Cope with Commodity Shortages," p. 186.

5. USDA, *Agricultural Statistics, 1975* (GPO, 1975), p. 133.

6. Statement by David J. Steinberg, executive director, Committee for a National Trade Policy, in *Export Control Policy,* Hearings before the Subcommittee on Foreign Agricultural Policy of the Senate Committee on Agriculture and Forestry, 93 Cong. 1 sess. (GPO, 1973), p. 224.

7. USDA, *Agricultural Statistics, 1967* (GPO, 1967), p. 166; USDA, *Agricultural Statistics, 1975,* p. 129.

8. USDA, Statistical Reporting Service, Crop Reporting Board, *Agricultural Prices: Annual Summary, 1974* (USDA, June 1975), pp. 18, 149.

were organizing meat boycotts amid vehement concern about skyrocketing food costs.

For President Nixon, who had dramatically lifted most price controls in January, food price inflation was a policy crisis and a major political embarrassment. So it was, also, for Shultz, who had strongly favored the easing of controls. Pressure for action mounted on Capitol Hill—in April the Senate narrowly defeated a bill providing an across-the-board price freeze, and on June 4 the Senate Democratic caucus called for a ninety-day freeze on prices, wages and salaries, profits, rents, and consumer interest rates.[9] But it was not at all clear how effective renewed price regulation would be in the now-booming economy, and the agricultural sector was particularly difficult to bring under control.

One obvious possible short-term expedient was to protect domestic supplies by limiting exports, an approach viewed with sympathy by Cost of Living Council Executive Director John Dunlop though opposed by other senior economic policy advisers, including Shultz and Secretary of Agriculture Earl Butz. So when Nixon responded to the economic crisis (and to his larger, Watergate-related, political crisis) by ordering on June 13 a sixty-day freeze on all prices except those of raw agricultural products, economic logic dictated some action against the danger that export demand would continue to bid up the prices of these products and squeeze U.S. livestock producers. The president declared therefore that "a new system for export controls" was needed to hold down "the price of animal feedstuffs and other grains in the American market."[10] Two weeks later, on June 27, Secretary of Commerce Frederick B. Dent declared a complete, temporary embargo on U.S. exports of soybeans, cottonseeds, and the products thereof.

This was, according to press reports, the first time the United States had imposed such an embargo except in war or threat of war. And though it proved short-lived, it had a serious negative impact on farm and foreign policy by calling into question the dependability of the United States as a world supplier of farm products and (because prior international consultation had been minimal) by raising serious doubts in Europe and Japan about whether American economic policy would take account of their needs when crises arose. In Tokyo the "soybean shock" took its place alongside the "Nixon shocks" of 1971, when the

9. *Congressional Quarterly,* June 16, 1973, p. 1484.
10. "Address to the Nation Announcing Price Control Measures, June 13, 1973," *Public Papers of the Presidents: Richard Nixon, 1973* (GPO, 1975), p. 586.

United States had, within thirty-one days, announced a presidential visit to China and unveiled a tough new international economic policy without advance consultation with the deeply affected Japanese government.

And the crowning irony was that subsequent evidence made export controls appear totally unnecessary. Once the embargo was imposed, it became clear that much of the apparent export demand was speculative. On August 1, 1973, the Commerce Department announced that it would license the export of up to 100 percent of the soybeans contracted for before June 13, though it retained tighter restrictions on oil cake and meal; the following month, as the harvest of the record U.S. 1973 soybean crop began, controls were effectively lifted.[11] Major importers ended up getting the soybeans they needed, and U.S. exports from the 1973 crop topped the record set for 1972. And the domestic supply crisis receded. Prices dropped to well under the June peak of $12.90 a bushel, though they remained high by historic standards.

Why then was the embargo imposed? Three questions in fact require answers. Why did the administration not know the actual export demand for soybeans, when the crisis had been building for months? Why did it choose export restraint? And why such extreme restraint—first a total embargo, then a ceiling on private export contracts allowing delivery of only 50 percent of what they provided?

The Failure to Know

In an editorial of July 2, 1973, *The Washington Post* labeled the embargo "a staggering confession of incompetence." The "lesson" of the Russian sale, it argued, was "that a prudent and competent government does not voluntarily leave itself in total ignorance regarding the sales of its crops to foreign buyers." But, it added, "having sat on its hands last year while the traders sold off the nation's wheat stocks, the [Agriculture] department naturally continued to sit on its hands this year while they proceeded to sell off the soybean stocks." By contrast, "a reasonably foresighted administration would have required, last fall, that traders publicly register all foreign sales." Yet Deputy Assistant Secretary of Agriculture Richard E. Bell could tell a Senate subcommittee that sum-

11. For a concise description of these actions, see United States–Japan Trade Council, "Trade Roundup No. 11," August 10, 1973, pp. 5–6, and "Trade Roundup No. 13," September 13, 1973, p. 2.

mer only that Agriculture had been working on a "voluntary reporting system in export sales" which they were moving to put into effect in mid-June.[12]

There were apparently several reasons why USDA officials were reluctant to monitor export contracts closely. It is costly; it requires information that exporters prefer to keep secret for competitive reasons; it smacks of interference with the "free market." For those reluctant to employ controls, there is also the danger that information-gathering will help precipitate them. One reason is intrabureaucratic—the very availability of contract data in short-supply situations may strengthen the arguments of those inside government advocating controls, since the data are likely to indicate strong demand, yet the ultimate magnitude of sales remains uncertain. And information-gathering may also affect the commodity market. As a Commerce Department official put it, "if we had started to gather information on a particular commodity in February, anticipating that we would have a comfortably long period of time to evaluate what was occurring in that commodity before imposing controls . . . people in the market [might] start becoming concerned that the Government was anticipating the imposition of controls and, therefore, the flow would begin to accelerate and we would reach that trigger threshold a lot sooner than we ultimately did reach it."[13] Such a prospect was particularly inhibiting for an administration overwhelmingly disposed against strong government regulation of agricultural markets, international as well as domestic.

Thus as prices skyrocketed and other signals of an exceptionally tight market accumulated—including "intense pressure" from soybean processors[14]—officials in Agriculture (and the Council of Economic Advisers) resisted information-gathering, which they saw as a step in the direction of export control. Not until June 13 was a comprehensive survey of outstanding export contracts undertaken (by the Commerce Department), pursuant to President Nixon's decision to employ export controls where necessary to "put the American consumer first." At this point there was a clear need to get the best available data, as quickly as possible. Moreover, such data was legally required before a formal ex-

12. *Export Control Policy*, Hearings, p. 49.

13. Steven Lazarus, deputy assistant secretary of commerce for East-West trade, ibid., p. 49.

14. GAO, "U.S. Action Needed to Cope with Commodity Shortages," p. 29.

port control could be undertaken, since the existing export control authority (which Nixon was seeking to have broadened) required that a controlled commodity be in short domestic supply and under serious inflationary pressure from abnormal foreign demand.

And the hasty, eleventh-hour way the data was gathered almost guaranteed that it would be unreliable. Shortly after becoming deputy assistant secretary of agriculture in March, Bell began to develop a system of voluntary registration of export contracts. He encountered resistance inside the department: some people thought it technically impossible to obtain reliable information, since some contracts would not be consummated; others believed that companies needed to keep their contracts secret for competitive reasons (a need that was greater in the pre-1972 buyers' market than in the sellers' market that had emerged). Thus the reporting system established on June 13 had not been pretested. The weakness of the data was exacerbated by the fact that the Department of Commerce sent out the questionnaires. (The secretary of commerce was legally responsible for imposing export controls, with agriculture secretary's concurrence on farm products.) For Commerce amended the Agriculture draft of the questionnaire to conform more closely to the format it had used three weeks earlier to report exports of ferrous scrap. In the eyes of Agriculture officials, this made it even less likely to produce reliable findings.

The results of the questionnaire were alarming. They "showed exports of soybeans and soybean meal running 6 and 27 percent, respectively, above previous estimates for July and September 1973," with soybean exports estimated at "92 million bushels for July 15 to August 30."[15] This estimate was reduced to 66 million bushels, after elimination of double-counting, but was still double the 33 million bushels estimated to be "available for export after fulfillment of domestic requirements."[16]

Although Agriculture Department officials were very skeptical of these findings, believing they sharply overestimated actual export demand,[17] their reputation within the government for knowledge of food

15. Ibid., p. 187.

16. Lazarus, *Export Control Policy*, Hearings, p. 56.

17. Secretary Butz quickly sought a different reading. He telephoned executives in the major soybean processing firms to determine how much of a current supply squeeze they were feeling, but their replies were not definitive. They seemed as uncertain as government officials as to what the real supply situation was.

markets had sunk very low by mid-1973. Agriculture officials had clearly misread world commodity markets in 1972. And by the spring of 1973 their assurances that food price inflation was ebbing became a standing joke among economic policy officials. On February 13, the department had forecast a 6–6.5 percent rise in food prices for 1973. One week later, Butz disclosed an increase of 2–3 percent for January alone. By the end of the first quarter, they had shot up more than the forecast for the year —about 7.5 percent. On May 8, USDA acknowledged that retail food prices that year might be as much as 9 percent above 1972; by June 22 it raised the estimate to 12 percent.[18]

The credibility of the "expert" agency thus evaporated just at the time that expertise was most important as a check on the alarming, but misleading, data the government had just gathered. So Secretary Butz reluctantly endorsed the embargo order, and an ignorant government took unnecessary, damaging export control action. There was a mitigating circumstance—the tight supply situation was very new. A dependable export reporting system takes time to develop, and there had been no evident need for one for at least twenty years before the fall of 1972. Still, an earlier effort by the responsible agency, prodded perhaps by economic policy officials alert to the possibility of a crisis, could surely have produced better data and thus a better basis for an intelligent decision.[19]

Why Export Controls?

The purpose of soybean export controls, of course, was to protect the U.S. economy from inflation pressures. Domestic economic policy pre-

18. *New York Times*, February 14, February 21, April 24, May 9, and June 23, 1973. In fact, the food price index rose about 20 percent from January 1973 to January 1974, and another 11 percent from then until January 1975; see *Economic Report of the President, January 1975*, p. 300. The annual average for 1973 was about 15 percent above 1972; that for 1974 was about 14 percent above 1973.

19. Thereafter USDA, both burned and determined not to let the Commerce Department control agricultural export reporting in the future, did develop more effective means of monitoring though its credibility problem continued in 1974 and 1975. And the monitoring responsibility exercised by Commerce was formally transferred to USDA in the Agriculture and Consumer Protection Act of 1973, which became law in August.

vailed over foreign and food policy, the converse of 1972. Yet most
Nixon administration economic policy officials saw it not as a victory
but as a defeat; as earlier noted, George Shultz offered his resignation
when the June 13 price freeze that led to the controls was announced.[20]

Senior Nixon administration economic officials were strongly predisposed against controls over private economic transactions. They saw
government's role as facilitator of the free market and believed controls
distort the free market without curing the ills they addressed. "I think
no one should aspire to manage the economy," said Shultz.[21] And the
president shared their orientation, his distaste for price controls dating
from his service as a junior lawyer in the wartime Office of Price Administration. When he reluctantly imposed controls in August 1971, over
Shultz's opposition, it was at least partly because dramatic economic
policy action then was likely to improve his prospects for reelection.

Once reelected, the president and Shultz moved quickly to end controls: on January 11, 1973, they announced removal of most mandatory
wage and price controls, though controls over food processors and re-
tailers were retained in modified form. Whatever the economic logic of
this action, it was politically disastrous, for that was just the time the
consumer price index began to shoot up at a pace faster than any U.S.
inflation since the late forties, with food prices leading the way. Nixon
and Shultz were thrown on the defensive and remained there.

On March 29, Nixon ordered the Cost of Living Council to impose
price ceilings on beef, lamb, and pork. Senate and House members began to press for a price freeze across the board, with House Ways and
Means Committee chairman Wilbur Mills calling the need more urgent
now than in 1971. Administration economic policy officials fought
against this pressure. They also opposed export controls, which they saw
as the logical and likely outcome of a price freeze given the tight agri-

20. Interview, *Washington Post*, April 14, 1974. Shultz added: "I have to say
in retrospect I think it [the freeze] was a great thing. Yeah, it was terrific. It was so
bad that even the most hardened advocates of freezes and controls could see that
there were limitations on what you could accomplish by that means . . . it turned
out to be a great educational experience for everybody." At Nixon's urging, Shultz
temporarily withdrew his resignation but did leave government in the spring of 1974,
at which time the *Post* interview was granted. For further discussion of his experience in the soybean embargo see George P. Shultz and Kenneth W. Dam, *Economic
Policy Beyond the Headlines* (Stanford Alumni Association, 1977; Norton, 1978),
pp. 8–9, 81.

21. *Washington Post*, April 14, 1974.

cultural commodity markets. So when John Dunlop had suggested either controlling or, at least, monitoring exports in February and March, he met strong resistance. But by early May, it was clear that inflation was continuing. Dunlop succeeded in having the staff work begun on a possible overall freeze on retail food prices, and a group was formed, under the direction of Gary Seevers of the Council of Economic Advisers, to explore specifically the ramifications of export controls. Represented on this group were the Departments of Agriculture and Commerce and the staffs of the Council on International Economic Policy and the National Security Council. The State Department was not represented.

Members of the Seevers group were generally opposed to export controls. However, their economic analysis concluded that controlling feed exports would dampen feed prices, and such dampening might prove essential to keep many U.S. livestock producers in business as long as meat price ceilings were maintained. And the predominant political pressure on the president was not just to keep these ceilings on but to impose others also. Since for legal and practical reasons, specific export data were needed to institute controls, the Seevers group advised that exports be monitored, and George Shultz recommended an export monitoring system to President Nixon.[22]

Nixon was also getting advice for stronger action. Dunlop was deeply concerned about food price rises and the likelihood that they would generate increased union wage demands and thus fuel further inflation. He saw food retail price controls and agricultural commodity export controls as mutually reinforcing means of combating them. And as Dunlop, an exceptionally sharp advocate, was making the economic case in administration councils, Nixon was being pushed by advisers like Melvin Laird, John Connally, and Bryce Harlow to take strong action for political reasons. The president had just suffered through the worst spring of his political life—Watergate disclosures had transformed his standing from that of ascendant president with a near-record electoral mandate to a besieged president struggling to hold onto what remained of his personal credibility and capacity for leadership. And the thought cannot have escaped him that he might recoup politically, rekindle faith in himself as a strong president, if he executed another dramatic policy shift.

22. Graziano, "Commodity Export Controls," pp. 19–20; also GAO, "U.S. Action Needed to Cope with Commodity Shortages," pp. 29–30.

So Nixon decreed a sixty-day freeze on prices on June 13, 1973, in a dramatic television address to the nation. After claiming credit for the "phenomenal" economic growth since August 1971 (real U.S. output had increased by 11.5 percent), he moved quickly to the "one great problem that rightly concerns every one of us . . . rising prices, and especially rising food prices." To combat this, he was "ordering a freeze on prices" (excepting unprocessed products at the farm level), which would "last for a maximum of sixty days" and be followed by "a new and more effective system of controls," albeit one that would "not be designed to get us permanently into a controlled economy." Then turning to the export question, he said:

One of the major reasons for the rise in food prices at home is that there is now an unprecedented demand abroad for the products of America's farms. Over the long run, increased food exports will be a vital factor in raising farm income, in improving our balance of payments, in supporting America's position of leadership in the world. In the short term, however, when we have shortages and sharply rising prices of food here at home, I have made this basic decision: In allocating the products of America's farms between markets abroad and those in the United States, we must put the American consumer first.

Therefore, I have decided that a new system for export controls on food products is needed—a system designed to hold the price of animal feedstuffs and other grains in the American market to levels that will make it possible to produce meat and eggs and milk at prices you can afford.

I shall ask the Congress, on an urgent basis, to give me the new and more flexible authority needed to impose such a system.[23]

With this decision and declaration, some form of government effort to restrain soybean exports became very likely, if not inevitable. The domestic economic crisis had generated political pressure, which led to a presidential decision to impose a freeze. Shultz's opposition notwithstanding, domestic economic concerns had clearly prevailed. Both farm policy concerns over the country's reputation as a reliable food supplier and foreign policy concerns about relations with importing countries and broader effects on world trade were given short shrift. Indeed, they were not prominently raised in the closed intragovernmental forums at

23. "Address to the Nation Announcing Price Control Measures," pp. 584–86. Apparently the language about putting the American consumer first was Nixon's own. According to one official, CEA chairman Herbert Stein (who wrote the speech) took it to the president, who was recuperating from pneumonia in the hospital, and returned with only that one change. The president, though committed to liberal trade in principle, could not resist appealing to pro-American market discrimination in practice.

which the questions were discussed and the staff work, however reluctantly, was completed.[24]

Why Such Severe Controls?

One study of the soybean episode concludes, "From June 13 onward, export controls were a foregone conclusion."[25] Strictly speaking, they were not—controls on any commodity would depend on the situation for that commodity and on the results of export monitoring; and in fact no export controls were imposed on the other major U.S. feed-grain export, corn.[26] But the United States was now committed, by presidential declaration, to the use of export controls in case of serious economic need. The president did promise, in a phrase misinterpreted overseas, "We will keep *the export commitments we have made as a Nation.*"[27] This caused grain traders and overseas customers to conclude, erroneously, that pre-June 13 contracts would be honored. Nixon also promised consultation with other countries "to seek their cooperation in resolving the world-wide problem of rising food prices." But, he concluded, "we will not let foreign sales price meat and eggs off the American table."

But even if supply and price forced some form of export limitation, it did not have to be the type of control action ultimately taken—a total embargo, followed by cutting across contracts, by licensing for export only 50 percent of the amount of soybeans in each pre-June 13 export contract. And the embargo came as a total shock to importing countries, who were not consulted as promised. It also shocked many in Wash-

24. In a qualified defense of the failure to take these values more fully into account, one senior official argued that policy officials could not have anticipated that "the President was going to go bananas and slap on the freeze." But Nixon was anything but alone in favoring a freeze, as foregoing discussion shows. Thus it is not unreasonable to believe that these economic policy officials—and, indeed, agriculture policy officials—might have anticipated earlier that they could be forced into some form of export controls against their will. Had they anticipated this they might have turned their attention to reducing the international and domestic costs.

25. Graziano, "Commodity Export Controls," p. 21.

26. Controls were imposed on close substitutes for soybeans (cottonseed, simultaneously with soybeans, and forty-one other commodities several days later). See ibid.

27. "Address to the Nation Announcing Price Control Measures," p. 586. Emphasis added.

ington: five minutes before its announcement the State Department's senior food and commodity policy specialist, for example, learned of it for the first time!

With the hindsight knowledge that the alleged shortage evaporated once controls were in place, it is obvious that the government could have taken more moderate forms of action: persuading foreign governments to work to limit imports to short-term needs as long as the tight market continued; or allowing existing contracts to be filled but over a stretched-out time period. For it was a short-run crisis; the record new soybean crop, though delayed by late planting, was to be harvested by October, and futures prices for 1973-crop soybeans were running at half of those for what remained of the 1972 crop.

The general reasons that moderate action was not taken have been cited—the newness of the problem; the lack of information on exports actually planned; the ignorance on the part of many of the way the private soybean trade worked and the concentration of what knowledge there was in a department whose expertise was discredited. Another important factor was the closed decisionmaking process, inevitable to some degree on any issue where government action may have dramatic impact on commodity markets. Moreover, those controlling the process concentrated on particular economic values and did not bring into the process others (like the State Department) who would have emphasized other values.

The formal economic policymaking group in mid-1973 was the Council on Economic Policy (CEP), headed by George Shultz, and this was the organizational umbrella under which export control deliberations took place. This was appropriate, for its role was to coordinate overall economic policy, international as well as domestic. Shultz assigned formal responsibility for further work on export controls to an interagency task force chaired by a staff member of the Council on International Economic Policy, the official institution responsible for foreign economic policy coordination. This task force formed three subgroups, which set to work examining the various possible export control systems, the legal and constitutional issues, and the question of international consultations. The State Department participated in this task force.

But as its work was proceeding, a far more restricted, emergency process was also proceeding which involved mainly the Cost of Living

Council and the Council of Economic Advisers. And this smaller ad hoc group ended up controlling the analysis and the action.[28] One internal CEA memo of June 25 reached an alarming conclusion:

> The combination of high feed prices and the freeze, if continued for 3 or 4 months until new crops are harvested, will force the livestock, dairy & poultry industries through a major contraction during which their capital base (breeding flocks and stock) will be eroded. If this happens, it will be mid-1975 before we get out of the food price problem.[29]

And though its author had formerly opposed export controls, he now concluded that it would be necessary to "act this week to control exports of soybeans, soybean meal and perhaps corn"; there was "no other way of avoiding the contraction in the livestock-poultry sector unless we abandon the freeze." The ad hoc group concluded that it would be necessary to have enough soybeans available domestically for the soybean-crushing industry operating at maximum capacity; even better, *more* than enough for full capacity, because sellers would then compete for the crushers' business, pushing soybean prices down.

With this foreboding and with this computation of domestic need, CEA and CLC officials received, apparently on Monday, June 25, the first results of the Commerce Department's export contract survey. It showed that soybean exports would total at least twice the amount necessary for domestic use by the criteria discussed above. The reaction was panic—officials were skeptical of the data but had no good way to check it before taking action, which seemed to be required immediately.

Dunlop pushed hard for quick action. His earlier warnings about exports wreaking domestic havoc seemed vindicated, and since the new statistics were, in effect, the only statistics in town, no one in the group felt they were on solid enough ground to oppose him. And for-

28. As the GAO report described things: "Although the primary decisionmakers reviewed some incomplete interagency analyses, they did not have the benefit of well-thought-out, formal decisionmaking options. Most option papers on legal and constitutional implications; consultations with foreign governments; alternative export control systems; and relationships between export controls, export promotion, and concessional export programs were not finalized before it was decided to impose controls. In the wake of the decision, some limited analyses of these subjects were completed and made available to decisionmakers, should a similar short-supply situation recur. These options papers also helped in implementing the controls." GAO, "U.S. Action Needed to Cope with Commodity Shortages," p. 34.

29. Internal memo obtained from CEA. Stein and Seevers discussed these possibilities publicly on June 25 but without the strong prescriptive tone of the internal memo. *New York Times,* June 26, 1973.

eign policy concerns went largely unvoiced. The State Department was not included in these emergency deliberations; the National Security Council representative, an experienced economist personally skeptical about the data, was new to his position and to the specific issues involved.

Thus on June 27, 1973, an ad hoc group of economic advisers, not fully representative of all U.S. interests, possessing misleading data and pressed for time, made the decision to advise an embargo on exports of soybeans. The actual decision was made by George Shultz, as CEP chairman, with President Nixon's concurrence. The formal action was taken, as required under the law, by Secretary of Commerce Dent. Publicly, Butz termed the action "drastic" but necessary. Dunlop said it "puts first the dinner table of the American consumer." Dent said it had been imposed "because of the extremely tight supply situation . . . until the present soybean crop is harvested"[30] and promised that the administration would announce by July 2 what quantities would be available for export and what method would be used in allocation of the available export supply.

In the several days after June 27, administration officials worked intensively with soybean exporters to devise a reasonable and workable means of allocating available supplies[31] and consulted with foreign governments to assuage their apprehensions.

The system chosen for allocating exports, however, was to some officials at least as damaging as the initial embargo announcement to the credibility of the United States as a supplier. Several alternatives were considered (including allocation by country of destination based on its historical market share or its own estimates of its minimum needs, giving priority to contracts with the earliest delivery dates, and so forth), but time and data were insufficient, apparently, for developing such a system. So on July 2 a simple method of allocation was established. Because only 33 million bushels of soybeans would be available for export that summer and the estimated total needed to fulfill contracts concluded before June 13 was 66 million bushels, a policy

30. *New York Times,* June 28, 1973; United States–Japan Trade Council, "Trade Roundup No. 9," June 28, 1973. "Reports from various parts of the country that farmers are destroying chickens and selling breeding sows because their cost of feed has risen to a point where they will lose money on the sale of the fed animal" forced the decision, according to the *Times.*

31. For the transcript of discussions with exporters see *Export Control Policy,* Hearings, pp. 329–63.

of issuing licenses for just 50 percent of the amount in each contract was established.[32]

Cutting across contracts not only caused legal problems but undermined a principle to which the administration was deeply committed both domestically and internationally—the sanctity of the private economic contract. In addition, it discredited the dependability of the United States as a supplier and gave other countries, too, an excuse to renege on contracts because of changed circumstances. There was no way to avoid some interference with existing contracts, of course, given the goal of reducing the amount of soybeans to be shipped that summer. But, as one official suggested, a better course might have been to license the full amounts of all contracts but require that half the amounts be filled from the 1973 crop—thus stretching out the delivery time but assuring that face amounts would eventually be provided. In fact, Cargill proposed such a plan just after the July 2 order was issued, citing the way Peru had handled its anchovy export problem.[33]

As things turned out, the data and assumptions supporting the embargo were wildly inaccurate. And, in retrospect, the effect of the controls seems to have been the opposite of that desired. They were meant to be a short-term measure to tide the United States over a difficult period but in fact had only a limited impact on summer 1973 soybean exports. The fact and form of their imposition, however, sent an enduring message to major U.S. markets. It would be harder for the United States to argue persuasively that the European Economic Community should import more food from the United States and rely less on subsidized domestic production; and it would be easier for a Japanese minister of agriculture and forestry to urge greater food production at home and diversification of overseas sources of soybean supply. It is particularly disturbing, therefore, that the officials sensitive to these costs, and involved in the inevitable repair work, were not involved in the embargo decision.

32. For soybean meal exports, a similar procedure led to a decision to license 40 percent of the amount in pre-June 13 contracts; for cottonseed oil cake and meal, 100 percent of pre-June 13 contracts were licensed (ibid., pp. 56–58).

33. "Recommendation for Altering the Export Control Program," draft proposal made available by Cargill, Incorporated (no date).

CHAPTER FIVE

The Struggle over Food Aid, 1974 and 1975

THE TIGHT SUPPLY SITUATION put the Public Law 480 program through a major squeeze. Spending dropped to the lowest since the program's inauguration, and the actual amount of food provided fell to a fraction of former levels. Yet despite continuing tight grain markets, the program's supporters showed unexpected strength in their campaign to reverse this decline in aid volume and to direct the food provided to the hungriest nations. In December 1974, Congress enacted a statutory requirement that the bulk of food aid be allocated to countries most in need. In fiscal year 1975, Public Law 480 spending recovered to the highest level since 1968. But for Bangladesh, the country most affected by the world food crisis, the expanded U.S. shipments came after the time of maximum need.

Background

Soybean prices eased in the summer and early fall of 1973, but the broad trend of farm and food prices remained sharply upward. Consumer food prices leaped an incredible 6.1 percent in August alone, following the end of the price freeze; they leveled off for the remainder of 1973 and then rose about 14 percent more in 1974.[1] Wheat prices jumped to an unheard-of $4.45 a bushel in August 1973 and were generally above $4—and occasionally above $5—through the end of 1974. Corn prices rose above $2 a bushel and kept rising.[2] Thus despite record

1. *Economic Report of the President, February 1975*, p. 300.
2. U.S. Department of Agriculture, Statistical Reporting Service, Crop Reporting Board, *Agricultural Prices: Annual Summary, 1974* (USDA, June 1975), pp. 12, 13.

U.S. harvests of wheat, corn, and soybeans in 1973, the food situation in the United States (and therefore in the world) was precarious. The plight of the poorest food-importing countries was particularly severe, and the drain on their foreign exchange increased after the Organization of Petroleum Exporting Countries quadrupled the price of oil in late 1973 and early 1974.

But just as their need grew, the U.S. food aid program shrank. The program had long been declining in importance: the value of products shipped dropped from a peak of $1.6 billion in fiscal year 1965 to an average of $1 billion annually in 1969 through 1972. And whereas Public Law 480 had financed 33 percent of U.S. agricultural exports in 1957, this proportion dropped to 20 percent in 1966 and to 13 percent in 1972. After 1972, the decline was precipitous. Food aid exports were only 7 percent of total farm exports in fiscal year 1973 and only 4 percent in 1974. Shipments of wheat, long the major food aid commodity, had at least equaled commercial sales for most pre-1972 years. But these shipments dropped from 317 million bushels in 1971–72 to 57 million bushels in 1973–74, while commercial sales jumped from 316 million bushels to 1,092 million bushels. Funds for the food aid program dropped below $1 billion, the lowest level since the program's first year.[3]

And allocation was sharply altered. Every year from 1957 through 1971, India had been the largest recipient. But by 1973 title 1 food aid (low-interest credit sales) for the hungriest nations had virtually disappeared; the United States gave priority instead to political purposes. In fiscal year 1973 South Vietnam and South Korea alone received almost half of all title 1 food aid; in 1974 South Vietnam and Cambodia alone received 69 percent.[4]

The conditions that produced these changes continued through 1974—tight and costly commodities and pressure for their "political" allocation. Yet the U.S. government gradually altered its policies, both increasing the amount of food in the Public Law 480 program and allocating a greater share to the countries most in need. In his April 1974 speech to the Sixth Special Session of the UN General Assembly, Secretary of State Henry A. Kissinger promised a "major effort to increase the

3. *FATUS* (Foreign Agricultural Trade of the United States), December 1975, p. 16; USDA *Agricultural Statistics, 1975* (Government Printing Office, 1975), p. 4.

4. *FATUS*, December 1975, pp. 40–43; Daniel J. Balz, "Agriculture Report: Politics of Food Aid Presents U.S. with Policy Dilemma," *National Journal*, November 23, 1974, p. 1764.

quantity of food aid over the level we provided last year."[5] Addressing the UN General Assembly the following September, in the wake of the worst drought in the U.S. corn belt in twenty years, President Gerald R. Ford promised that the United States would increase "the amount it spends for food shipments . . . this year."[6] And finally, in early February 1975, Secretary of Agriculture Earl L. Butz announced a food-aid target of $1.6 billion for the fiscal year already more than half completed. The amount actually spent was somewhat smaller—a bit over $1.2 billion. But there were increases in the quantities of wheat and rice shipped, and Bangladesh and India headed the list of recipients.[7]

Why then did the United States expand food aid for fiscal 1975? And how successful was this response in effecting a timely provision of food to countries most in need?

The Decision(s) to Expand Food Aid

In April 1974, Lyle P. Schertz wrote in *Foreign Affairs* that "no major political force in the United States is embracing the food needs of most of the lower-income countries for whatever reason—charity, security, or economic self-interest."[8] And events of the preceding year offered ample evidence to support this conclusion. Food-importing poor countries had been largely ignored in both the Russian wheat purchases of 1972 and the soybean embargo the following year, decisions that went strongly against their interests. And while in contrast to those cases, the process of food aid policymaking was relatively open and certainly drawn-out, the pressures in 1973 were overwhelmingly to restrict aid to minimal amounts. They underscored the built-in contradiction in the structure and politics of the food aid program—that when countries need food the most, the program tends to provide the least.

For food-short developing countries, a ton of grain had become more costly to import; hence their need for concessionary finance, other

5. "The Challenge of Interdependence," in *Department of State Bulletin*, vol. 70 (May 6, 1974), p. 480.

6. "Address to the 29th General Assembly of the United Nations, September 18, 1974," in *Public Papers of the Presidents: Gerald R. Ford, 1974* (GPO, 1975), p. 160.

7. *New York Times*, February 4, 1975; *FATUS*, December 1975, pp. 12–13, 17, 31.

8. "World Food: Prices and the Poor," *Foreign Affairs*, vol. 52 (April 1974), p. 534.

things being equal, had increased. Yet Public Law 480 funds were budgeted in dollars, so the money provided for food aid bought much less food: in 1971, $655 million bought about 9.1 million tons of Public Law 480 grain; in 1974, $727 million bought only 3.4 million tons.[9] But more important than budgetary ceilings were the limits on commodities available. The food aid program was established to dispose of surpluses, and although the 1966 amendments removed the requirement that a commodity be declared surplus in order to be used for food aid, they substituted a requirement that a commodity must be declared available by the secretary of agriculture after domestic and overseas commercial needs had been met. Thus Public Law 480 had only a residual claim on American food resources, and "during the early months of 1974," for example, "concern about domestic supplies and carryover stocks of wheat resulted in reduced programing levels of wheat and wheat flour."[10]

Assuming that the United States did not impose export controls (subsidized sales of soybean oil had to be suspended, for example, after the embargo) there were no absolute rules for determining availability of commodities. Decisions were made by balancing values: program needs against impact on prices, stocks, the federal budget, and so on. But whereas the economic policy community had a particularly strong interest in limiting food outflows in this inflationary period, the program had lost its main supporting constituency. With commercial exports booming, the farm policy community had no urgent current need for it. Secretary Butz dramatized this new situation by sending his proposed Agriculture Department budget over to OMB with a zero figure for Public Law 480; when officials there responded that he must have left something out, he replied that he didn't need the program any more —"If Henry needs it, let the money come out of his budget!"[11]

And Henry Kissinger did need it; because Congress was cutting back other foreign aid funding—particularly for Indochina—and for food-importing countries, Public Law 480 could substitute, up to a

9. Totals for wheat and products, feed grains and products, and rice calculated from USDA, Economic Research Service, *U.S. Agricultural Exports under Public Law 480*, Foreign Agricultural Report 395 (USDA, October 1974), pp. 7–8, 16–18; and *FATUS*, December 1975, p. 17.

10. *Food for Peace Program: 1974 Annual Report*, H. Doc. 94-352, 94 Cong. 2 sess. (GPO, 1976) p. 5.

11. Some of his subordinates objected to this stance, not because they favored expanding Public Law 480 but because they thought it invited stronger State (and weaker USDA) influence over the program.

point, for other forms of financial support.[12] Kissinger also had developed a secondary interest in humanitarian food aid. And in the food-short summer of 1973, he took two actions which started the U.S. government along the road to expanding the program well before farm and economic policy concerns would have brought about such expansion.

The first step was to commission, as national security adviser, an interagency study on the foreign policy implications of food policy.[13] The soybean fiasco had made it clear that domestic food policy decisions could have international implications, and that officialdom had not yet sorted out these implications thoroughly and systematically. Moreover, the State Department had strongly protested its exclusion from that decision, and ordering a study with a major State role was one way that he and his National Security Council staff could respond constructively to this complaint. By this time, moreover, the future of food aid was uncertain: with prices skyrocketing and commercial demand at record levels, even *wheat* export controls were not out of the question, and this would have deprived the program of its most important commodity. So in that same summer, Kissinger's staff urged him to seek from President Nixon a decision to (1) impose no further export controls but (2) hold down food aid amounts to essential levels. And Nixon apparently agreed, though this decision was not formally disseminated.[14]

The second step that Kissinger took was to propose, in his first major address as secretary of state, "that a World Food Conference be convened under United Nations auspices in 1974."[15] The forum was the UN General Assembly; the apparent source of the idea was Senator Hubert H. Humphrey, who urged in the hearings on Kissinger's nomi-

---

12. Conversely, needy countries could have bought food if financing had been available, and such financing could have come from countries other than the major food exporters. Japan and Saudi Arabia, for example, could share the burden of combating world famine even though they were major grain importers. Needless to say, U.S. officials made this point frequently in international forums, arguing that responsibility for alleviating famine rested not so much with those who produced food as with those who could help finance its transfer.

13. *Nomination of Henry A. Kissinger*, Hearings before the Senate Committee on Foreign Relations, 93 Cong. 1 sess. (GPO, 1973), pt. 1, p. 19.

14. The 1974 report of the Council of Economic Advisers reports, among the "supply-increasing actions of the Federal Government" in 1973, the following item: "July 6—exports of food under P.L. 480 reduced to minimum levels" (*Economic Report of the President, February 1974*, p. 95). The exact form of this "action" is unclear from the report and other sources.

15. "A Just Consensus, A Stable Order, A Durable Peace," speech delivered September 24, 1973. *State Department Bulletin*, vol. 69 (October 15, 1973), p. 472.

nation as secretary of state that he "initiate . . . a discussion amongst the main exporting nations and the main importing nations as to what we are going to do in the coming year to relieve conditions of human misery and, in some areas, famine, in the light of the world food supply situation."[16] Kissinger was receptive. He was awakening to the foreign policy importance of food issues and may also have been looking for ways to involve himself more in economic issues as he assumed his new post. Agriculture Department leaders were reluctant, fearing (correctly) that such a conference would increase international pressure on U.S. food policies. But they and others were pleased when the conference date was set for late 1974, for they believed (incorrectly) that the expected bumper harvests of the following summer would ease the supply situation and the United States could then be more generous with food aid.

In the ensuing months, the approaching conference generated pressure on the United States to expand food aid, though its agenda dealt mainly with longer-term problems of expanding world food production. And it tended to increase State Department influence. Though Secretary Butz was designated chief of the U.S. delegation, Secretary Kissinger was to give the major American speech. And Ambassador Edwin M. Martin was appointed, apparently at NSC staff initiative, as coordinator of U.S. participation in the conference with a State Department office.

But through the fall and winter, policy on food aid remained to minimize it. New agreements were sharply limited except with "essential" recipients.[17] Holding down shipments took somewhat greater time, but they too dropped rapidly.[18] Since supplies were deemed too tight to

16. *Nomination of Henry A. Kissinger,* Hearings, pt. 1, p. 148.

17. Of those concluded in the second half of 1973, the six largest (and eight of the largest ten) were with Cambodia and Vietnam; in the first half of 1974, the five largest were with the same two countries. USDA, Foreign Agricultural Service, "Public Law 480, Concessional Sales Agreements Signed Through December 31, 1975," pp. 25, 27.

18. The following shipments of title 1, Public Law 480, commodities are illustrative. Figures are for total shipments, thousands of metric tons.

July–December 1972	3,020
January–June 1973	1,966
July–December 1973	1,016
January–June 1974	786
July–December 1974	472
January–June 1975	3,103

USDA, Foreign Agricultural Service, "Title I, Public Law 480: Total Amounts Shipped Through June 30, 1975, By Country and Commodity," p. 169.

permit longer-run planning, an interagency committee chaired by the Office of Management and Budget was created to determine, on a quarterly basis, the amounts that were available and to make tentative allocations among countries before specific agreement proposals (developed under the Interagency Staff Committee chaired by USDA) were prepared and negotiated. Officials remember the process as difficult—it was hard to get good analyses from USDA (or from anybody else) about the effect of different food aid levels on prices, on recipient countries, and so on. And interagency conflict was frequently sharp. State officials responsible for particular country relationships pressed for increases; economic policy officials were strongly restrictive. The Agriculture Department took a more detached position, not opposing increases if they did not come out of other USDA budget items but not pushing them either. When the commodity supply situation seemed to improve in the spring of 1974, however, Agriculture officials showed more interest in expanding the program, seeing it as a safety valve if commodity prices began to fall.

Nor had the interagency study been effective in clarifying U.S. policy priorities and choices, either because of the complexity of the issues or the way questions were framed. An official who helped get the study started called it a "disaster," with "pedestrian" analysis. By around the beginning of 1974, it was superseded by two more specific studies under the general responsibility of the Council on International Economic Policy (CIEP)—one (led by OMB) on food aid, the other on food reserves.

But it was not these studies but the pressure of specific events that forced officials to address food aid in 1974. One such event was Kissinger's April speech to the Sixth Special Session of the United Nations General Assembly. The months before this session had been dominated by the OPEC embargo and the fourfold oil price increase that followed, and there was some belief that a generous U.S. position on food could undercut U.S. efforts to press for lower oil prices. As Leslie Gelb and Anthony Lake describe the situation:

> Schultz [sic] and Kissinger spoke of rising food costs for the LDC's as a lever on OPEC. The more pressure the LDC's would feel from the food and fuel squeeze, the more likely they would be to put pressure on OPEC to roll back prices. . . . The idea seemed to be: let the poor countries feel the pinch, so the Arabs could hear the yell.[19]

19. "Less Food, More Politics," *Foreign Policy*, no. 17 (Winter 1974–75), p. 180. They refer to George Shultz, secretary of the treasury.

But by early April, Kissinger had turned from such a confrontation strategy to one in which the United States would dramatize its responsiveness to world concerns on food as part of its campaign to get OPEC to make its commodity available at less burdensome price levels. Moreover, grain prices had begun to drop from their early 1974 peaks and were expected to drop further with all U.S. grain acreage restraints removed for 1974. Thus Kissinger, overcoming resistance from economic policy officials on a matter over which he had maximum leverage (the wording of his speech), promised "a major effort to increase the quantity of food aid over the level we provided last year."[20] But this did not mean a decision to increase the administration's fiscal 1975 budget for Public Law 480, though State had pressed for one. The target remained at $891 million, or about what was actually provided in fiscal 1973 and 1974. Rather, the anticipated further declines in U.S. grain prices were expected to make it possible to ship more commodities for the same amount of money.

Then came the summer drought in the midwest corn belt—the worst in twenty years—and unfavorable weather for wheat as well. The Agriculture Department's estimate of the corn crop plummeted as the drought continued, from a record of over 6.5 billion bushels projected in May, to around 6 billion in July, to 5 billion in September.[21] The wheat crop was not 2.1 billion bushels, as projected in March, but 1.8 billion bushels.[22] Heavily influenced by this drop in U.S. crops, total world grain production for 1974–75 declined about 5 percent from the previous year, much larger than the drop two years earlier.[23]

The effect on U.S. food prices was severe. The Council of Economic Advisers reported in early 1975:

The predicted leveling off [of U.S. food prices in 1974] began in the spring and continued until midsummer, but it was short-lived. . . . Instead of the

20. "The Challenge of Interdependence," p. 480. One official involved in drafting the speech remembers a careful effort to word this section so that it could mean an increase over either the calendar or the fiscal year, whichever proved easier for the United States to accomplish.

21. Seth S. King, "Good Planting Prospects in Midwest Point to Record Corn and Wheat Crops," New York Times, May 1, 1974; New York Times, July 13, August 13, and September 12, 1974. The final harvest, 4.7 million bushels, was by far the smallest since the corn blight year of 1970, and yields per acre averaged slightly below that year.

22. Economic Report of the President, February 1975, p. 164.

23. Ibid., p. 163. World production in 1974–75 was still slightly above that of 1971–72, because of a large increase in production in 1973–74. For figures see USDA, Economic Research Service, The World Food Situation and Prospects to 1985, Foreign Agricultural Report 98 (USDA, December 1974), p. 4.

bumper harvests that had been forecast, crop production as a whole suffered the largest setback in nearly 40 years. Instead of substantially slower increases in the second half of 1974, retail food prices advanced at a 13.4 percent annual rate between June and December 1974.[24]

For administration economic officials, determined to minimize inflation *and* avoid repeating the export control fiasco of 1973, the situation dictated continued tightness on food aid. At the same time, with the World Food Conference in Rome approaching and the food situation worsening in areas like South Asia, a world hunger coalition of private church groups, voluntary agencies, and key senators was pushing to increase food aid; the Senate unanimously passed a resolution for more aid introduced by Hubert Humphrey.[25] The emphasis was consistent with the new directions mandate that Congress had enacted in 1973, which shifted priority from economic development toward "basic human needs"—toward helping the "poorest countries" and the "poor majority of people within those countries."[26]

The food policy government seeking to make these difficult trade-offs operated in at least three separate, though related, organizational frameworks. The broadest formal role was played by the President's Committee on Food established in June 1974 (with the phasing out of the Cost of Living Council machinery) to review and coordinate domestic and international food policy activities "significantly affecting food costs and prices." The committee itself was not very active, but under it was the Food Deputies Group chaired by CEA member Gary Seevers, which worked very actively that summer and fall to develop and implement a strategy for informally allocating U.S. food supplies among foreign buyers. The coordination of Public Law 480 allocations and the decisions on overall program levels continued to be the responsibility of the OMB-chaired working group, which (like the Seevers group) operated mainly at the assistant secretary level. These two groups were dominated by economic policy officials, who sought to constrain both USDA (on commercial exports) and State (on food aid); indeed, a strong CEA-OMB-Treasury alliance was working to this end. These agencies were willing to consider increases in food aid if the market crisis eased and prices fell, but they strongly opposed an-

24. *Economic Report of the President, February 1975*, p. 160.

25. William Robbins, "U.S. Crop Losses Dim Prospects for Large World Food Program," *New York Times*, September 22, 1974.

26. For a brief summary of implementation of the mandate, see *International Development and Food Assistance Act of 1978*, H. Rept. 95-1087, 95 Cong. 2 sess. (GPO, 1978), pp. 5–6.

nouncing an increase publicly, for fear that would drive commodity prices up further. Moreover, the new president, Gerald Ford, was embarking on his first major policy initiative, the Whip Inflation Now (WIN) program, and he saw holding down government spending as a prime means to this end.

At the same time, U.S. planning for the food conference continued under Ambassador Edwin Martin. Secretary Kissinger was pressing for a forthright U.S. declaration on food aid—an open commitment to do more—setting the stage for a six-month battle over the size and visibility of the food aid budget and over the amounts of food in the program. The first action-forcing event was Ford's scheduled September speech to the UN General Assembly, his first major presidential foreign policy address. At Kissinger's urging (and over OMB and CEA resistance), Ford promised that "the United States will not only maintain the amount it spends for food shipments to nations in need but it will increase this amount this year."[27] But reflecting the strong concerns of these domestic economic officials, who were staring at bad crop reports and rising grain prices, Ford did not mention specific amounts of food, though Kissinger had pressed for a commitment to greater volume.[28] Thus the U.S. position of April—more food but not necessarily more money—was turned on its head.

With economic policy officials opposed and Agriculture strangely on the sidelines, Kissinger renewed his effort to put the United States on record for increasing the amount of food aid. The action event this time was his conference speech scheduled for November 5, in which he wanted to strike a posture of maximum U.S. leadership. His tactics were similar to those he had used before; he had his speech prepared quietly by a small group within State, he worked directly with the president for clearance, and he shared the draft with cabinet colleagues only at the eleventh hour. This created problems for delegation chairman Butz, who had difficulty planning his role without knowing what, exactly, the authoritative statement of the U.S. position was likely to contain.

Kissinger wanted to promise a significant increase in quantity, one that would add at least $500 million to the $891 million budget figure. But the economic policy advisers fought back. When Treasury Secre-

27. "Address to the 29th General Assembly of the United Nations."
28. For details on this episode see Gelb and Lake, "Less Food, More Politics," p. 183. They report a general commitment by Ford at this time to a $1.5 billion food aid budget for fiscal 1975.

tary William Simon received a draft for his personal review, he distributed it to other top Ford economic aides. At an executive committee meeting of the administration's new Economic Policy Board on Thursday, October 31 (to which neither State nor Agriculture was apparently invited), Simon, new CEA chairman Alan Greenspan, and others urged the president to reject a specific commitment to increased quantity. Ford agreed. Kissinger—who was overseas—was most upset about the meeting and the decision. He managed to get another White House meeting convened, the following Saturday, with State represented, though Ford—who was on the West Coast—did not attend. But the economic advisers stuck to their position and Ford to his acceptance of it.[29]

Secretary Kissinger's speech to the World Food Conference, therefore, went only slightly further than Ford's September speech. Acknowledging that "an expanded flow of food aid will clearly be necessary," he declared, "during this fiscal year, the United States will increase its food aid contribution, despite the adverse weather conditions which have affected our crops. The American people have a deep and enduring commitment to help feed the starving and the hungry."[30]

Advocates of a stronger U.S. effort to deliver on this commitment continued their campaign at the conference itself, where the presence of a large number of church, international welfare, and "world hunger lobby" representatives were present as observers. On November 7 Senator Dick Clark and other congressional members of the U.S. delegation in Rome who wanted increased food aid targeted toward the hungriest nations convinced Secretary Butz to sign a cable to President Ford calling for a "minimum one-million-ton increase current FY 75" over the amount provided the previous year. But the Ford White House did not approve the request. Though press secretary Ron Nessen emphasized that it had not been rejected, Butz explained that Ford

29. This account, based on interviews, is essentially consistent with the account in Balz, "Agriculture Report: Politics of Food Aid," p. 1762. There were two other interagency meetings that Thursday, without Ford, that also dealt with the issue. One was the regular EPB executive committee session at 8:30 a.m., with two State, two NSC, and three Agriculture attendees. The other was a deputies' meeting held while the principals were with Ford; Assistant Secretary of State Thomas O. Enders attended. Roger B. Porter, executive secretary of the EPB, reports a board decision the day before that "the EPB Executive Committee with the addition of the Secretaries of Agriculture and State" would handle food issues. See "Organizing U.S. Food and Agricultural Policy Making," unpublished paper, p. 17.

30. *Department of State Bulletin*, vol. 69 (December 15, 1974), p. 826.

feared an increase "would have a bullish effect on the market," and might drive prices up so that available funds could purchase less grain.[31]

So as the World Food Conference closed in mid-November, the United States still had made no clear decision on the amount of food aid it would provide for a fiscal year already four and a half months old. State had won a presidential commitment to an apparently substantial, unspecified increase; the economic advisers had won on the principle of flexibility, to adjust to the domestic price situation, and on no immediate public announcement; USDA had apparently won the assurance it most coveted, that any Public Law 480 expansion would not come out of the rest of the Agriculture budget.

It took almost three more months, however, for the final decision to be made and announced.[32] Over this period, grain prices declined, and other foreign demand seemed to wane as the Soviet Union and China announced they would not take delivery on about 800,000 tons of grain they had contracted for. So the economic policy community's resistance to increased food aid waned also. The administration reviewed options ranging from $1 billion to $1.6 billion. It reviewed also the implications of a new congressional provision that 70 percent of concessional food aid go to the countries most in need. This provision increased Kissinger's pressure to expand the program, for as humanitarian food aid increased, political food aid could also increase. Finally, on February 3, 1975, Secretary Butz announced that the Ford administration would increase international food aid to a total of $1.6 billion, including transportation costs.

To set a target does not mean it will be fulfilled: Public Law 480 is a cumbersome program to administer. Actual food aid for fiscal 1975 fell well below $1.6 billion. Even so, the $1.2 billion actually expended was the largest amount since fiscal 1968.[33] And the grain tonnage, at 4.5

31. Clyde H. Farnsworth, "Food-Rich Lands Weigh Plan to Fight Hunger," *New York Times,* November 8, 1974; William Robbins, "U.S. Commitment to More Food Aid Rejected by Ford," *New York Times,* November 16, 1974. For one eloquent plea for action by a spokesman of a private organization, see James P. Grant, "Food and Famine: Seizing the Initiative," *Washington Post,* November 12, 1976.

32. This paragraph based on *Washington Post,* December 6, 1974; and *New York Times,* December 9, 1974; January 21, 1975; January 23, 1975; and February 4, 1975.

33. In the first three months of 1975, $393.4 million in new title 1, Public Law 480, agreements were signed, more than for all of calendar year 1974; and as shown in note 18, title 1 shipments for January–June 1975 were over six times the volume of the previous July–December. USDA, FAS, "Public Law 480, Concessional Sales Agreements," pp. 27, 29; USDA, FAS, "Title I, Public Law 480; Total Amounts Shipped," p. 169.

million, was slightly above the minimum 1 million ton increase sought by Clark and his colleagues at Rome.[34]

The Fight over Allocation

As these last developments illustrate, within the issue of how much food aid there was to be was the issue of which countries should receive it. And allocation came increasingly to dominate the question of what the total amount should be.

Public Law 480 food moves under two titles. Under title 1, recipient governments buy U.S. food on credit subsidized by the U.S. government, with the interest rates and repayment terms negotiated separately in each bilateral sales agreement. The recipient government is then responsible for getting the food to people through sales at prevailing market rates, or at government subsidized prices, or through other special programs. Under title 2, the U.S. government donates food directly to other countries, through the Food and Agriculture Organization of the United Nations or through voluntary private relief agencies like CARE. The food then goes directly to recipients in school feeding programs, emergency or famine relief, food-for-world development projects, and so on.

In recent years, title 1 had been around 70 percent of total food aid, and it was the allocation of this food that was being disputed. It had always been employed for foreign policy as well as development and welfare policy purposes. However, India's position as the primary food aid market from 1957 through 1971 illustrated the important role that actual food need did play in food aid distribution.[35] But India, encouraged by agricultural production increases and anxious to escape the role of international supplicant, announced with some pride that its food self-sufficiency program had progressed to the point where it would need no American grain in 1972 and would not renew the Public Law 480 agreement that expired in June of that year.[36] These announce-

---

34. *FATUS*, December 1975, pp. 16–17.

35. In each year during this period, India received more Public Law 480 wheat (and more overall U.S. food aid, measured in dollars) than any other country. USDA, ERS, *U.S. Agricultural Exports under Public Law 480*, pp. 60–61, 210–27.

36. For contemporary references, see *New York Times*, September 7, 1971; and January 24 and April 30, 1972. In the April reference, Kasturi Rangan strikes a somewhat euphoric note: "Officials believe that India never again will have to depend on foreign countries for food."

ments were related also to the U.S. "tilt" toward Pakistan in the war which led to the creation of Bangladesh. India continued to receive substantial title 2 food aid—23 percent of the world total in fiscal 1974, for example.[37] But it dropped out of the title 1 program and in fact supplied a large amount of food to Bangladesh in the period immediately after it gained independence.

Thus, even before the events of 1972 and 1973 reduced the food aid program, allocation had become very different from that of the sixties. In fiscal 1973, Cambodia, South Vietnam, and South Korea received 67 percent of all title 1 aid; Indonesia received 8 percent, Pakistan 6 percent, and Bangladesh 5 percent.[38] The program had become, essentially, a means for buttressing client states and U.S. relations with these states.[39] The foreign policy community, led by Henry Kissinger, had become its prime constituency, and the "minimum levels" to which food aid was reduced beginning in mid-1973 were set with foreign policy purposes preeminent. The development policy community was a weak internal voice; Agriculture had little stake in humanitarian food aid in a tight commodity situation. Moreover, now that U.S. troops had withdrawn from Indochina, the Congress was limiting other aid to Vietnam and Cambodia, and food was something Kissinger could use to compensate. As long as a country was a grain importer, Public Law 480 credits were money that could replace money Congress was taking away. And Public Law 480 was a flexible program, with far less congressional control over what was spent or who received it than the general foreign assistance program.

But as the world food situation worsened in 1974, voices outside the executive branch rose to protest what they viewed as a grotesque, callous policy. Senator Mark Hatfield denounced a "food aid policy" in which "preserving puppet regimes is more important . . . than preserving the lives of millions of people."[40] And 1974 saw the reemergence of the broad coalition of individuals and private groups to whom world hunger was a crucial problem and who wanted larger U.S. resources directed toward alleviating it. In the lead were senators like Humphrey

37. Balz, "Agriculture Report: Politics of Food Aid," p. 1765; *FATUS*, December 1975, pp. 16, 31.

38. Balz, "Agriculture Report: Politics of Food Aid," p. 1763.

39. It was also increasingly skewed toward countries that could take Public Law 480 rice, since the program continued to finance over one-third of U.S. rice exports throughout this period.

40. *Congressional Record* (December 4, 1974), p. 38149.

and Clark, who combined liberal voting records with agricultural constituencies. Developing countries that were both food importers and oil importers had been hit with a double blow in 1973–74, as wheat prices tripled and petroleum prices quadrupled. And food production was lagging once again in the largest food-deficit area, South Asia: India's self-sufficiency proved short-lived as production leveled off while population and demand continued to grow; Bangladesh still required large grain imports but had depleted its foreign exchange and could no longer rely on India for food assistance.

The United Nations developed estimates for the World Food Conference that the countries "most seriously affected" by the world economic crisis would require 7 million to 11 million tons of food aid in fiscal 1975. The conference itself brought a world spotlight on the deepening crisis. A representative from Bangladesh told conferees that 1 million people would die in his country within six weeks unless additional food was provided. Congressional members of the U.S. delegation used the Rome conference to exhort the president and Secretary Kissinger to take a more generous posture. Columnists like Tom Wicker and Anthony Lewis of the *New York Times* underscored the gap between U.S. food aid rhetoric and practice.[41] Bill Moyers pressed Kissinger on food aid allocation in the first interview of his new public television series.[42]

As Kissinger pushed for expanded food aid, he became, it appears, more sensitive to its humanitarian uses—and even more sensitive, perhaps, to the value of taking a humane public stance. Hence he titled his World Food Conference address "The Global Community and the Struggle Against Famine," and included in that comprehensive treatment of the world food problem not one mention of the relation of food to other U.S. foreign policy objectives. But the positions his department took one month later left little doubt that the secretary continued to see Public Law 480 primarily as a tool for political influence. Earl Butz might have played the public role, dramatizing the foreign policy uses of food (telling the Rome conference that food was a "tool in the kit of American diplomacy" and taking a side trip to Cairo during the

41. Tom Wicker, "Now It's Food for Politics," *New York Times*, November 12, 1974; Anthony Lewis, *New York Times*, January 23, 1975.

42. Kissinger replied, remarkably enough, that "the vast majority—the considerable majority—of our food aid goes for humanitarian purposes" (Lewis, *New York Times*, January 23, 1975).

conference to sign an agreement for 200,000 tons of wheat as part of America's Middle Eastern diplomatic efforts),[43] but it was Kissinger who pressed privately for foreign policy priorities—with Butz on the sidelines.

On December 5, 1974, at a meeting held at Agriculture, the State Department presented three food aid options for the 1975 budget. Each included a total amount and the allocation of that amount. And each allocation gave overriding priority to countries with political or security value.[44] A National Security Council staff official was even unwise enough to declare, "to give food aid to countries just because people are starving is a pretty weak reason." Interestingly, it was officials from OMB who pressed for consideration of an allocation alternative giving greater priority to the neediest countries; they wished to demonstrate that these needs could be met without spending the large total amount favored by State. The paper prepared for the president several days later included a low option of $1 billion and a high option of $1.4 billion but also two middle options of $1.2 billion, one with State's preferred allocation and one (OMB's) with greater humanitarian emphasis. And the internal battle was heated; in fact, one press account was avowedly based on documents "made available by officials making a last-ditch effort" to shift the program's emphasis in the humanitarian direction.[45]

Meanwhile, the Senate was watching—and taking action on its own. On December 3, the fiscal year 1975 foreign assistance authorization bill came to the Senate floor. On December 4, Senator Humphrey, the bill's floor manager, introduced an amendment placing a ceiling on the amount of concessional food aid that could go, in fiscal 1975, to countries not on the UN's list of the thirty-two "most seriously affected" by the world economic crisis. The amendment was adopted by voice vote. The Senate–House conference rewrote it, incorporating a percentage formula: no more than 30 percent for countries not on the list. A colloquy between Humphrey and Hatfield clarified the point, somewhat

43. Clyde H. Farnsworth, New York Times, November 17, 1974; Balz, "Agriculture Report: Politics of Food Aid," p. 1760.

44. Under the middle option, $612 million in title 1 aid was to go to Cambodia, Vietnam, South Korea, Indonesia, Chile, Pakistan, and the Middle East; $194 million to India, Bangladesh, and Sri Lanka.

45. Dan Morgan, Washington Post, December 9, 1974; William Robbins, New York Times, December 9, 1974. These published reports are consistent with, and substantiated by, interview sources. See also Martin Kriesberg, "Food Aid and Foreign Policy," unpublished paper, USDA, Economic Research Service, February 5, 1975.

ambiguous in the amendment itself, that it applied to title 1 rather than to overall food aid.[46]

By changing the language to a percentage formula, Humphrey was in effect bargaining with the executive branch; the larger the total program, the more the allocation for foreign policy purposes. And though the amendment further delayed the final budget decision, as the administration sorted out its meaning and Kissinger bargained with Humphrey on interpretation,[47] it ultimately increased the aid total and raised the share allocated to humanitarian purposes. In terms of actual food aid received in fiscal 1975, three of the "most seriously affected" countries—Bangladesh, India, and Pakistan—led the list. And concerning compliance with the amendment, the Agriculture Department's report on 1975 shipments concluded:

The Foreign Assistance Act of 1974 directs that at least 70 percent of U.S. concessional food aid in fiscal 1975 go to those countries which the United Nations designates as meeting certain criteria. In 1975, the criteria included countries with a per capita income in 1971 of under $400 and with a balance-of-payments deficit equal to 5 percent or more of imports. By the end of fiscal 1975, 41 countries met these conditions. About 70 percent of U.S. food aid did move to UN designated countries in 1975; however, over four-fifths of the total shipped to countries on the UN list went to just five— Bangladesh, India, Cambodia, Pakistan, and Egypt. Most of the remaining countries on the UN list are in Africa.[48]

46. *Congressional Record* (December 17, 1974), pp. 40383–84. Of the thirty-two countries, six had received title 1 aid in fiscal 1974: Bangladesh, Cambodia, Guinea, Pakistan, Sri Lanka, and Sudan. Four others received it in 1975: Haiti, Honduras, India, and Tanzania.

47. Kissinger wanted to be able to count Vietnam as a "most seriously affected" country, arguing that it met all the criteria and would have been so designated had it been in the United Nations. Humphrey's reply was, "If the President gives us a more liberal over-all program, he can have more liberal treatment on definitions." Leslie H. Gelb, *New York Times*, January 21, 1975.

48. *FATUS*, December 1975, p. 13. According to the same source (pp. 31, 38–39), the top ten recipients in fiscal 1975 (in millions of dollars of all food commodities) were as follows:

Country	Total food aid	Title 1 share of total
Bangladesh	212	206
India	211	103
Pakistan	100	79
Israel	95	50
Khmer Republic (Cambodia)	92	88
Egypt	89	76
Korea, Republic of	78	74
Chile	52	48
South Vietnam	30	23
Sri Lanka (Ceylon)	23	19

But the 70–30 requirement was a cumbersome instrument for achieving its humanitarian objectives. It was suited to the particular circumstances of 1974–75: a region (South Asia) urgently needing substantial amounts of food and a secretary of state relentlessly and successfully emphasizing foreign policy priorities instead—a grievous anomaly in American policy which required redress. By 1976, the amendment (redrafted, but with the same allocation purposes) was causing administrative problems and bringing lesser apparent humanitarian gains. Bangladesh no longer required massive amounts of concessional food aid; evidence suggested, in fact, that "bumper domestic crops combined with a large volume of imported food" were "overtaxing the storage capacity and managerial capability of the Government of Bangladesh," resulting in large-scale spoilage.[49]

The amendment not only reduced title 1's flexibility as a foreign policy tool, it hampered its use as a tool of domestic agricultural adjustment. It was (according to critical officials) a wheat bloc amendment, which made it very hard to move rice under the program. The South Asian countries didn't want rice—it was expensive, and their institutions for marketing food aid were built around wheat. Korea, a major rice market, wasn't poor enough to meet the revised criteria; and Indochina had gone communist. But U.S. rice growers, whose acreage allotment had been expanded particularly for the food aid program (mainly for Indochina), were now facing a glut and demanding action.

The Humphrey amendment is thus an apt example of the desirability, effectiveness, and limitations of congressional efforts to intervene in foreign policy administration. It sought to limit executive discretion that was, in congressional eyes, being used to pursue a mistaken (or at least out-of-balance) policy. And in the short run, the intervention was effective. In the longer run, however, it added another constraint to a program already very difficult to administer, even as it no longer effectively served the goal for which it was established.

The Case of Bangladesh

There remains one other critical allocation question—whether the food allocated to the hungriest nations arrived when the need was

49. Rudolph Rousseau, *Commodity Storage Conditions in Bangladesh,* staff report for the Subcommittee on Foreign Assistance of the Senate Foreign Relations Committee, 94 Cong. 2 sess. (GPO, 1976), p. 1.

greatest. Here the Bangladesh example requires closer examination. For while statistics show that country to be the largest food aid recipient in fiscal 1975, and by far the largest title 1 recipient, they also show that most of the food arrived after the hour of maximum need had passed.

To have met Bengali needs in a timely, effective manner would not have been easy. The aman rice crop, harvested between mid-November and mid-January, accounts for 60 percent of annual production. Hence, the period of greatest need is the months immediately before this crop is harvested and marketed—September to November. But this is also a period of major flooding, when much of Bangladesh is under water and internal transport is difficult. Food for rural areas should arrive at the ports by August or early September. Moreover, Bengali ports are physically limited and inefficiently managed, creating a congestion problem: shippers don't like to go there because they lose money waiting. And inside the country, food distribution and storage are inefficient.

Compounding these problems is the fact that the Bangladesh government channeled much of the food aid it received to groups other than the very hungriest. As a Senate staff report put it in 1976, "the ration system through which this food is distributed is designed to subsidize the food supplies of the most politically significant portions of the population: urban residents, the military, civil servants, police, students, etc."[50] These priorities held even in 1974; Donald F. McHenry and Kai Bird point to the rise in starvation "because the Dacca regime of Rahman was unwilling to divert foreign food aid from the urban ration system into the famine districts."[51]

In this context, the most responsive and humane U.S. food aid policy imaginable could have only limited the human damage of the food shortage. But U.S. policy was not responsive and humane. Of the 308,000 metric tons of food grain aid that arrived in Bangladesh during the crucial August–November 1974 period, the U.S. food aid supplied 68,000—less than one-quarter of an inadequate total.[52] Bengali grain

50. Ibid., p. 4.

51. "Food Bungle in Bangladesh," *Foreign Policy*, no. 27 (Summer 1977), p. 75. But even if no title 1 food went directly to the poor, it might *still* have helped them indirectly by dampening grain prices.

52. In the same period, the Bangladesh government purchased 137,000 metric tons from the United States on commercial terms; Saudi Arabia also financed 48,000 tons of U.S. wheat. "Schedule of Vessels Arrived/Expected at Bangladesh Ports Carrying Foodgrain, Other Foods, and Fertilizers, August 1974–January 1975," annex G to report from the U.S. agricultural attaché in Bangladesh, December 13, 1974.

imports dropped from 220,960 tons in August to 27,525 in September and 75,700 tons in October.[53] Not until October did the United States sign a general title 1 agreement with Bangladesh which (as progressively enlarged through April 1975) provided for amounts of wheat and rice proportionate to Bengali needs.[54] In the critical months before October, commercial imports totaling 300,000 tons were canceled when the Bangladesh government could not obtain enough short-term credit to finance contracts with American grain companies.[55]

The human cost was apparently high. Precise measurements are almost by definition unavailable in such a situation, but a report "for official use only," which was circulated within one respected international development organization, estimates that from September to November, 20,000 to 30,000 people died of starvation because food "came too late." A rough calculation by Lester R. Brown, extrapolating from a district that keeps good birth and death records, indicates that a "nationwide increase in deaths of 333,000" could have occurred in the fall of that year.[56]

Why was the United States so tardy in its response? The primary reason was that nobody was really paying Bangladesh very close attention. In 1965–67, India-watching was a major preoccupation within the U.S. government, from the top down. President Lyndon B. Johnson could cable Prime Minister Indira Gandhi, "I suspect I follow almost as closely as you the course of the rains, the Indian harvest, and new seeds, and the figures on fertilizer application,"[57] and if his words came across as paternalistic and offensive, there was considerable truth in them. No one above the country desk level was giving Bangladesh comparable scrutiny in 1974.

(BD-4094). The following pages draw substantially from attaché reports and other USDA documents, as cited at particular points.

53. "Bangladesh: Monthly Foodgrain Arrivals," report from the U.S. agricultural attaché in Bangladesh, June 6, 1975 (BD-5023), p. 5.

54. USDA, FAS, "Public Law 480, Concessional Sales Agreements," pp. 27–29. The October 4 agreement as amended provided for 550,000 metric tons of wheat and 300,000 metric tons of rice. "Bangladesh: Annual Grain Report, FY 1975," report from the U.S. agricultural attaché in Bangladesh, July 30, 1975 (BD-5032), p. 3.

55. Reports from the U.S. agricultural attaché in Bangladesh, August 1, 1974 (BD-4069), pp. 2–3; and June 26, 1974 (BD-4058); Emma Rothschild, "Food Politics," Foreign Affairs, vol. 54 (January 1976), p. 296.

56. "Hunger," New York Times, October 27, 1976.

57. Lyndon Baines Johnson, The Vantage Point: Perspective of the Presidency, 1963–1969 (Holt, Rinehart, and Winston, 1971), p. 231.

Another reason was that global development and welfare policy had become much less important to senior American officials in the near-decade which separated the two episodes. A related reason was that Bangladesh, for well-known historical reasons, was not considered a state for which the United States had any particular responsibility. The United States had "tilted" toward Pakistan in 1971, when the Bengalis had won their independence in a bloody civil war capped by Indian intervention. During the last month of that war, Kissinger had responded to the suggestion that the new country would be "an international basket case" with the comment that "it will not necessarily be our basket case."[58]

So though the country was a food-deficit, financially strapped entity from its creation, it initially looked elsewhere for aid. The United Nations mounted a massive relief operation, and India provided considerable food aid during the early months. But the first title 1 agreement was not signed until August 6, 1973—for 80,000 tons of wheat, later amended to add about 70,000 more. The fact that the United States provided even this much wheat in a tight period was evidence of some responsiveness to that country's needs—hence the memory of some food aid officials that that country's needs were reasonably accommodated. And Bangladesh did get a very large share of the very small amount of the Public Law 480 wheat shipped from the United States in July–December 1974.

But most of this wheat arrived at the very end of December or early in 1975, after the crisis had passed. The crisis had come suddenly, in the summer of 1974, with the exhaustion of the Bangladesh government's ability to pay and an unfavorable turn in the weather. Throughout the spring, Bengali officials had been pressing for increased food aid and for advance commitments they could count on—both hard to come by in 1974. They had also contracted for large commercial imports, but by June the U.S. agricultural attaché reported that the Bengali government was having difficulty paying for 450,000 tons contracted from Continental, Cargill, and Cook. If the country did not find the money, he continued, the grain companies might cancel all or part of the contracts—as in fact they subsequently did. Bengali officials asked for title 1 credit for this wheat and were told that U.S. regulations forbade

58. Paraphrased in Joint Chiefs of Staff minutes of the Washington Special Actions Group meeting of December 6, 1971, made public by Jack Anderson and published in the *New York Times,* January 6, 1972.

this and that a new authorizing agreement needed to be signed before any new food aid could be provided.[59]

In July and August abnormally high floods reduced the harvest of the aus rice crop just coming to market and disrupted the transplanting of the aman crop. This both increased food demand for relief purposes and reduced domestic production (though contemporary reports seem to have exaggerated these losses).[60] The Bengali government increased its total import estimate for fiscal year 1975 from 1.7 million to 2.3 million tons. Pledges from donors were now separated in world food program listings into preflood and postflood categories. And while the U.S. agriculture expert in Dacca was skeptical about the extent of flood damage, he did report on August 1 that "there may be a serious shortage of foodgrains in the next few months."[61]

Negotiations on a new food aid agreement dragged on. A provision of U.S. law barred sales to countries trading with Cuba, and this issue was resolved only after the Bangladesh government canceled further jute exports to that country.[62] Once the agreement was finally signed on October 4, normal delays of placing orders, shipping, and so on, practically guaranteed that food would not arrive before late December. (Interestingly, the Saudi government managed to purchase 48,000 tons of U.S. wheat and deliver on *its* postflood pledge in November. And the government of India purchased for its own food needs about 500,000 tons of U.S. wheat a month during October to December 1974.)[63]

Thus the U.S. government employed business-as-usual methods to deal with a serious, fast-developing food emergency; there was not among top officials enough urgency attached to the crisis to pull Bangladesh out of channels, to cut red tape as it was typically cut for Cam-

59. Reports from the U.S. agricultural attaché in Bangladesh: BD-4058; BD-4068; and BD-4069.

60. The *New York Times*, August 18, 1974, for example, reported that 80 percent of the aus crop was destroyed and that in sum, "at least" 40 percent of annual food production was lost. The World Food Programme office in Dacca estimated a few months later that the aus crop had been reduced by 700,000 tons, to 2.5 million long tons (enclosure to report from U.S. agricultural attaché in Bangladesh, December 13, 1974, BD-4094). The final figure from the government of Bangladesh was 2.86 million long tons.

61. Attaché report BD-4069.

62. Rothschild, "Food Politics" p. 296; McHenry and Bird, "Food Bungle in Bangladesh" p. 82.

63. Annex G, attaché report BD-4094, pp. 1–2; report from the U.S. agricultural attaché in New Delhi, IN-5002, p. 19.

bodia or Vietnam, to get the food there in time. And the outside pressure, which ultimately brought the increase in humanitarian food aid, was effective too late to meet this particular crisis.

Ironically, the United States was to pour title 1 grain into Bangladesh thereafter. By 1976, a Senate subcommittee staff report was criticizing a "highly questionable" decision to send Bangladesh 150,000 additional tons of wheat and 50,000 tons of rice "despite the overflowing storage facilities" and the resultant "increased spoilage."[64] One reason cited was that "many of these same officials were criticized when U.S. assistance was not immediately available during a recent famine in Bangladesh"; they "did not wish to be placed in that situation again." Another was that USDA was once again, as in pre-1972 days, "under pressure to move PL 480 commodities, particularly rice."

64. Rousseau, *Commodity Storage Conditions in Bangladesh,* pp. 5–6. Eventually the 150,000 tons of wheat were not shipped; the rice was.

CHAPTER SIX

The Grain Reserves Proposal, 1975

THROUGH MOST OF THE 1972 TO 1975 PERIOD, while the world was enduring the successive crises in food supply, the world community was actively deliberating the issue of international grain reserves. Proponents
argued that reserves could dampen price fluctuations, help guarantee
market access for commercial importers, and would be available for
famine relief and other critical needs. Indeed, had reserves with agreed-
upon rules of access and allocation in time of shortage existed during
those years, the trade-offs faced by U.S. policymakers in the crises treated
in the foregoing chapters could have been mitigated or avoided altogether. But the U.S. government moved very slowly on the reserves
issue. Finally, after at least two years of internal debate, Washington did
propose to the International Wheat Council in September 1975 the creation of an international system of nationally held wheat and rice stocks.
But the system proposed was limited in size, uncertain in efficacy, and
not very responsive to the views of the other national governments
whose collaboration would be required to put it into effect.

Background

From the turnaround in the world food situation of late 1972 until
early 1974, the U.S. government took a negative approach to food reserves. Secretary of Agriculture Earl L. Butz recognized some need to
have food available "to lessen genuine hardship and prevent starvation,"
and recognized also that "maintaining reserve stocks of food for commercial use [was] wise and necessary,"[1] but he was equally determined

1. "A Realistic Look at Food Reserves," address of December 11, 1973, in *Vital
Speeches*, vol. 40 (January 15, 1974), pp. 197–98; Butz quoted in Daniel J. Balz,

that the government role in bringing about such stocks should be minimal. "The U.S. government has now gone out of the commodity business," he said with pride after the exhaustion of Commodity Credit Corporation (CCC) stocks, "and we want to stay out of the business of managing stocks of farm products for the nation and the world." He added: "We must get over the idea that there is something evil about rises and falls in food supplies and prices."

In 1974, however, more positive statements from those in authority began to be heard. In his speech to the Sixth Special Session of the UN General Assembly, April 15, 1974, Secretary of State Henry A. Kissinger declared American readiness "to join with other governments in a major worldwide effort to rebuild food reserves."[2] The following September, before the UN General Assembly, President Gerald Ford made this into a commitment to "negotiate, establish, and maintain an international *system* of food reserves."[3] More detailed information about what such a system would entail was offered by Kissinger in his World Food Conference speech that November. He set forth six elements: international sharing of information on production, stocks, and trade; agreement on the size of the reserves; sharing responsibility for holding the reserves; guidelines for managing the reserves to protect against famine and excessive price fluctuations; a preference for cooperating countries in the distribution of reserves; and procedures for adjusting targets, settling disputes, and dealing with noncompliers. And the secretary suggested that "a worldwide reserve of as much as 60 million tons of food above present carryover levels may be needed to assure adequate food security."[4]

It took almost another year, however, for the U.S. government to agree on what is, on balance, a very modest proposal. On September 29, 1975, Richard E. Bell, deputy assistant secretary of agriculture, presented a proposal for an international grain reserve system to the International Wheat Council. The United States proposed accumulation of

"Economic Report: World Food Conference Prompts U.S. Farm Policy Review," *National Journal*, June 1, 1974, p. 804.

2. "The Challenge of Interdependence," in *Department of State Bulletin*, vol. 70 (May 6, 1974), p. 480.

3. "Address to the 29th Session of the General Assembly of the United Nations, September 18, 1974," in *Public Papers of the Presidents: Gerald R. Ford, 1974* (Government Printing Office, 1975, p. 81. Emphasis added.

4. "The Global Community and the Struggle Against Famine," in *Department of State Bulletin*, vol. 71 (December 16, 1974), p. 828.

a 30 million ton reserve—25 million tons of wheat and 5 million tons of rice—"adequate to offset at least 90 percent of production shortfalls."[5] In addition, the proposal said that "consideration should be given as to whether stocks of coarse grains are needed." Responsibility for holding reserves would be "equitably shared among participants," taking into account "measures of trade in food grains, gross domestic product, and variance in production." Reserves would be "nationally held," with each government determining "how its reserves will be maintained." But all would be required to follow "internationally agreed rules or guidelines" regarding when stocks were to be acquired or released. Specifically, these guidelines would be tied to "a quantitative indicator based upon stock levels and deviations in production from the long-term production trend." Participants in the system would "receive assured access to supply at market prices"; nonparticipants "would not be assured of obtaining access to reserves held by others." And should participants be forced to apply export restraints in a very severe shortage, they would "give preferential treatment to other complying participants."

The U.S. proposal was coolly received. One reason was that European countries preferred price triggers for acquisition and release of stocks, since the Common Market agricultural policy was based on price indicators. Moreover, European countries wanted reserves to be part of a comprehensive commodity arrangement, with prices kept high and within a narrow range, an approach the United States resisted. But another reason for the cool reception was that by the time the United States got its proposal together, the international food crisis had receded. With grain prices falling and stock replenishment beginning in any case, the issue had lost its urgency. Importing countries could now afford to take their time about negotiating—to wait and see how trade negotiations went at Geneva before bargaining seriously in London; to see if a new American administration might modify the stand of the old. For they no longer needed to worry about access to grain in the short term. The international buyers' market was returning.[6]

Why did it take so long for the U.S. government to respond to what

5. For summaries of the proposal, see Philip H. Trezise, *Rebuilding Grain Reserves* (Brookings Institution, 1976), pp. 52–55; and Daniel J. Balz, "Economic Report: Export Controls Possible Under U.S. Grain Reserve Plan," *National Journal*, November 11, 1975, p. 1427.

6. See U.S. Department of Agriculture, Economic Research Service, "World Grain Situation Improving," *World Agricultural Situation* (USDA, December 1976), pp. 16–28.

many outside governments saw as an urgent need? And why was the
U.S. proposal not stronger, or better adapted to the international diplomatic environment?

The Slow Pace of Policymaking

Calls for a system of reserves to insure world food security had become
standard public fare by mid-1973.[7] But to many in the farm policy
community, reserve stocks were the very thing they were at long last
escaping *from*. For most of the postwar period there was no food reserve
problem. Surplus U.S. stocks, a by-product of price support programs,
had brought stability to the domestic consumer price index and assurance that supplies would be available to meet world production shortfalls. In the marketing year 1965–66, for example, world stocks of wheat
and coarse grains were drawn down almost as much as they were in
1972–73. But because world (mainly U.S.) grain reserves were higher in
1965 than in 1972, the price effects of the first drawdown were minimal,
whereas those of the second were dramatic.[8]

During the postwar period, food stocks were regarded as not a blessing but a curse. Farmers saw them "overhanging the market" and de-
pressing prices. To Agriculture Department officials they not only depressed prices but were a drain on the budget as well—a concern more
than equally shared in the Treasury and the OMB. Thus U.S. policy
under both Democratic and Republican administrations in the sixties
and early seventies was aimed at stock reduction. This policy had had a
measure of success up to 1972; thereafter the Russian sales and expanded
overall world demand completed the job.

7. See, for example, the proposal by Senator Hubert H. Humphrey for "consumer
and marketing reserves," outlined in *Export Control Policy,* Hearings before the
Subcommittee on Foreign Agricultural Policy of the Senate Committee on Agriculture and Forestry, 93 Cong. 1 sess. (GPO, 1973), pp. 20–39; the proposal for "internationally supervised stockholding of major farm products" in *Toward the Integration of World Agriculture,* a tripartite report (Brookings Institution, 1973), pp.
23 ff.; and "World Food Security Proposal of the Director-General," Food and Agriculture Organization of the United Nations, August 1973, in Library of Congress,
Congressional Research Service, *International Food Reserves: Background and Current Proposals,* prepared for the Subcommittee on International Organizations and
Movements of the House Committee on Foreign Affairs, 93 Cong. 2 sess. (GPO,
1974).

8. Trezise, *Rebuilding Grain Reserves,* p. 1.

Suddenly prosperous farmers recognized well that their prices would have risen far less in 1972–73 had U.S. and world reserves been greater; they associated ongoing reserve stocks with the depressed market conditions of the two previous decades.[9] And Secretary Butz encouraged this association. Though he had been slow to exploit the free market opportunity the Russian grain sale had afforded, by early 1973 he was a strong spokesman for a commercial agriculture liberated from government constraints. He saw price fluctuations, not governmental stock management, as the appropriate adjustment mechanism for balancing food supply and demand. And because he was reluctant to offer farmers the assurance of economically meaningful price supports to brake falling prices, he could hardly call on them to accept the restraint on market price rises which an effective reserve system would enforce.[10] So his farm policy depended, doctrinally and politically, on a considerable range of price fluctuations. Butz argued, moreover, that if the U.S. government stayed out of the commodity business, farmers and traders would accumulate greater stocks themselves, as would importing countries.

Thus the agricultural policy community was generally skeptical of reserves, notwithstanding the more positive views of many agricultural economists[11] and the stakes of certain agriculture interests (for example, livestock producers) in more stable grain prices. The foreign and development policy communities, on the other hand, were strongly interested. For foreign policy officials, a food reserves system not only might prevent shocks (like the soybean embargo) to bilateral relations and provide a means to assuage world food emergencies; it could also be a breakthrough for international cooperation in the long-abrasive sphere of agricultural trade, and a constructive response to pressure from developing countries for a "new international economic order" responsive to their interests and needs. Development advocates supported it for the latter reason and because it could contribute to more generous food aid policies in time of need.

Foreign policy concerns got the U.S. government moving on the

9. This association, while valid in certain respects, neglects the fact that the accumulation of reserves strengthens farm prices. This of course was the reason for the old Commodity Credit Corporation stocks.

10. Federal commodity programs remained in effect throughout the Butz regime, but the secretary resisted raising support levels from 1973 levels to accommodate sharply increased production costs; thus they offered little protection.

11. One was Butz's chief economic policy official, Don Paarlberg.

issue; in the wake of the soybean embargo, a comprehensive interagency study of international food policy was ordered in the summer of 1973.[12] When this analysis proved inconclusive, a study of food reserves was ordered, under the oversight of the Council on International Economic Policy (CIEP) staff, with USDA responsible for the specific staff work.[13] By early 1974, a minimal consensus had emerged within the government that there *should* be some international stock arrangement and that it *should not* be controlled by an international agency. This was reflected in a modification of Butz's public stance. By March, he was conceding that "we may well need a better set of guidelines for individual nations to consider following" in maintaining carryover food supplies and that "stockpiling policy" was a problem that must "be faced during the course of negotiation" on agricultural trade; he continued to oppose "government-held" reserves in the United States and to emphasize that, for food security, "the answers begin with production."[14] Kissinger was at the other end of the consensus range, prepared, he said, to join "in a major worldwide effort."[15]

But progress toward greater specificity came hard. One reason was the disappearance of leadership as Nixon became enveloped in Watergate and as the staff under him went through changes. George P. Shultz, Nixon's economic czar, left government in May; he was replaced by Kenneth Rush as White House economic coordinator and William E. Simon as treasury secretary. Peter M. Flanigan, whose Council on International Economic Policy staff had been jockeying with the National Security Council staff on international economic policy issues, left government at about the same time, to be replaced as CIEP executive director by William D. Eberle, the special trade representative. In June (at about the time two National Security Council staff members active on food issues were moving to the Treasury Department), the President's Committee on Food was established, chaired by Rush and including the top officials of State, Treasury, Agriculture, CEA, and OMB;

12. See chapter 5.

13. Leslie H. Gelb and Anthony Lake, "Less Food, More Politics," *Foreign Policy*, no. 17 (Winter 1974–1975), p. 178.

14. Earl L. Butz, "Food Security Is Everybody's Business," speech delivered to the annual meeting of the National Grain and Feed Association, March 13, 1974 (USDA press release 705–74); and testimony, March 6, 1974, *The Trade Reform Act of 1973*, Hearings before the Senate Committee on Finance, 93 Cong. 1 sess. (GPO, 1974), pt. 2, pp. 379, 421.

15. "The Challenge of Interdependence."

it replaced the Cost of Living Council food committee.[16] But Rush's role ended when Nixon gave way to Ford in August, and the committee was supplanted by the Economic Policy Board (EPB), created by Ford on September 30 to coordinate general economic policymaking.

A second reason for lack of movement on reserves was the ambivalent position of the economic policy community. In February 1974 the CEA had generally endorsed stockpiling, to help ensure that the United States could be "a reliable supplier of food for the world," and "to provide a measure of domestic price stability."[17] It favored "the examination of multilateral approaches," and concluded that under likely near-future market conditions, "accumulation of contingency reserves would . . . require that the Government purchase commodities in the market or have ready access to farm-held stocks under the Government loan program." But if senior economic policy officials were more positive than Butz about the price-stabilizing potential of reserves, they did not actively champion them. For they shared his preference for free-market approaches over government management, an orientation that continued from Shultz to Simon, and at CEA from Herbert Stein to Alan Greenspan.

Finally, food reserves policymaking moved slowly because there was no way a system could be established in 1974 which would alleviate current food shortages. Had greater reserves been held in 1972, under an arrangement that protected them against sudden, massive drawdowns like the Russian purchases, there would certainly have been less instability in grain and soybean markets thereafter. But even if agreement on a system could be quickly reached—and no one argued that it could—actual replenishment of reserves had to wait until production grew and/or consumption fell because of higher prices. Thus reserves were essentially a long-run proposition, and the government was overloaded with short-run food policy concerns.

Without strong White House leadership and support from economic policy officials, and with reserves being largely irrelevant to the immediate crises, it was difficult for State to move the issue forward against the resistance of USDA. The Agriculture Department had more than an equal claim to the issue and had direct jurisdiction over critical matters

16. The Cost of Living Council was being abolished, but Dunlop and others felt it important to continue executive office oversight of USDA. The official action was "Economic Stabilization—Termination of Activities," Executive Order no. 11788, *Federal Register*, vol. 39 (June 18, 1974), p. 46824.

17. *Economic Report of the President, February 1974*, pp. 134–36.

like how U.S. reserves would be accumulated and released, by whom, and at what prices.

State's one important source of leverage was the upcoming World Food Conference. Since reserves were prominent on the agenda, State could demand that the United States take a diplomatic *posture,* even if no agreement could be reached on a concrete *program.* Ambassador Edwin M. Martin was effective in pushing the issue as U.S. coordinator for the conference, and Kissinger won clearance from other agencies for a speech outlining six elements of an international reserve system. But the effort to define these elements provoked greater interagency conflict in the months ahead.

The Proposal's Content: The Mountain Labored . . .

Kissinger's strong endorsement of an international reserve system at Rome seemed a clear victory for those favoring strong U.S. action. But eight months later, a careful contemporary analyst concluded that "nearly everything has gone Butz's way."[18] State did ultimately prevail on one key issue, but the final U.S. proposal, outlined in September 1975, was for a relatively weak system, and it elicited little interest from other countries.

Of the six elements proposed by Kissinger at Rome, three occasioned little controversy within the U.S. government. The "exchange of information" on stock levels, crop prospects, and trade intentions was universally supported; so was "sharing of the responsibility for holding reserves," since all wanted to share a burden which had, up to 1972, been primarily carried by North America. And there clearly had to be "procedures for adjustment of targets and settlement of disputes and measures for dealing with noncompliance."[19]

Nor was there strong disagreement on two other issues—whether U.S. reserves should be governmentally or privately held and whether reserves should be negotiated at the International Wheat Council in London or the Multilateral Trade Negotiations at Geneva. Senator Hubert Humphrey pressed for government-owned and government-managed stocks, and Senator George McGovern believed that "a

18. Daniel J. Balz, "Economic Report: State-Agriculture Feud Delays Grain Reserve System," *National Journal,* June 28, 1975, p. 951.
19. "The Global Community and the Struggle Against Famine."

reserve in private hands is no reserve at all."[20] But Secretary Butz was adamantly opposed to government-held stocks, and by early 1975, if not before, State Department officials had concluded that the United States could play its part in an international system with privately held stocks, provided that appropriate rules and incentives were established for their acquisition and release.

On the locus of negotiations, the office of the special trade representative wanted reserves to be taken up at the Multilateral Trade Negotiations (MTN), where the United States could trade access to U.S. supplies (which a reserves system would help assure) for reductions in European Community agricultural trade barriers.[21] But both State and Agriculture preferred the International Wheat Council. Agriculture officials, only lukewarm about reserves anyway, feared that by pushing for a reserve proposal at Geneva the United States might lose leverage on other agricultural trade matters; State shared this concern, and also did not wish to have a reserve agreement delayed until an overall MTN package was negotiated—1977 at the earliest. Moreover, both agencies wanted to involve the Soviet Union in the talks, since the Russians were the primary source of trade instability in world grain markets. The Soviet Union was not a party to the General Agreement on Tariffs and Trade (the umbrella for MTN), but it was a member of the International Wheat Council. Hence, at an ad hoc meeting in February with ten other governments, the United States won a decision that "examination of the need for a formal reserves agreement should be undertaken within the framework of discussions taking place within the International Wheat Council on bases for a new agreement to succeed the International Wheat Agreement of 1971."[22]

The three "elements" that remained as sources of contention were, in ascending order of importance: "agreement on the size of global reserves"; "preference for cooperating countries in the distribution of reserves"; and "guidelines on the management of national reserves, de-

20. *Washington Post*, September 15, 1974.

21. Such a connection was urged in *Toward the Integration of World Agriculture*, pp. 22 ff. For a discussion of how trade liberalization can reduce the size of world reserve stocks required, by making consumption adjust more rapidly to price changes, see Robbin S. Johnson, "The World Grain Economy and the Food Problem," *World Development*, vol. 5 (May–July 1977), pp. 549–58.

22. Letter to Senator Hubert H. Humphrey from Thomas O. Enders, January 21, 1976, reprinted in *Who's Making Foreign Agricultural Policy*, Hearings before the Subcommittee on Foreign Agricultural Policy of the Senate Committee on Agriculture and Forestry, 94 Cong. 2 sess. (GPO, 1976), p. 33.

fining the conditions for adding to reserves and for releasing from them."
And because of an internal dispute over these issues, a fourth became
important—whether a reserve should be designed for overall market
stabilization or for the more limited goal of alleviating the threat of
famine in developing countries.

Even as the World Food Conference was meeting, Kissinger and his
aggressive assistant secretary for economic affairs, Thomas O. Enders,
moved to gain the initiative in the interagency struggle that lay ahead.
The secretary of state persuaded President Ford to create a new interagency committee, the International Food Review Group (IFRG) under
the National Security Council. The IFRG's purpose was to coordinate
U.S. follow-up to the World Food Conference; Kissinger was chairman
and Enders was head of the working group. This initiative was of course
opposed by both agriculture and economic policy officials, but Kissinger
managed to define food reserves as a foreign policy problem and thus
won presidential acquiescence.[23]

The IFRG was, like most such cabinet committees, a formal umbrella rather than an active forum—it met only occasionally during its
sixteen-month existence. But Enders's working group met often, bringing together State, the Office of Management and Budget, the Council of
Economic Advisers, STR, Treasury, and CIEP. In these meetings, Enders
pushed very strongly his ideas on the content of the U.S. proposal, particularly on the most important and controversial issue, guidelines for the
acquisition and release of reserve commodities. He sought as tight a system as possible, with stocks large enough and guidelines specific and
binding enough to provide maximum supply insurance and market stabilization. The system would be built around agreed price indicators.
When the prices approached the upper end of an agreed range, participants would consult and then release grain from stocks in a coordinated
manner; when prices were down, the parties would accumulate stocks.
To ensure that nonparticipants did not disrupt the system with large
grain purchases in time of shortage (or failure to build stocks in time of
surplus), participants would give one another preference over outsiders
in access to supplies during time of shortage.

23. Kissinger apparently won President Ford's approval during a three-hour
private meeting at Camp David, November 10, when the secretary reported on his
trip (which had included a swing through the Middle East). One reason the economic policy advisers disliked the new institution was that it was outside the framework of the Economic Policy Board, which Ford had established six weeks earlier to
coordinate all domestic and international economic policy decisions.

To Enders, a tight structure was necessary for a reserve system to work; to Butz and Bell, a tight structure would require domestic supply management, to which they were doctrinally opposed. Price-based international rules would compel them to intervene in commodity markets when they did not wish to. And commodity policy was *their* turf; they had no intention of yielding all or part of it to an international system that State would play a large role in managing. So, lukewarm at best to any proposal, they gained the one they would settle for by simply resisting the one that was offered. This put State in a bind, for absent a strong presidential decision in its favor, there would be no U.S. proposal unless State yielded to USDA. Agriculture, in the words of one of its most involved officials, "outlasted them."

Agriculture reiterated its objections: that the plan was a price-fixing arrangement contrary to free-market principles and policies; that stocks would overhang the market and depress prices; and that the farm community wouldn't accept any reserves scheme. To State officials, USDA was "highly ideological," and its arguments could be effectively rebutted; indeed, they felt they *had* rebutted them. But State's problems were not limited to USDA, for economic policy officials were also ideologically opposed to Enders's plan.[24] To them it looked very much like the type of price-regulating international commodity arrangement for which the developing countries were pressing. In addition, OMB staff officials were unhappy with any plan because neither State nor Agriculture seemed able or willing to provide cost estimates.

Gary Seevers, the agricultural specialist on the CEA, was increasingly skeptical. While recognizing the potential benefits in price stabilization and sharing of the costs of stockholding, he thought Enders aspired to manage the international market more tightly than was possible or desirable. The CEA staff agricultural economist, G. Edward Schuh, was even more skeptical. Thus while the February 1974 CEA annual report was generally favorable to an international effort, the February 1975 report dwelled on the difficulties and predicted that international "negotiations on grain reserves are likely to be protracted."[25]

As an alternative Seevers and Schuh developed a proposal for a more

24. Two Treasury officials actively involved at the staff level were strong supporters of a tight reserve system, and thus a real "thorn in our side" to Agriculture. But their leverage was limited because they were not believed to have the support of Secretary Simon. Balz, "Economic Report: State-Agriculture Feud," p. 957.

25. *Economic Report of the President, February 1975*, p. 182.

limited reserve, earmarked explicitly for developing countries. This proposal was opposed by both State and Agriculture—by State because it wished to stabilize agricultural relations among the advanced industrial nations and with the Soviet Union; by Agriculture because the proposal looked like food aid, which Agriculture wanted to keep separate from grain reserves. The CEA responded to State that the Soviet problem should be resolved through a bilateral agreement (or an exporters' cartel that regulated Russian purchases); and that the solution to the problem of agricultural relations with the European Community and Japan was trade liberalization, which would reduce world price fluctuations by spreading the burden of adjustment to them.

Enders's price-based system was not without economic logic,[26] but bureaucratically it was counterproductive. It gave USDA a pretext for continued resistance to any grain reserve proposal, and it alarmed economic policy officials, whose support Enders needed to overcome the resistance of USDA. Nor was Enders's commitment to a tight system entirely shared by his deputy, longtime State commodity specialist Julius L. Katz, who was skeptical about its efficacy. And Kissinger, not involved in the detailed economic debate, wanted agreement on a specific U.S. position. Thus Enders pulled back from his drive for price triggers and accepted quantitative guidelines early in 1975.

The question of the size of the reserve also moved closer to resolution. Kissinger had spoken at the World Food Conference of "as much as 60 million tons of food above present carryover levels."[27] But part of this was to be feed grains, and further interagency staff work concluded that the demand for feed grains adjusted rapidly to price changes—when prices went up, livestock producers moved more cattle to market. So the debate was now narrowed to how much food grain, mostly wheat, should be held. State wanted 35 million tons. Agriculture favored 20 million tons, to encourage greater price fluctuations.

But there remained the thorny question of how to deal with countries that did not join the system, especially the Soviet Union. United States officials were at best uncertain whether the Russians would accept the

26. "For U.S. reserve stock management, price rules are preferred to quantity rules." Jerry A. Sharples and Rodney L. Walker, "Grain Reserves: Price Instability and the Food Supply," in USDA, Economic Research Service, *Agricultural-Food Policy Review* (USDA, January 1977), p. 91. Trezise argues, similarly, that "the most generally suitable" guidelines "would be prices in world markets." *Rebuilding Grain Reserves*, p. 59.

27. "The Global Community and the Struggle Against Famine."

obligations for information-sharing and reserve management which a multilateral scheme would call for. For State, it was essential that the system give preference to members in time of shortage—and thus discriminate against those who had not shared the burden of maintaining the reserves. To Agriculture, such preference meant export controls, which they opposed for reasons of both economic doctrine and self-interest. In particular, they did not want to risk alienating the Russian market, which had helped make possible Butz's "policy of plenty."

Faced with the continuing stalemate, Kissinger and Enders resorted to the now-familiar device of a secretarial speech to press for a policy breakthrough. The occasion was a scheduled speech to the Kansas City International Relations Council on May 13, 1975, which Kissinger employed to address the growing demands from developing countries for a new international economic order.[28]

Kissinger spoke of seven principles which would govern "a comprehensive international system of reserves" that the United States would "formally propose" in "meetings later this month." One principle dealt with size ("large enough to meet potential shortfalls in food grains production"), a second with burden-sharing ("fair allocation" between "exporters and importers" based on "wealth, grain productive capacity, and trade"). Three of them covered guidelines, and here the influence of Agriculture was evident. Enders had wanted to say "agreed international rules" for buildup and drawdown of stocks; USDA had insisted on "agreed international rules *or guidelines*" (emphasis added). Drawdowns would be "triggered by shortfalls in world production," the quantitative trigger. And "each participating country should be free to determine how its reserves will be maintained and what incentives to provide for their buildup, holding, and drawdowns." The sixth principle provided that "the system must assure access to supplies for countries that participate in it." (State had wanted to say *"priority* access," signaling discrimination against outsiders, but USDA had resisted.) The seventh, uncontroversial in Washington, was that "the system must encourage expanded and liberalized trade in grains." Finally, Kissinger held forth hope that "if others join us in negotiating such a system, the

28. Henry A. Kissinger, "Strengthening the World Economic Structure," *Department of State Bulletin*, vol. 72 (June 2, 1975), pp. 713–19. See Balz, "Economic Report: State-Agriculture Feud," pp. 957–59. Enders managed to win USDA clearance for the specific language on reserves by talking directly with Butz (who was frequently more accommodating in private than his subordinates were, or than Butz's public rhetoric would suggest).

outline of an international reserves agreement can be completed before the end of the year."

But this effort to force a consensus was unsuccessful; the predicted proposal "later this month" did not materialize, though Kissinger repeated essentially the same language in his address to the Organisation for Economic Co-operation and Development on May 28.[29] As a State official put it, after the Kansas City speech, "everybody fell off the wagon." The Council of Economic Advisers continued to push for a smaller reserves system for developing countries. (Schuh was now acting chairman of the Food Deputies Group, Seevers having left the council in April.) Agriculture was unhappy, partly because of the discrimination against outsiders, partly for reasons outlined by Assistant Secretary Clayton K. Yeutter:

The rhetoric doesn't conform to a loose system. It provides the opportunity for other countries to perceive a system other than what we want. The European Community will unquestionably read the speech as an opportunity to negotiate commodity agreements on grains.[30]

With the stalemate still unbroken, the Enders working group was no longer a productive vehicle for reserves decisionmaking; it had forced attention to the issue and had narrowed several interagency differences, but it was too much on State's side of the issue, and thus too little trusted by the agricultural and economic policy communities, to bring the issue to resolution.

Instead, the final decision was forced by economic policymakers. At a June 11 meeting of the Economic Policy Board, James Lynn and presidential economic assistant L. William Seidman pressed Katz for a resolution and the board ordered State to prepare a new options paper. On June 13, Seevers's position on the Council of Economic Advisers was filled by Paul W. MacAvoy, who thereby became chairman of the Food Deputies Group. MacAvoy, who generally did not sympathize with State Department efforts to meet developing countries partway on commodity issues and was initially very skeptical of the idea of an international food reserves system as well, was persuaded that the issue was not price-fixing but buffer stocks. The issue was thus recast as an economic analysis problem. Econometric studies ordered by MacAvoy's group showed that a system of reserves would have a favorable effect on the world food situation. They also concluded that in practice the system

29. *Department of State Bulletin*, vol. 72 (June 23, 1975), pp. 853–54.
30. Balz, "Economic Report: State-Agriculture Feud," p. 959.

would move other countries to share, at least slightly, the burden of food reserves. Based on this study, a consensus was reached in mid-July and pinned down at a cabinet session led by Kissinger later that month.

The rudiments of the agreement were made public in Kissinger's September 1 speech to the UN Seventh Special Session and its complete form in the proposal submitted to the International Wheat Council on September 29. The amount of reserves was a compromise between State and Agriculture: "30 million tons of wheat and rice,"[31] predominantly wheat. It proposed a two-stage system of guidelines for cooperation in reserve management based on a compromise put forward by Yeutter, now deputy special trade representative: a relatively loose system in times of plenty, tighter in periods of short supply. State won on the discrimination issue—participants would "receive assured access to supplies . . . nonparticipants or participants not complying with the agreement would not be assured of obtaining access"; if a shortage were "so severe that participants were forced to apply export restraints . . . they would give preferential treatment to other complying participants."

The final proposal was stronger than it might have been had not State persisted. But in pressing for a tight, price-based system of grain stock management, State had moved too far into the spheres of economic and agricultural policy, and (more important) had proposed arrangements at variance with the values of officials who led USDA, CEA, OMB, and Treasury in 1974 and 1975. Kissinger had strong leverage with President Ford, and Enders was very adept bureaucratically, but since they were unable or disinclined to forge alliances with key economic or agriculture policy officials, their effectiveness was limited to issues and occasions that they could define as *foreign* policy rather than *economic* or *agricultural* policy. Had they not exploited the World Food Conference and Kissinger's role as foreign policy spokesman, there might not have been any U.S. reserves proposal; but their lack of a shared perspective with either the economic or agriculture policy community limited the substance of the proposal. What was critical was not only that each community emphasized different questions—international system-building, domestic economic management, commodity politics—but also the fact that the Nixon-Ford economic and agriculture officials gave different *answers* to the questions, more conservative answers than foreign policy officials.

31. For a summary of the proposal, see Trezise, *Rebuilding Grain Reserves*, pp. 52–54.

CHAPTER SEVEN

The Russian Grain Purchases, 1974 and 1975

WHILE THE FOOD AID AND GRAIN RESERVES debates were being brought to their conclusions, American food policymakers were also confronting anew the problem of Russian grain purchases and their effect on domestic prices. But this time neither the Russians nor the grain companies went unconstrained. Farm policy values were reined in to accommodate economic and foreign policy goals. In October 1974, a White House meeting called by President Ford led to the cancellation of Continental Grain Company and Cook Industries sales contracts with the Soviet Union and a renegotiation to make the commodity mix more consistent with limited U.S. corn supplies. In July 1975, the administration suspended grain sales to Russia until the size of the 1975 U.S. corn crop could be known and a bilateral agreement negotiated regulating future Soviet purchases in the U.S. grain market.

Background

After their large purchases of 1972, the Russians stayed out of the U.S. grain market until late 1974. Soviet grain production for 1973 was a record 212 million tons. But their 1974 crop was down to 184 million tons, and that fall they again entered the U.S. market suddenly, although for smaller amounts and not without some prior diplomatic consultation. On Thursday, October 3, they contracted with Continental for 1 million tons of corn; on the following morning they signed a deal with Cook for 1.3 million tons of corn and 900,000 tons of wheat. The Department of Agriculture was notified immediately, under reporting procedures then in operation, and (as previously instructed) the department passed the information on directly to the White House.

As noted in chapter 5, U.S. grain supplies were very tight that fall, in the wake of the corn belt drought. Corn prices received by farmers in October reached a peak of $3.45 a bushel; the price for a bushel of wheat reached $4.85.[1] Consumer prices were again rising rapidly after some leveling off the previous spring. There was also evidence the Russians were in the market for at least 2 million additional tons. And everyone remembered 1972.

Thus, though the amounts were quite small compared to 1972,[2] the administration responded quickly. On Friday afternoon, one day after the first of the grain contracts was signed, Secretary of the Treasury William Simon summoned representatives of the grain companies to a White House meeting set for 9 A.M. Saturday. At the meeting, in the presence of Simon, Earl Butz, and other officials, President Ford told the company representatives that the sales should not go forward, citing U.S. political pressure and the danger that Congress might force export controls if the sales were not stopped.[3] The following Monday, Butz summoned grain company representatives to a meeting at the Department of Agriculture at which he announced to an overflow audience the enforcement of a new, "voluntary" system under which companies would obtain "prior approval" at USDA for all sales in excess of 50,000 tons to any country.[4] Shortly thereafter, Secretary Simon led a mission to Moscow to renegotiate the contracts, which ended up with the same total volume of grain but reversed the amounts of wheat and corn.

For the next few months the government monitored grain exports with great care. But as market conditions eased and prices fell, the process

1. U.S. Department of Agriculture, Statistical Reporting Service, Crop Reporting Board, *Agricultural Prices: Annual Summary 1975* (USDA, June 1976), pp. 12–13.

2. The 2.3 million tons of corn and 900,000 tons of wheat were less than 2 percent of U.S. production. The 1972 wheat sales had been about 25 percent of U.S. production.

3. Edward W. Cook, chairman of the board of Cook Industries, asked that the government put its "request" in writing, and Simon sent him a mailgram: "These contracts are *not in the national interest at this time* and Cook Industries should not proceed to implement them" (emphasis in original). A similar mailgram was sent to Continental. For the full text, see *Sales of Grain to the Soviet Union,* Hearings before the Permanent Subcommittee on Investigations of the Senate Committee on Government Operations, 93 Cong. 2 sess. (Government Printing Office, 1974), pp. 20, 37.

4. To explain what he meant by a voluntary system, Butz told a story about a worker who, after years as the lone holdout in his plant, had "voluntarily" joined the union following a call from the president of the company. Why had he changed his mind? "Nobody ever explained it to me before the way he did." How did the boss explain it? "He said if I don't join the union I'll be fired tomorrow."

was relaxed, and on January 29, 1975, Secretary Butz announced the lifting of the requirement for prior approval for wheat and soybean sales. On March 6, similar requirements for other grains were ended, though companies still had to report sales contracts after they were signed.

Then, in late spring and early summer 1975, evidence mounted of Russian crop problems that would eventually bring estimates of that year's grain harvest well below the 1972 level.[5] On July 16, USDA announced the first 1975 sale of U.S. grain to the Soviet Union. Eight days later, with 10 million metric tons of grain already under contract, Agriculture asked exporters to give advance notice of any further grain sales to Russia and indicated that the United States expected no more sales until the August 11 corn crop report was in. With that report showing some deterioration in crop estimates, Butz announced that the "temporary suspension" of sales to Russia would continue until the September crop report.[6] Everybody remembered 1974 and what happened to U.S. corn that year.

At this point, the U.S. labor movement made a dramatic public entrance into the issue. Maritime unions wanted the Russians to pay higher shipping rates and use U.S. bottoms for a larger proportion of their shipments, and the U.S.-Soviet maritime agreement was to expire at the end of the year. Aligning their interests with those of consumers fearing a repeat of 1972, AFL-CIO President George Meany announced on August 18, 1975, that members of the International Longshoremen's Association would refuse to load grain bound for Russia unless the administration promised that the interests of consumers—and the shipping industry—would be protected. Meany also urged that a "wheat board" outside USDA be established to manage exports.

On August 26, as the unions moved to implement their boycott (and with court orders temporarily blocking them), President Ford, John T. Dunlop, now secretary of labor, James T. Lynn, director of OMB, and L. William Seidman, Ford's economic adviser, met with Meany and five other labor leaders at the White House. On September 9 they met again (with Henry Kissinger and Earl Butz also present) and tentative agreement was reached: the unions would suspend their boycott for a month; the moratorium on new sales to Russia would be extended until mid-

5. Russia produced an estimated 168 million tons of grain in 1972, and 133 million tons in 1975.

6. Daniel J. Balz, "Economic Report: Soviet Grain Purchases Prompt Informal Export Controls," *National Journal*, September 6, 1975, p. 1261.

October; and the administration would seek "a longer-term and more certain purchase understanding with the Soviet Union, providing, among other features, for certain minimum purchases" of grain.[7] On that same day yet another food policymaking unit was established to oversee the negotiations, the Food Committee of the Economic Policy Board and the National Security Council, chaired jointly by the secretary of state and the secretary of the treasury.

On September 10, as Charles W. Robinson, under secretary of state for economic affairs, left for Moscow to begin negotiations, the State Department quietly requested, through its Warsaw embassy, that Poland stop buying grain in U.S. markets, and Poland did so. On September 19 a new U.S.-Soviet agreement on shipping rates was announced. But conclusion of the grain purchase arrangement was delayed because of an unsuccessful Kissinger-Robinson effort to extract a simultaneous Soviet commitment to sell oil to the United States at below OPEC prices![8] On September 29 Secretary Butz and the Polish minister of agriculture reached agreement on regularizing Polish purchases over a five-year period (a formal exchange of letters confirmed this in November). On October 10 President Ford announced the United States was resuming sales to Poland because of record U.S. wheat and corn crops. Finally, on October 20, he announced the end of the moratorium on sales to Russia and the signing of a five-year grain trade agreement, beginning October 1976.

The agreement committed the Soviet Union to purchase at least six million tons of wheat and corn each year. It also guaranteed that the United States would not impede Soviet purchases of up to eight million tons unless U.S. supplies were extraordinarily low.[9] If the Russians wished to buy more than eight million tons, intergovernmental consultations were required. For 1975–76, the Russians agreed to consult if they wished to purchase more than 7 million tons beyond the 9.8 already contracted for.

7. *New York Times*, September 10, 1975. This summary draws heavily on contemporary press accounts; a Congressional Research Service chronology in *Who's Making Foreign Agricultural Policy*, Hearings before the Subcommittee on Foreign Agricultural Policy of the Senate Committee on Agriculture and Forestry, 94 Cong. 2 sess. (GPO, 1976), pp. 126–29; Robert G. Kaiser, "Old Grain Policy Unworkable, U.S. Officials Found," *Washington Post*, September 11, 1975, reprinted ibid., pp. 111–13; and Balz, "Economic Report: Soviet Grain Purchases," pp. 1259–64.

8. See Dan Morgan, *Merchants of Grain* (Viking Press, 1979), chap. 11.

9. Specifically, U.S. grain supplies (stocks plus new production) had to be below 225 million tons; they were 226 million in 1974, the lowest in fifteen years.

The Rocky Road to Balanced Policy

The outcome in both 1974 and 1975 was a balancing of food policy goals and interests, a far better balancing than had occurred in 1972 and 1973. The domestic economy was protected from unlimited Soviet grain purchases, but sales to Russia were continued and regularized and there was the diplomatic achievement of getting Russia to behave more cooperatively in international markets. These accomplishments were limited, but, given the difficult trade-offs and strong political pressures, they were significant. Perhaps most important, the U.S. government had effectively avoided the sins of 1972 and 1973—all major policy values were taken into account, and all were to some degree protected.

But the farm community was up in arms. The previous spring, vetoing a bill to raise price support levels, President Ford had declared (on Agriculture Department initiative), "We have now eliminated all restrictions on exports and we are determined to do everything possible to avoid imposing them again. Our farm products must have unfettered access to world markets."[10] Now the administration was denying farmers their market reward; the Russians had gone to other markets during the three-month embargo, and the summer rise in farmers' grain prices gave way to a decline.

A galling symbol of farmers' losses was the evidence that their voice in the federal government—the Department of Agriculture—had been either ignored or overridden in these decisions. There was the Food Committee, with Butz but one of eight members; there was a photograph in newspapers throughout rural America of George Meany and Gerald Ford negotiating grain export policy at the White House; there was the State Department negotiating suspension of exports to Poland. Asked, "Have you lost the power to make agricultural decisions in the Administration?" Butz replied, "No, sir. I am free to decide what time we set our office hours."[11] Senator Robert Dole said the following January, "I am not certain President Ford will ever recover from that in rural

10. *Weekly Compilation of Presidential Documents 1975*, vol. 13 (May 5, 1975), p. 475.

11. White House press conference of October 20, 1975, on the Soviet grain agreement, reprinted in *United States Grain and Oil Agreements With the Soviet Union,* Hearings before the House Committee on International Relations, 94 Cong. 1 sess. (GPO, 1976), p. 61.

America."[12] Embargoes became a prominent issue in the 1976 election campaign.

Thus two questions demand further analysis. How was it possible for the U.S. government to achieve a more balanced policy on agricultural exports in 1974 and 1975 than it had in 1972 and 1973; what processes, managed by which people, were responsible? And were any of the costs of this policy (like the farm belt insurrection) products of these processes (as distinguished from the inevitable unhappiness of particular groups with the substance of the decisions that were taken)?

Any explanation of why the Soviet sales of 1974 and 1975 received more balanced official treatment must begin with 1972 and 1973.[13] Even for the purest free marketeers in Agriculture, 1972 established the need to have some monitoring of Russian purchases and, under certain circumstances, to regulate them. And the Agriculture and Consumer Protection Act of 1973 in fact required that any export sale above 100,000 tons be reported immediately to USDA. The 1973 crisis established, especially for domestic economic policymakers, the need to avoid formal export controls if at all possible. Even though officials continued to give different weights to competing values, the determination to avoid repeating these two mistakes was widespread. This reduced the chance of certain food policy interests riding roughshod over others.

As noted in chapter 5, the institutional umbrella for bringing greater balance to food policymaking in mid-1974 was the President's Committee on Food, established June 18. Its actual working unit, the Food Deputies Group chaired by Gary Seevers of the Council of Economic Advisers, continued to function after the committee was supplanted by the creation of the Economic Policy Board in October. Agriculture, State, Treasury, and OMB were active members of the group. During the summer of 1974, the group first met biweekly, then weekly, to review the deteriorating U.S. crop situation and the rising export demands. As the extent of the shortfall became clear, the group developed an export-restraining strategy.[14] They did not *tell* foreign governments explicitly how much grain they could purchase, but U.S. officials sought to *learn*

12. *Who's Making Foreign Agricultural Policy*, Hearings, p. 15.

13. These and subsequent paragraphs draw substantially on interviews and *Sales of Grain to the Soviet Union*, Hearings, pp. 45–69.

14. There were those in Treasury who felt that corn export controls might be required, but Agriculture and State aligned effectively against them (as they had not done in June 1973).

their intentions and asked them not to make "large early or unnecessary purchases," but rather "to limit their purchases" to what they required.[15]

As part of this strategy, Secretary Butz asked the Russian ambassador, Anatoly Dobrynin, in late August what grain purchases the Soviet government was contemplating, and when his question did not elicit immediate information, the U.S. embassy in Moscow, and later Butz, asked again. They told the Russians that the United States wished to remain a reliable exporter, but that supplies would be tight and it was hoped that Soviet purchases would be "modest" and "reasonable."

To USDA, "modest" meant about 1 million tons of corn. When Continental Grain Company sold the Russians this amount on October 3, and Cook Industries sold them 1.3 million tons the following day, alarm about the economic and political impact spread quickly to the White House.[16] William Simon—who had become treasury secretary in May with a narrower mandate than George Shultz and was seeking to widen it—seized the initiative and called the meeting at which the grain companies, under presidential pressure, agreed to suspend the contracts until they could be renegotiated.

The tightened export management system that grew out of this crisis —prior approval and informal negotiations with foreign buyers to limit their purchases—was overseen by a new White House-based committee, which Gary Seevers also chaired. The other members were Clayton K. Yeutter, assistant secretary of agriculture (and in his absence, Richard E. Bell), Julius Katz, State's commodity specialist, Harald Malmgren, deputy special trade representative, and Robert Hormats, chief National Security Council economic aide. What they were implementing amounted to informal export controls—they set an overall export target and oversaw official communications with both grain companies and foreign governments to keep total sales within that target.

The export restraint system was not at all popular in the farm belt (as Ford discovered when he campaigned in the Midwest before the November midterm elections). And USDA, while recognizing the need

15. Assistant Secretary of State Thomas O. Enders, *Sales of Grain to the Soviet Union,* Hearings, p. 48.

16. USDA advised Continental Grain Company of its view. Bernard Steinweg, Continental Grain Company, ibid., p. 33. See also Edward W. Cook, ibid., p. 16. The Cook sale was apparently not monitored as stringently by USDA and/or that company resisted monitoring more strongly. For more on confusion in communications with the Russians and the grain companies, see the next section.

for (or at least the political inevitability of) some form of export management, wanted a system not only less stringent but under its own control. Seevers, who had been made chairman while he was traveling overseas, thought the role too operational for the CEA. So Agriculture proposed that Bell be made chairman, which he was, in early 1975. The committee continued to function for a while but met less frequently as the supply situation eased (partly because U.S. farmers sharply reduced corn feeding to livestock) and the export target was raised.

By the time the Russian issue reemerged in July 1975, then, Agriculture was once again in control of export monitoring. And with farm prices declining steadily through the winter and spring and bumper crops likely, the department badly needed new Russian sales to bolster the market.[17] But Butz and Bell both recognized also that exports could not be open-ended. And both the Soviet Union and the grain companies wanted to avoid a replay of 1974 and were looking for guidelines.

When signs accumulated that the Russians might be reentering the market, and on the scale of 1972 rather than 1974, Butz and Bell set a quantity—10 million tons—and communicated it to the Russians and the grain companies without getting formal interagency clearance. They surfaced the number publicly as a *prediction* of what Russia might buy, but enforced it privately as a *limitation*. "It was quite clear," said a grain executive. "Mr. Butz and Mr. Bell said we could spare 10 million tons."[18] By the end of July, Bell was telling Congress that the Russians had in fact contracted for 9.8 million tons of grain out of the 1975 U.S. crop and that no more sales were expected before the August 11 crop report.[19] And around the end of August, Bell could say with some justification, "This thing has unfolded just about as we had intended."[20]

Thus in the summer of 1975 the Department of Agriculture was playing a much more active export management role than was evident from the public statements of Butz and Bell. Operating to be sure under the threat of having responsibility once again wrested from them, they pur-

17. USDA estimated on July 31 that the sales to Russia contracted during that month would increase the average price of wheat in 1975–76 by 75 cents a bushel above what it would in the absence of such sales. The comparable figure for corn was 30 cents. *Grain Sales to the Soviet Union,* Hearings before the Permanent Subcommittee on Investigations of the Senate Committee on Government Operations, 94 Cong. 1 sess. (GPO, 1975), p. 31.

18. Balz, "Economic Report: Soviet Grain Purchases," p. 1262.

19. *Grain Sales to the Soviet Union,* Hearings, p. 14; Balz, "Economic Report: Soviet Grain Purchases," p. 1261.

20. Balz, "Economic Report: Soviet Grain Purchases," p. 1264.

sued a rather flexible and sophisticated policy course. USDA was doing what the department had long been criticized for *not* doing—restraining commercial agribusiness interests in the name of other food policy values. And because of the monitoring system, department officials had far better information on current grain sales than they had had in 1972. But grain and food prices were beginning to rise again, and George Meany and the maritime unions were about to insert themselves forcefully into the fray. As a result, USDA would lose "the action" once again, and more visibly than ever.

Early that spring, several maritime union leaders had asked for a meeting with Secretary Butz to discuss rising food prices. At the meeting they pressed their real concern, the expiring U.S.-Soviet maritime agreement and their dissatisfaction with the terms of the agreement. The threat was unstated but clear—they might hold up ships bound for Russia unless they got the terms they wanted. They knew that if the United States had a bumper crop in 1975, American farmers would be depending on substantial Russian sales to keep prices strong. And they knew that USDA leaders knew this as well. Bell contacted Hormats and emphasized the urgency of the problem. Hormats in turn contacted USDA's archadversary, John Dunlop.

Dunlop was concerned not only with the union problem but with the impact of unrestrained exports on inflation and with what he considered an irresponsible and perhaps incompetent USDA approach to the price problem. Thus when Bell indicated that the United States could raise the Russian sales figure to 14 million and that USDA was planning to do so,[21] Dunlop countered that this might have a major impact on prices and was properly the subject of interagency study. Other economic policy officials and institutions shared Dunlop's concern. Federal Reserve Board chairman Arthur F. Burns, for example, was predicting that the sales already made would have substantial inflationary impact.

An interagency study was made: Paul MacAvoy of the CEA worked with Bell and others to estimate what impact exports of several million tons more would have on U.S. food prices and concluded that, given a good 1975 corn crop, there would be no "substantial price increases at the farm, in the futures markets and, therefore, in the CPI."[22] But when dry weather in the corn belt brought the August 11 corn crop estimate

21. *Grain Sales to the Soviet Union,* Hearings, p. 14. See also *Washington Post,* July 16, 1975.

22. *Grain Sales to the Soviet Union,* Hearings, p. 46.

down from 6.045 to 5.85 billion bushels, evoking memories of the 1974 summer's deterioration, USDA was overruled in its push for more exports. So on August 11, Butz announced that the now-acknowledged suspension of grain sales to Russia would continue until the September crop report, though he added, "We do want to sell more to the USSR, and if this crop materializes it will be easily within our capacity to do so."[23]

A week later, the maritime unions entered the issue publicly. As their initial boycott was being halted and then tested in the courts, Dunlop, an experienced labor mediator, moved to the center of the issue, using the unions' pressure as a vehicle to achieve better protection of the U.S. economy against massive Russian grain purchases. It was he who met first with the union leaders on the morning of August 26 and brought them to the ninety-minute session with Ford that afternoon. The White House announcement signaled that the Ford-Meany "summit" would continue to be a prime forum for grain policy, much to the outrage of farm groups.[24] But the president was in a bind, for not only did the farm economy depend considerably on sales which the unions could block; a sustained boycott could also do serious damage to his administration's détente policy. He formalized and strengthened Dunlop's role by assigning him the responsibility of finding a way out of the bind. Thus when the issue was tentatively resolved two weeks later, it was after another White House meeting for Meany and his maritime colleagues, with Dunlop playing a central role. Between Ford and Meany, the outcome was more a cease-fire than a final settlement: the boycott was temporarily suspended while the administration sought long-term agreements with Russia.

As for the struggle between Dunlop and Butz, the labor secretary won a clear victory, in strong alignment with both economic and foreign policy officials.[25] Treasury and the CEA wanted to regularize Russian impact on the domestic food economy. The State Department (and

23. *New York Times,* August 12, 1975.

24. The announcement, in its entirety, was, "The meeting explored the matter of grain exports, living costs and maritime issues. This was a preliminary meeting. No decisions were made. There will be further meetings between Administration officials and Mr. Meany and his associates. The President will participate in the future meetings as appropriate." *New York Times,* August 27, 1975.

25. Asked where the September 9 plan came from, Dunlop replied, "Very simple. It came from me." Kaiser, "Old Grain Policy Unworkable."

Kissinger personally) had long been interested in broadening the web of negotiated arrangements with the Soviet Union on matters of mutual concern, and Dunlop won Kissinger's assent to the initiative early in September, when Kissinger returned from a Middle East diplomatic mission. With the selection of Charles Robinson to lead the negotiation, State's interest and role were recognized and strengthened. (So also was the personal role of Robinson, who was competing with Thomas Enders for economic primacy at the State Department.)

Butz and USDA were not opposed to a bilateral Soviet grain arrangement—in fact it was a logical extension of what they had done informally that summer by enforcing a grain purchase ceiling. But Butz was certainly unhappy about being so completely and publicly shunted aside in decisionmaking, and unhappy about the continuation of the sales suspension as leverage to win Russian agreement and labor peace.[26]

Operationally, the Food Committee of the EPB and the NSC, created as part of the September 9 policy package, proved insignificant. Its membership was essentially identical to the Economic Policy Board, and in practice it simply reaffirmed the board's food policy authority. Symbolically, it damaged the Ford administration in the farm belt since it lent substance to the charge that the secretary of state (cochairman of the committee), who knew little about agriculture, was now dominating farm policy. And the EPB hardly had full control over Kissinger and Robinson, whose futile efforts to win a quid pro quo in the form of Soviet oil sales to the United States delayed conclusion of the grain package, notwithstanding the economic advisers' (and Ford's) apparent coolness toward this linkage strategy.

Moreover, farmer reaction constrained the negotiations on the grain deal that the foreign and economic policy pressures had brought about. The six weeks between the September 9 announcement and the October 20 agreement were weeks when the world grain situation was easing, U.S. grain prices were falling, and American farmers were bringing a record corn crop to harvest. Thus when Robinson pressed for further concessions, his Soviet counterpart could respond (as recounted by a

26. The best defense of the embargo Butz could muster upon its termination was that "it was proper in view of the tremendous emotional reaction in this country that occurs almost with a knee jerk emotional reaction when you sell anything to the Soviets." White House press conference, October 20, 1975, reprinted in *United States Grain and Oil Agreements with the Soviet Union*, p. 61.

Soviet diplomat), "We of course would prefer to buy from you, but we cannot wait indefinitely and will have to buy elsewhere if the embargo continues. Your farmers will not like this. Is your President aware of these facts? Well, perhaps you should remind him of them once again." In fact, the Russians were purchasing grain elsewhere during the U.S. embargo, American officials knew it, and the Russians knew they knew. This could only weaken Robinson's ability to win tighter provisions governing Soviet grain sales to other countries, not to mention the effort to exploit U.S. "food power" to win concessions on oil.[27]

But despite these serious limitations, the U.S. government managed its 1974 and 1975 grain export crises far more effectively than those of 1972 and 1973. The process was confusing and sometimes chaotic, but the policy product was a middle course between the open spigot of 1972 and the sudden embargo of 1973. Organizationally, it was a product of formal institutions designed to balance policy—the Food Deputies Group, the Economic Policy Board. It was even more, perhaps, a result of the fact that particular senior officials—Simon in 1974, Dunlop in 1975—perceived that their interests were served by active leadership to avert a replay of 1972. The food price inflation of 1973 and 1974 had underscored for them the importance of grain supplies for domestic economic stability and the considerable public political backing they would get for taking stands counter to agricultural export interests.

Finally, food policy concerns had moved the Department of Agriculture to manage exports in a much more sophisticated and balanced way than could have been expected from the record of 1972 and 1973. By this time, of course, Butz and Bell were on a rather tight White House leash; but they did enforce informal export limits before the Soviet issue was taken from their hands.

But if the ultimate product was more balanced policy, the disorder on the road to achieving it had costs of its own. For the changing of priority among objectives, and the shifts in (or confusion of) responsi-

27. While the agreement prohibited Soviet resale of U.S. grain to other countries, it did not prohibit export of an equivalent amount of Russian grain in time of plenty. Nor did it constrain Soviet purchases from other exporters. Thus it controlled the net Soviet impact on world grain markets far less than it controlled direct U.S.-Soviet trade. For the text of the agreement, see ibid., pp. 51–52.

On the oil linkage issue, see Morgan, *Merchants of Grain,* chap. 11; and Roger B. Porter, "Presidential Decisionmaking: The Economic Policy Board" (Ph.D. dissertation, Harvard University, 1978), chap. 5.

bility for achieving the objectives, meant that inconsistent or vague signals were sent to Russia, and to the American farm community.

The Disruptive Political Effects

Analyzing the 1972–75 period in which he played such an active role, Gary Seevers concluded that a "major source of new uncertainty" for the food industry (farmers, food processors and traders, and so on) derived "from governmental policy: unexpected government interventions have become more frequent, and the absence of a political consensus on food issues leaves the most probable future policy in doubt." About 1974–75, he noted, "In a twelve-month span, the government intervened to restrain exports, acted to discontinue all restraints, and then intervened again." Such shifts, he concluded, "have had very disruptive market effects."[28]

In the 1974 and 1975 Soviet grain episodes, such shifts in the content of policy were accompanied (partly as cause, partly as effect) by shifts in the locus of responsibility for policy. And this combination of shifts in power and policy had disruptive political effects, both within the executive branch and in the broader national political community. These effects, in turn, made it harder for the government to achieve whatever food policy goals it settled upon. It was inevitable and in some respects desirable, of course, that power should ebb and flow as policy pressures and priorities shifted—and since power generally shifted in the direction of the new priorities and pressures, the system did in this sense prove adaptive, flexible. But though policymaking tidiness has no particular virtue as an abstract ideal, the concrete costs of lack of tidiness, of incoherence, should not be neglected.

In both October 1974 and August 1975, strong intervention by actors outside USDA shifted policy toward greater responsiveness to economic and foreign concerns, but in each case the shift proved temporary, for two related reasons.

The first reason was that, as the crises receded, economic and foreign policy officials turned their attention to other issues, while the farm policy community continued to concentrate on food. The second was the

28. Gary L. Seevers, "Food Policy: Implications for the Food Industry," *American Journal of Agricultural Economics*, vol. 58 (May 1976), pp. 270, 273, 274.

reaction from the farm policy community, which was split on Earl Butz and his free-market policies but relatively united against these particular interventions in export markets.[29]

Thus in early 1975 Richard Bell won the chairmanship of the export management committee, as the issue began to lose its urgency to others. And thus, in March 1976, with farm prices falling and the autumn election approaching, Secretary Butz succeeded in persuading President Ford to announce in a speech to the Farm Forum in Springfield, Illinois, that he was replacing the EPB/NSC Food Committee and the International Food Review Group with the new Agricultural Policy Committee, chaired by Butz. (The Food Deputies Group became the committee's working group and was subordinated to it.) Ford was fighting for nomination and election, and farmer support was crucial, so he decided, he told a questioner on March 5, that "this particular subject was so vital that we ought to take it out from underneath the coverage of what we call the Economic Policy Board." He was "absolutely confident that this bolstering of agricultural policy within the executive branch will benefit the farmers of Illinois and the entire United States."[30] A key official of the Economic Policy Board, who was traveling abroad at the time of this change, reacted strongly against it. But even the EPB staff recognized that the existing interagency committee structure was no longer politically viable, that the secretary of agriculture had to have a more visible role. The more drastic change was accepted as inevitable in an election year, tolerable in the short run because no 1976 food crises seemed likely, and perhaps temporary because coordinating procedures would be reviewed in 1977 anyway.

29. Organizations favoring the Butz approach (American Farm Bureau Federation, Great Plains Wheat, Inc.) denounced export restraints as contrary to that approach. As a Great Plains Wheat representative put it, "moratoria and the fear they may be imposed [played] havoc with U.S. commodity markets and farmer income [and destroyed] farmer incentives to produce." The National Farmers Union, which advocated a strong government supply management role, declared itself "unalterably opposed" to what it considered one-sided intervention, to "any form of export controls or restrictions that are not directly limited to effective measures which will protect farmers against the collapse of prices in times of surpluses." *Who's Making Foreign Agricultural Policy*, Hearings, pp. 109, 139. Both the American Farm Bureau Federation and the National Farmers Union testified against the U.S.-Soviet Agreement. *United States–Soviet Grain Agreement, S. 2492, and Other Matters*, Hearings before the Subcommittee on International Finance of the Senate Committee on Banking, Housing, and Urban Affairs, 94 Cong. 1 sess. (GPO, 1976), pp. 2–41.

30. *Weekly Compilation of Presidential Documents*, vol. 12 (March 15, 1976), p. 344.

Thus efforts to institutionalize food policy coordination around economic and foreign policy officials aligned against USDA did not outlast the crises which generated them. Conversely, USDA's venture into active export restraint in 1975 was undone by the onset of crisis. Once the stakes of consumers and domestic economic policy officials rose, once the unions moved forcefully into the issue, the Butz department could not function as the broker of these interests. Although this was in part because of Butz's personality and style, it was more a result of the way Butz and his subordinates conceived their public role and their constituency. To consumers he might have appeared outrageous and irresponsible, to his cabinet colleagues rather narrow in his policy focus, but for many commercial farmers Earl Butz was the secretary of agriculture who championed *their* cause, *their* access to markets, and under whom *their* exports had tripled and their income more than doubled.

Butz gloried in this role and (once the 1972 election had passed) identified himself totally and unabashedly with the free market. So when he and Bell enforced a lid on Russian sales in July and August of 1975, they had to do so semicovertly. After the 10 million ton level was reached, USDA asked grain companies "to advise the Department before beginning negotiations of large export sales." But while it used this procedure to enforce the sales moratorium, it was slow in revealing there was one; Bell told Senator Lawton Chiles, of Senator Henry Jackson's Permanent Subcommittee on Investigations, on July 31, 1975, "We have no cutoff point," though he emphasized, "we do not expect the Soviets to make any purchases of grain in this market during the next 3 or 4 weeks."[31]

A contemporary *National Journal* article concluded that "the Ford Administration had instituted a strict, if not strictly legal, system of export controls designed to deny grain to the Soviet Union." But it recognized also the risks of the political tightrope Butz and Bell were walking: in "choosing not to explain in any detail the approach they are taking, Administration officials risk a perpetuation of the uncertainty that exists any time the Russians move into the market."[32] For in the wake of 1972, the 1975 Russian grain purchases generated newspaper headlines and Senate investigations. Ambiguous messages, from the department that had allowed excessive sales in 1972 and 1974, were hardly reassuring. Indeed, Senator Chiles interpreted Bell's statement to mean

31. *Grain Sales to the Soviet Union*, Hearings, p. 26.
32. Balz, "Economic Report: Soviet Grain Purchases," pp. 1263, 1264.

that "once we did have sort of a cutoff," but "We have taken the cutoff off" and expressed alarm on behalf of the "housewife" who had "paid through the nose in 1972."[33] Reuben L. Johnson of the National Farmers Union said, "I don't trust any behind the scenes hanky-panky between Butz and the grain companies to protect the consumer."[34] Such distrust pervaded the executive branch as well, as it had in the 1973 soybean embargo, exacerbated this time by USDA's covertness and by the department's known readiness to export somewhat more grain than others felt prudent.

A brokering role requires trust from the major parties at interest, especially when an issue heats up; USDA was widely distrusted. George Meany played on this distrust to achieve his objectives. John Dunlop played on it, and on Meany's intervention, to achieve his: the reorganization of food policymaking and the subordination of USDA's interest to a broader public interest. President Ford adopted the Dunlop's plan; in that political context, almost any president probably would have.[35]

Secretary Butz's Department of Agriculture could not coordinate when crisis came and prices rose, or threatened to; others could not coordinate once crisis faded and prices fell. The policies that resulted from this ebb and flow of power did respond, sometimes belatedly, to changing circumstances. But this pattern had disruptive political effects.

One effect was poor communication with the Russians and less negotiating leverage with them than might otherwise have been the case. In August and September 1974, two channels were used to convey the message that purchases should be modest—Butz's meetings with Ambassador Dobrynin, and State Department cables to Moscow. The particulars of these communications were closely held by each department and colored, it appears, by their interests. The USDA didn't want to be too tough and threaten that golden Russian market. State didn't want to discourage détente; according to one Executive Office of the President official, the State cable could easily be interpreted as "the market is tight, we want to sell to you, so please get your claim in now." Thus

33. *Grain Sales to the Soviet Union*, Hearings, p. 27. Chiles was not mollified when Bell observed, accurately, that 1972 was not the year when she paid through the nose.

34. Balz, "Economic Report: Soviet Grain Purchases," p. 1264.

35. Ironically, farm belt reaction then pushed him back. In the Farm Forum speech, he threatened to out-Butz Butz in playing to the farm galleries, with his rhetoric about stored grain creating "a great overhang of food" and his promise never to "use our exports to implement or be a pawn for international politics." *Weekly Compilation of Presidential Documents*, vol. 12 (March 15, 1976), p. 341.

after the event, Kissinger felt obliged to concede that "a strong possibility exists that we may have misled the Soviet Union as to what we thought we could deliver"; it was a "misunderstanding between bureaucracies."[36] An opportunity was lost for a move toward a better method of handling Soviet grain transactions—such as was accomplished the following year.

Part of the problem in 1974 was the desire to handle the Russian situation without an explicit ceiling. As Thomas Enders put it, "We would probably have been much more effective with the Soviet Union if we had initially gone to them and said we can allocate to you x million tons of grain this year." But "that would have been tantamount in our view to the imposition of export controls."[37] Such a specific signal might have been conveyed informally had one agency had a clear and trusted lead, but none did. One USDA official involved recalled the essence of U.S. policymaking this way: he phoned State about the anticipated Russian purchases, saying that the United States needed to give Russia a figure—how much they should buy. State disagreed; that would be a commitment and a control. In their view, the United States should ask Russia how much it needed, emphasizing that it be a modest amount. The cable that went out asked simply, How much do you need? The Russian reply was, How much do you want us to buy? When Russia finally entered the market, the U.S. reaction was, "You dumb ninnies, that's not a modest amount."

Divisions within the government damaged negotiations with Russia again in 1975 when Robinson went to Moscow. As Bell noted later, the fact that not Bell but a lower-level USDA official accompanied Robinson "may have contributed to feeling among the agricultural sector that the agreement was totally the State Department's idea even though the concept of the agreement had originated from joint work by Bell and Don Novotny."[38] To the degree that the Russians also got this misleading message (either directly or through farm belt reaction), U.S. leverage was weakened.

Another problem of ad hoc policymaking was that it treated private actors unequally. Grain companies received different signals from USDA in 1974, advantaging some and costing others. Continental was asked by

36. "Secretary Kissinger's News Conference of October 7," *Department of State Bulletin*, vol. 71 (October 28, 1974), p. 568.

37. *Sales of Grain to the Soviet Union*, Hearings, p. 50.

38. "USDA and Food Policy Decisionmaking: A Report of the Agriculture Department's 1976 Young Executives Committee" (USDA, January 1977), p. 24.

Butz to inform him before concluding a sale, then was told it could sell 1 million tons of corn but should hold back on wheat. The next day Cook, which was not asked by Butz to provide prior information, sold additional corn and 900,000 tons of wheat. The four companies who sold no grain to Russia, according to one non-USDA official who contacted them after the crisis broke, were "sore as hell" because they thought they had been explicitly told by USDA not to complete any deal. The difference between Cook and Continental may be explained by the fact that, to judge by their Senate testimony, the former was considerably more resistant to government sales management. But such inequities increased resentment about the arbitrariness of government controls and thus the resistance to them.

But the largest cost of the way the U.S. government made food policy trade-offs in 1974 and 1975 was the alienation of the farm community. Without the support or at least the tolerance of this community, a viable longer-term system for balancing theirs and other policy values is very hard to achieve, for they are the most affected by food policy day-to-day. It is they, in the main, who continue to write farm bills;[39] it is they whose understanding and support is probably indispensable for establishing an adequate reserve policy. But partly because USDA was pushed aside, consultation with farm groups on the 1975 U.S.-Soviet agreement was apparently very limited.[40] The Ford administration coped with food crises better than its Nixon predecessor. But because of the approach of the secretary of agriculture, and public reaction to this approach, the problem of creating a political base for a long-term, balanced food policy was left to its successors.

39. On the likelihood of this practice continuing in 1977, see Daniel J. Balz, "The Coming Debate on Food—Will All the Issues Be Faced?" *National Journal,* September 25, 1976, pp. 1338–43. The article proved prophetic.

40. Bell acknowledged this failing. See "USDA and Food Policy Decisionmaking," p. 24.

CHAPTER EIGHT

Food Policy Begins at Home

FOOD POLICY REQUIRES reconciling a range of conflicting but legitimate policy concerns. There is no generally accepted set of priorities among these concerns, because different policy communities weight them differently. One would therefore expect the food policy process to be untidy, especially in a period when sharp price rises increase the stakes of governmental policymakers and their outside constituencies.

This expectation is amply confirmed in the episodes examined in the preceding chapters. These accounts suggest, moreover, that untidiness can also be desirable. Newspaper headlines and the clash of competing advocates give visibility to particular issues, reducing the chances that an important policy concern will be excluded from the debate.[1] Perhaps the tidiest of the five cases in terms of regularity of procedures and clarity of responsibility is the response to the first Russian grain purchases—at least until January 1973. In terms of outcome, it is probably the worst.

Food policymaking in 1972–76 was further complicated by the newness of the situation. Officials who addressed it had no experience with a world that might buy more grain than America could afford to sell and with a market where corn and soybean prices tripled and wheat prices quadrupled in periods of seven months to two years. In such circumstances serious miscalculations are inevitable. One reassuring conclusion from the experiences examined is that learning did in fact take place. The episodes of 1974 and 1975 were better handled in the limited but

1. For an argument stressing the value of politicization and controversy in drawing attention to neglected concerns, see Robert O. Keohane and Joseph S. Nye, "Organizing for Global Environmental and Resource Interdependence," *Murphy Commission Report*, vol. 1, app. B, pp. 52–54. See chapter 1, note 1, for full reference.

important sense that no areas of policy concern were as grossly slighted as domestic economic policy was in 1972, farm and foreign policy in 1973, and development policy in both. The least-common-denominator compromise on food reserves is a reminder that balanced policymaking does not assure creative or effective policy in terms of the problem addressed. But it *was* a gain that the substantively and politically difficult crises of fall 1974 and summer 1975 were handled without either formal export controls or open-ended export sales and that officials coping with them *knew* more—about what the Russians and the grain companies were doing and about the informal means available for influencing international grain transactions.

But the learning was limited. In every episode examined except food reserves, policy and power shifted too suddenly and too late. The return to a more humanitarian food aid policy came too late for Bangladesh; the White House takeover of farm policy in January 1973, and the soybean controls imposed the following June, came after time had sharply narrowed the options. And in these two cases, as in the grain sales reprises of 1974 and 1975, the eleventh-hour shifts in power and policy were products, in important part, of the actual and perceived insensitivity of the primary food policy department to anything but farm policy concerns, rather narrowly construed. For other actors, interest in food policy is intermittent, a function of how it affects their nonfood concerns. But for the Department of Agriculture, food and agriculture are the primary, ongoing business. It has the in-depth expertise; it has the day-to-day ties with the farm community and those interest groups for whom agriculture is also the central preoccupation.

For this reason, it seems futile to try to institutionalize food policy leadership in a specialized office outside the Department of Agriculture. Such a step is frequently proposed. On February 27, 1975, for example, Senator Mark Hatfield introduced legislation "to create an Office of Food Administration in the Executive Office of the President to be headed by an administrator appointed by the President by and with the consent of the Senate." Such a reform, he argued, could end "bureaucratic delay" in providing needed food aid and bring broader coherence to international food policy. This food office was to "formulate and recommend" to the president policies for adequate food production and nutrition at home and abroad. The bill "specifically direct(ed)" cabinet officials involved in food policy to "cooperate fully with the Administration."[2] And in June 1977, the National Academy of Sciences came for-

2. *Congressional Record* (February 27, 1975), pp. 4552–53.

ward with a proposal for "the establishment of . . . two entities in the Executive Office of the President: one to develop and maintain a coherent U.S. strategy for dealing with world food and nutrition problems; the other, subordinate to the first, to facilitate coordination of U.S. and international research activities on food and nutrition."[3]

Both proposals were motivated by a strong desire to make U.S. food policy more coherent and give greater priority to global welfare and development concerns. And on organization charts, they look appealing: as the NAS put it, such coordination would be buttressed by the "higher authority" of the executive office, served by "strong staff work independent of the special interests."[4] But experience with specialized executive office units is not encouraging. They are unlikely to be able to establish strong ties to the president—or to his principal staff aides—unless he is giving substantial personal time and priority to the issues they treat. And the real leverage within the executive office is exercised by those staffs that manage major decision processes with broad substantive reach, like the National Security Council for presidential foreign policy choices and the Office of Management and Budget for agency spending. Other EOP offices must be content with far more modest roles, particularly in periods when there is not a crisis in their policy areas. And in fact the idea of a top-level food office had a reasonably clear test in 1961, when President Kennedy appointed George McGovern White House director of food for peace. McGovern knew Kennedy personally, had his substantive and political support, and was energetic in promoting the program. But the major responsible agencies, particularly USDA, kept effective control of food aid policy out of his hands.[5]

In noncrisis periods, USDA is bound to predominate on food policy. But if it does not respond to food policy concerns broader than those of the commercial agricultural establishment, it will lose the action when crisis forces presidential intervention to assuage these other policy concerns.

It is normal, of course, for any department to be parochial, since each has, by definition, less than government-wide responsibilities and hence

---

3. Commission on International Relations, National Research Council, *World Food and Nutrition Study: The Potential Contributions of Research* (Washington, D.C.: National Academy of Science, 1977), p. 24.

4. Ibid., p. 152.

5. Manlio F. DeAngelis, "Foreign Aid: The Transition from ICA to AID, 1960–61," in National Academy of Public Administration, "Making Organizational Change Effective," *Murphy Commission Report*, vol. 6, app. O, pp. 142–51. For a more positive, indeed euphoric, assessment of this experience, see Arthur M. Schlesinger, Jr., *A Thousand Days* (Houghton Mifflin, 1965), pp. 170, 605.

less than a society-wide constituency. And to a degree such parochialism is useful, for the department head must retain credibility with his constituency (and the congressional committees responsible to it) if he is to be effective. An endemic problem of government organization is to build counterweights to parochialism. In the U.S. executive branch, such counterweights are generally interagency committees and/or analytic-coordinating staffs with links to the president. Those that entered the cases examined here fall into two categories—those created specifically for food issues and those with a broader mandate.

About the specific food groups, enough has already been said. Those at the assistant secretary level were essential for handling the post-1972 issues, and while the experience of each differed, their contributions were substantial. More uneven were the contributions of the general coordinating units—the National Security Council (NSC); the Council on International Economic Policy (CIEP); George Shultz's Council on Economic Policy (CEP); and President Ford's Economic Policy Board (EPB). Usually they broadened the range of policy values given consideration, as when the NSC opened food issues to interagency study after the soybean fiasco and when the EPB insisted that Kissinger's proposed food aid pledge be analyzed for its impact on domestic grain prices. But they also tended to weigh actions from their own particular perspectives, the NSC pressing for the political allocation of food aid, the EPB giving priority to the domestic economy. Only toward the end of the period reviewed here had the staff of a coordinating body—the Economic Policy Board—established itself as an honest broker, trusted, in the main, by officials in competing agencies such as State and Agriculture. And then, for political reasons, President Ford removed food problems from its formal jurisdiction, though it continued to play a role in monitoring food issues through the noncrisis year of 1976.

But there were limits to the ability of a central staff organization to promote coordinated, balanced food policies without Department of Agriculture leaders sensitive to the need for balanced policies, engaged in building a constituency for such policies, and willing to use the department's information, analytic talent, and expertise to develop such policies. The department will continue to be, by definition, farmer-centered and agribusiness-centered. But it is not beyond the realm of possibility for its leaders to include consumers in their constituency and international food institution-building among their responsibilities.

As nonfarm policy values became more at stake in 1972–76, it was probably inevitable that Agriculture would have to share food policy-making to a greater extent and that some power would shift to economic and foreign policy institutions, particularly to the former. But the belated, total, and even humiliating way that it shifted seems more the product of the particular parochialism of the Earl Butz regime. A secretary less determined to minimize government management of commodity markets and more concerned with the impact of food policy actions on economic and foreign and development policies could have made the process of adjustment far smoother. Orville Freeman in 1961–68 actively pursued such ends, even seeking (unsuccessfully) to have his bailiwick renamed the Department of Food and Agriculture.[6] With the attrition of Agriculture's political base in the Congress and the society and its consequent need to broaden its support, such a change may now be feasible.

What is important, of course, is not the name but the orientation—the way the secretary (and the president) conceives the role and builds and maintains Agriculture's constituency. Nor would major reorganization be necessary or even desirable. E. A. Jaenke, formerly a senior USDA official, has argued that "the increasing importance of food suggests the advisability of considering a basic re-organization of the governmental structure," transforming Agriculture into a Department of Food by removing its nonfood bureaus (for example, the Forest Service) and bringing within it certain food functions from other departments, like the international food negotiations responsibilities of State and the food aid responsibilities of the Agency for International Development (AID).[7] But while a broadening of USDA's perspective would need to be linked to an increase in its food policy influence, major consolidation seems unlikely to lead to the integrated, balanced food policies that Jaenke favors. Would not commercial agricultural interests continue to be the department's support base and constituency and therefore continue to receive priority? It is preferable that some of the formal responsibility for agricultural trade negotiations, food aid, and the impact of food on the economy remain outside USDA, to maintain the institutional links of other concerns to food policy and to counteract the inevitable USDA bias. But a reorientation would enable the secretary

6. Weldon V. Barton, "Food, Agriculture, and Administrative Adaptation to Political Change," *Public Administration Review,* vol. 36 (March/April 1976), p. 150.

7. E. A. Jaenke and Associates, "A National Food Policy: Requirements and Alternatives," paper prepared for the Office of Technology Assessment, U.S. Congress (December 1975), pp. 34–36.

and his chief subordinates to take the lead on more issues, both lightening the coordinating burden of the White House and making it easier for the White House and other departments to exercise food policy leadership in cases where it is impossible for Agriculture to do so.[8]

Such a reorientation depends importantly on the substantive views of the secretary and his staff. Constructive USDA leadership on food reserves, for example, requires belief in their potential value for farm, economic, and foreign policy purposes. Similarly, effective handling of short-supply crises depends on the substantive responsiveness of the department's leadership to the concerns of the nonfarm policy communities. Because reserves are closely linked to USDA's primary area of domestic concern—commodity markets—it is probably impossible for the government to develop strong policies on this issue without Agriculture in the forefront. And in supply crises, it is USDA which will be sending out most of the signals to food producers and food traders. If it fails to prepare them for food policy actions that accommodate nonfarm concerns at some cost to producers, the reaction of the farm community is likely to be a replay of 1975.

It was therefore a welcome development that Jimmy Carter's secretary of agriculture, Bob Bergland, came to office in 1977 seeking to serve a broad constituency. His orientation was aptly summarized by the heading of a *National Journal* interview with Daniel J. Balz, "Bergland Says the Farmer and the Consumer Should be Friends."[9] Seeking a sharp turn from the policies of Earl Butz, he chose a prominent consumer advocate as assistant secretary for consumer and nutrition services and a development-oriented agricultural economist for the post of assistant secretary for international affairs and commodity programs. Domestically, he sought to stabilize prices through meaningful support levels and a reserve stock program. And as a former Minnesota wheat farmer and popular member of the House agriculture committee, Bergland had the farm belt credentials to make this base-broadening easier for his prime constituents to accept.

8. Calls from within the Department of Agriculture for responsiveness to a wider range of concerns and constituencies include: Don Paarlberg, "The Farm Policy Agenda," speech delivered at the National Public Policy Conference, Clymer, New York, September 1975 (USDA press release 2621-751); and "USDA and Food Policy Decisionmaking: A Report of the Agriculture Department's 1976 Young Executives Committee" (USDA, January 1977). See also T. A. Stucker, J. B. Penn, and R. D. Knutson, "Agricultural–Food Policymaking: Process and Participants," in U.S. Department of Agriculture, Economic Research Service, *Agricultural–Food Policy Review* (USDA, 1977).

9. *National Journal*, March 12, 1977, pp. 385–88.

Unfortunately, he came to office just as grain farmers were learning anew that free markets move down as well as up. The average farm price for wheat, which had stayed generally above $4.00 a bushel from mid-1973 until early 1975, plummeted to $2.43 a bushel by January 1977. It would drop further—to $2.03 that June—before beginning to climb again. And while farm prices generally did not fall so sharply, net farm income had declined from the remarkable $33 billion of 1973 to $20 billion in 1976. Adjusted for inflation, net income per farm was back where it had been in the late sixties and early seventies.[10]

Economically, the farm bubble had burst. Grain farmers who had overinvested in the boom years were in severe straits; all felt the pressure as costs rose and receipts fell. Politically, this meant farm discontent. The National Farmers Union likened conditions to those which greeted Franklin D. Roosevelt in 1933, and before the year was out the new American Agriculture Movement would win headlines for its demands for parity prices and its well-publicized (if ineffective) call for a national farm strike. This created enormous problems for the secretary in terms of his primary political need—to build farm community confidence in him as its advocate in Washington. His task was made harder when the president rejected his early recommendations on grain price support levels, and he was forced into the position of defending proposals for price supports lower than he (and the Senate and House agriculture committees) felt economically fair or politically viable.[11] Nor was Bergland helped by the fact that, with world stocks growing and food prices temporarily stable, there was remarkably little congressional pressure from those espousing consumer or international welfare concerns.

Bergland recouped somewhat thereafter when he got Carter to accept higher support prices. His political problems were further eased over the next two years as the Carter administration returned to wheat acreage diversion, and as grain prices, responding again to Russian purchases on the 1972 scale, rose once more. But if the Butz experience underscored the pitfalls of narrow farm advocacy, his successor demonstrated how difficult it is to play a broader role, especially when there are hard times on the farm. Yet Bergland has been right to try.

10. USDA, Statistical Reporting Service, Crop Reporting Board, *Agricultural Prices: Annual Summary, 1977* (USDA, June 1977), p. 26; *Economic Report of the President, January 1978*, p. 362.

11. Bergland told the Senate agriculture committee, "What I'm doing today is not what I'd recommend privately if I were a private citizen." *Washington Post*, March 24, 1977.

For in the management of food policy the U.S. government faces a dilemma common to other policy areas as well. The department with most of the information and day-to-day action tends to emphasize one set of policy concerns to the neglect of others. Yet to transfer authority from it to a White House-based coordinating body would separate the making of policy from detailed information and operational responsibility, complicate communications with the Congress and the public, and undercut the department's performance of its ongoing, day-to-day functions. And once this "solution" is used in enough policy areas, the biases of departments and agencies and the boundaries between them merely become replicated in the organizational and jurisdictional divisions within the Executive Office of the President.

There is no perfect solution for food policy, any more than there is for the issue of whether foreign policy leadership (short of the president) comes best from the secretary of state's office or from the National Security Council staff. But the broader the constituency which a secretary of agriculture can make his own and the wider the range of policy concerns his department seeks to accommodate, the greater the share of governmental food policy leadership they are likely to be able to assume. And the better the overall food policy process is likely to function. Conflict will remain, but it will be less of a zero-sum game.

CHAPTER NINE

Trade Policy

TRADE POLICY, as treated here, includes all actions of the U.S. government directly affecting the movement of goods between nations, but it focuses primarily on *American* exports and imports. Like food policy, its boundaries are difficult to draw with precision. And the two obviously overlap. Trade policy is the broader in that it includes movements of all internationally traded goods; it is narrower in that it excludes national actions that affect trade and trade policy without being a part of it—farm and food price policy, for example.

Competing Trade Concerns

Like food policy, trade policy is shaped by concerns arising from both domestic economic interests and international relations. Unlike food policy, it is not characterized by the interplay of relatively distinct policy communities, but trade policymaking conflicts are similarly rooted in differing policy values. And these concerns, with bases in the broader society, are reflected (and to some degree generated or amplified) by particular government institutions.

Industrial Policy

International trade affects the domestic and international markets for particular U.S. industries. When producers of textiles, steel, or color televisions press for import restrictions, they argue that foreign competition is threatening their livelihood and that of their workers. Government actions that respond to these concerns are *industrial policy* actions insofar as they influence the development of particular industries and sectors within the country.[1] Trade policy affects the sectoral evolution of the U.S. economy in many ways: by excepting some tariffs from trade liberalization agreements; by establishing quotas and other nontariff barriers; by using the government's bargaining leverage to improve the access of certain U.S. products to foreign markets.

But the U.S government has never had strong, institutionalized industrial policy. Laissez faire is the norm, and the many breaches of this norm have been ad hoc: land for the railroads in the nineteenth century, facilities for the airlines in the twentieth. Out of the farm depression of the thirties came farm income support and supply management programs; out of the plight of the textile industry in the fifties came bilateral and multilateral quota agreements restraining textile imports. Out of the energy crisis of the seventies may come explicit policies to develop that sector. But the common criticism that the United States has no energy policy extends to most other sectors. There has never been a strong private or governmental interest in shaping the overall development of the U.S. economy through policies favoring particular industries or sectors at the expense of others.[2]

There is, therefore, no industrial policy community in the sense that there are farm and economic policy communities. And there is no U.S. governmental institution (like Japan's Ministry of International Trade and Industry) giving priority to industrial policy generally, though officials within the Department of Commerce occasionally aspire to such a role.[3] Critics of laissez faire have called for "establishment of a

1. Miriam Camps defines industrial policy as "those governmental policies that directly affect patterns of production: who produces what, where." *"First World" Relationships: The Role of the OECD* (New York: Atlantic Institute for International Affairs and Council on Foreign Relations, December 1975), p. 23. And industrial policy, generally, corresponds to those government economic policy activities with the objective of providing "protection and priorities to particular regions or industries." E. S. Kirschen and others, *Economic Policy in Our Time*, vol. 1 (Amsterdam: North Holland, 1964), pp. 6, 14.

2. Thus the U.S. system differs from those of countries like France and Japan, where government actively involves itself in sectoral planning and intervenes on a relatively systematic basis to favor particular industries whose development is seen as in the national interest. This does not mean, of course, that such intervention is always effective or produces the intended results. On Japan, see Hugh Patrick and Henry Rosovsky, eds., *Asia's New Giant: How the Japanese Economy Works* (Brookings Institution, 1976), especially pp. 44–45 and 792–805.

3. Theodore J. Lowi entitles his subchapter on the Labor and Commerce Departments "Economic Policy for Industrial Society: The Empty Houses." *The End of Liberalism: Ideology, Policy, and the Crisis of Public Authority* (Norton, 1969), p. 115.

national industrial and manpower policy" to "develop the areas of potential strength in our domestic economy."[4] But the many policy actors inside and outside government who ask how U.S. trade actions will affect domestic industry seldom take such an overall view; rather they ask with specific industries in mind. Sometimes they employ broader rationales. Advocates of orderly marketing argue that the impact of trade on national industries and workers is so inherently disruptive that it needs to be closely and carefully regulated. But despite the movement of most of organized labor behind this viewpoint, it has yet to become the basis for an effective cross-industry coalition.

Domestic Economic Policy

Trade policy is also linked to *domestic economic policy,* and increasingly so as the trade share of American gross national product increases. Shifts in the trade balance affect the rate of overall economic expansion; imports can help dampen inflation; an "unfavorable" balance of payments can "threaten" the dollar in a fixed-exchange-rate regime and can reduce its value in a floating regime. Domestic economic concerns can affect trade policy in another way, for those who favor government intervention in the domestic economy may be inclined also to support trade-restrictive actions. John Dunlop's support of the soybean embargo comes to mind; so does George Shultz's opposition. Historically, this relationship has not always held. William Graham Sumner, the stern nineteenth century preacher of laissez faire, might argue that free enterprise must mean open competition internationally as well as domestically, but the high-tariff Republican party was the advocate of minimal business regulation at home. And the low-tariff Democrats brought in the New Deal even as they moved import duties down from the historic highs of the Hawley-Smoot tariff.[5]

In the postwar period, economic policy officials' stances on trade issues reflected more their orientation (usually positive) toward free trade than their attitudes toward domestic economic intervention. Most subscribed to the classical comparative advantage theory, that free trade increases world welfare by allocating resources to their most productive uses. More recently U.S. economic officials have also emphasized the link between import restraint and inflation. And in times when America's in-

4. *Williams Commission Report,* p. 9. See chapter 1, note 11, for full reference. Also see elaboration by William R. Pearce and others, ibid., p. 317.

5. The classic treatment of the politics of Hawley-Smoot is E. E. Schattschneider, *Politics, Pressures, and the Tariff* (Prentice-Hall, 1935).

ternational payments balance has been unfavorable, they necessarily have been concerned with the balance of trade, to the point, sometimes, of supporting aggressive negotiating and marketing strategies to expand export opportunities.

Foreign Policy

Trade policy is also very importantly *foreign policy*. As Thomas C. Schelling has noted, "Aside from war and preparations for war, and occasionally aside from migration, trade is the most important relationship that most countries have with each other"; hence, "trade policy is national security policy," mainly because of "its implications for other countries and our relations with them."[6] In the 1945–67 period, foreign policy concerns were a major—perhaps the major—influence on trade policy. Officials saw trade barriers as a major contributor to World War II and linked a liberal world economic order to the maintenance of peace. Trade with Western Europe and Japan became a means of helping rebuild their economies and of cementing U.S. relations with them. Conversely, restrictions on trade with China and Russia were a means of conducting the cold war. And in relations with developing countries, trade policy is linked to development policy by the subsidization of exports to them and the preferences given (since 1974) to imports from them.

Foreign policy officials concerned with these three arenas—the advanced industrial countries, the developing countries, and cold-war adversaries—view particular trade policy issues in terms of their impact on these countries. Does an action strengthen or weaken the economies of U.S. allies; does it strengthen U.S. ties with them? Does it weaken U.S. adversaries, or does it build bridges? Does it strengthen U.S. relations with developing countries; does it improve their welfare and development by transferring resources to them?

Patterns of Trade Politics

Economic and foreign policy officials typically align in support of as liberal and open a trading regime as domestic and international politics permit. Arrayed against them are those who stand to benefit from trade restrictions on particular products. These interests gain strength from their very high stake in a particular tariff or quota, whereas the benefits

6. "National Security Considerations Affecting Trade Policy," *Williams Commission Report: Papers,* vol. 1, p. 737.

of *not* imposing restraints are usually dispersed. Consumers, for example, are unlikely to organize as effectively as the Zenith Corporation to influence color television imports. So the political problem for liberal trade advocates is to keep protectionist pressure within bounds. Above all, free traders seek to avoid a repeat of the logrolling experience with the Hawley-Smoot tariff of 1930, when product interests built a coalition that brought them record levels of protection.

One method of coping with industrial pressure is to buy off the strongest: successive administrations have acceded to the textile industry's desire for quotas to keep that industry from leading a broad protectionist coalition. Another method is to channel pressures into regulatory proceedings: firms claiming injury from imports, or alleging unfair foreign export practices, can bring their cases to the International Trade Commission (the Tariff Commission until 1975) or the Treasury Department, and may win relief if they meet certain statutory criteria. A third method, more promising in concept than yet in practice, is adjustment assistance—government subsidies to help workers and firms move out of import-threatened industries into other productive activities. Last but not least, liberal trade advocates use international institutions and international negotiations as rationales to block trade restrictions and to mobilize support for further liberalization.

The international institutional framework for postwar trade relations is the General Agreement on Tariffs and Trade (GATT) of 1948. A cornerstone of the GATT system is the most-favored-nation (MFN) principle of nondiscrimination—a country offers to all parties to the agreement its most favorable tariff rates. Negotiations are conducted to reduce trade barriers under the principle of reciprocity—an exchange of concessions—even though the classical economic theory holds that net benefits can come to a country that reduces import barriers unilaterally. The reason for the emphasis on reciprocity is, of course, political. As Ernest Preeg notes, "Protectionist resistance to tariff reduction on particular products is difficult to offset by widely dispersed gains in efficiency or consumer welfare. . . . The bargaining approach, on the other hand, through which gains for export industries are matched against increased imports, has greatly strengthened the appeal of trade liberalization."[7] And the word "reciprocal" was in fact incorporated in the title

7. Ernest H. Preeg, *Traders and Diplomats: An Analysis of the Kennedy Round of Negotiations under the General Agreement on Tariffs and Trade* (Brookings Institution, 1970), pp. 23–24.

of U.S. trade legislation aimed at tariff reduction, from the initiation of this approach by Secretary of State Cordell Hull in 1934 through the 1950s.[8]

In 1962, with very strong Kennedy administration backing, Congress enacted the Trade Expansion Act, which provided the statutory basis for the most comprehensive tariff negotiations yet undertaken. The act made it clear that foreign policy interests would no longer dominate, by creating a special representative for trade negotiations (STR), in the Executive Office of the President, to lead the United States in the new round, a responsibility that had previously been the State Department's. Influential members of Congress believed State was too prone to bargain away U.S. commercial interests for vague foreign policy gains. But no one could quarrel with the Kennedy Round's impact on industrial tariffs. As Preeg notes, "The average Kennedy Round reduction of 36–39 percent by all major industrial countries" finally achieved in 1967 "was fully in keeping with the ambitious initial objectives."[9] For the United States, this reduction was in addition to the drop in tariffs from an average of 54 percent in 1933 to 12 percent in 1963.[10]

The Crisis in Trade Policy

Since the end of World War II the volume of trade had increased markedly, both in absolute terms and as a proportion of overall production.[11] And this trade generated substantial vested interests: multinational corporations, which profit from an open world economic order,

8. The emphasis on reciprocity, however, can cut both ways. Those who value it strongly and believe that the existing trade regime does not actually provide it can turn against free trade, arguing for raising their own barriers in self-defense unless other nations make unilateral or disproportionate concessions to right the imbalance. Thus, in arguing for textile quotas, Maurice H. Stans, secretary of commerce in the Nixon administration, repeatedly stated that the United States was the only open textile market in the world, and U.S. industry could not take this disproportionate pressure. Advocacy of fair trade can thus become indistinguishable from mercantilism, in its determination to improve the *relative* position of the United States in the international trading order.

9. Preeg, *Traders and Diplomats*, p. 257.

10. Ibid., p. 15.

11. The ratio of trade to overall production had declined in the 1920s and 1930s. See Steven D. Krasner, "State Power and the Structure of International Trade," *World Politics*, vol. 28 (April 1976), pp. 326–29.

and exporters, including major segments of American agriculture. Nevertheless, the completion of the Kennedy Round in 1967 brought renewed and mounting pressure for trade restrictions. By early in the next decade, trade experts were writing regularly of "neomercantilism," or "coming trade wars," or a "crisis in U.S. trade policy."[12]

One reason was that international negotiations could no longer play the role of political counterweight. While they were in progress, congressmen and executive branch officials could deflect protectionist demands on the grounds that meeting them would undermine the country's position at the negotiating table. Now this powerful argument was unavailable. Thus, for example, the textile and steel industries intensified their campaigns for new quota restrictions in late 1967 and 1968.

A second factor was the weakening of the U.S. trade balance, which had moved from a record surplus of $7.1 billion in 1964 to a near-deficit by 1968. Not only did this reflect the growing foreign competition which many U.S. manufacturing firms were feeling in their home markets; it gave credence to the view that American industry was losing its competitiveness vis-à-vis Europe and Japan in particular—because of either wage differentials or unfair foreign practices.

Third, and related to the declining trade balance, was the movement of organized labor, which had strongly endorsed the Trade Expansion Act of 1962, away from the free-trade camp. By February 1970, the AFL-CIO economic policy committee was declaring that developments of recent years had "made old 'free trade' concepts and their 'protectionist' opposites increasingly irrelevant," and called for new policies emphasizing an "*orderly* expansion of world trade."[13] Labor saw jobs threatened by competition from low-wage workers abroad, some of them employed by U.S. multinationals who had "exported the jobs" of American workers to take advantage of these lower wage costs.

Fourth, there was uncertainty about the priorities of the Nixon administration throughout its first term. The president declared himself a free-trader, but his administration gave its primary trade negotiating energy in its first three years to fulfilling his campaign promise of quotas on synthetic and wool textiles for the U.S. industry. And though Nixon

12. See C. Fred Bergsten, "Crisis in U.S. Trade Policy," *Foreign Affairs*, vol. 49 (July 1971), pp. 619–35; and Harald B. Malmgren, "Coming Trade Wars? (Neo-Mercantilism and Foreign Policy)," *Foreign Policy*, no. 1 (Winter 1970–1971), pp. 115–43.

13. *New York Times*, February 22, 1970. Emphasis added.

emphasized foreign policy, he evinced a disinterest in foreign *economic* issues, which was shared by his primary aide, national security adviser Henry A. Kissinger. Moreover, Nixon's first-term foreign policy ended up deemphasizing relations with Europe and Japan in pursuit of détente with Russia and rapprochement with China. (Emphasis on the former would have meant greater priority for trade issues.) Finally, Nixon assigned textile negotiating responsibility to the cabinet official most sympathetic toward protection—Secretary of Commerce Maurice H. Stans—and allowed Stans to control the appointment of the special trade representative, Carl Gilbert, who proved a weak counterweight.

The stress on textiles and the neglect of broader trade policy fueled protectionism on Capitol Hill. Failure to achieve a textile agreement with Japan led to the administration's "reluctant" endorsement of statutory textile quotas in June 1970. The House Ways and Means Committee, lacking the usual executive pressure against *all* such quotas, added quotas for shoes and a general provision making quantitative restrictions available to other industries if imports were large and growing. This so-called Mills bill[14] passed the House in November and reached the Senate floor a month later, only to die in parliamentary maneuvers as adjournment neared. And in September 1971, Senator Vance Hartke and Congressman James A. Burke proposed their highly protectionist Foreign Trade and Investment Act, which provided thoroughgoing quantitative restrictions on imports and aimed also to discourage foreign direct investment by U.S. corporations. The bill had the outspoken support of AFL-CIO President George Meany. As Hartke later summarized its aims, it sought to control "the worst practices of transnational firms like the export of U.S. jobs, technology, and capital, as well as permitting American enterprise to compete with imports on an equitable basis."[15]

14. The bill was named for Wilbur D. Mills, chairman of the House Ways and Means Committee. Actually, Mills disliked the bill. He had introduced his quota bill to buttress the administration's efforts to negotiate export restraint agreements with Japan and other major textile exporters, a device he much preferred to statutory quota restrictions. When the administration, to his apparent surprise, endorsed it, he felt he had little choice but to move it forward lest he lose control of his committee. In early 1971, Mills ingeniously got himself out of this bind by negotiating his own trade restraint agreement with the Japanese textile industry, which he then argued made statutory quotas unnecessary. For further discussion, see I. M. Destler, Haruhiro Fukui, and Hideo Sato, *The Textile Wrangle: Conflict in Japanese-American Relations 1969–1971* (Cornell University Press, 1979), especially chapters 9 and 11.

15. *Trade Reform,* Hearings before the House Committee on Ways and Means, 93 Cong. 1 sess. (Government Printing Office, 1973), pt. 14, p. 5019.

The Nixon Administration Response

But these pressures for new restrictions were countered by an effort to regenerate momentum toward trade liberalization. In July 1971, the Commission on International Trade and Investment Policy (the Williams commission), which President Nixon had created "to produce recommendations designed to meet the challenges of the changing world economy during the present decade,"[16] submitted its final report. This commission found that the structure of the world economy had changed. Rising trade and capital flows, strong competition from Europe and Japan, and regional economic arrangements increasingly placed the United States at a disadvantage. This effect was magnified by other factors such as differential rates of growth and inflation and the influence on exports and imports of an overvalued dollar. Moreover, international and domestic rules and institutions were proving unable to cope with these developments.

The commission noted "a growing concern in this country that the United States has not received full value for the tariff concessions made over the years because foreign countries have found other ways, besides tariffs, of impeding our access to their markets."[17] It cited in particular the nontariff barriers imposed by the European Economic Community and Japan. But it concluded that efforts to deal with the problem by restricting trade and investment flows would not serve long-term U.S. interests. The adjustment problem would simply shift to the more efficient industries in the form of higher costs and reduced opportunities abroad as other countries closed their markets to them. The commission felt that it made more sense to preserve and expand the advantages of an open system by dealing with the underlying problems. It therefore called for "a major series of international negotiations . . . to prepare the way for the elimination of all barriers to international trade and capital movements within 25 years,"[18] particularly nontariff barriers.

The work of the Williams commission was paralleled internationally by the High-Level Group on Trade and Related Problems sponsored by the Organisation for Economic Co-operation and Development

16. *Williams Commission Report*, p. ix.
17. Ibid., p. 2.
18. Ibid., p. 10. This summary draws upon "Outline for Remarks by William R. Pearce before the Committee on Foreign Relations" (Des Moines: December 11, 1974), pp. 2–3.

(OECD). The group met monthly in late 1971 and early 1972 under the chairmanship of Jean Rey, former president of the European Community. The group concluded in August 1972:

> A new effort to secure greater liberalisation, achieved through negotiation, is needed not only for the direct benefits it will bring but because without it the divisive forces of protectionism will grow stronger, with the risk that the world will slip back into an era of restriction and ultimately of contraction of the international economic system.[19]

As one actively involved in building this antiprotectionist countermomentum put it later, "The idea caught on of using multilateral negotiations to solve some of the domestic complaints and to offer a positive alternative to protectionism."[20]

Finally, changes inside the government in 1971 and early 1972 made it far better able to develop a constructive response. In January 1971, President Nixon established the Council on International Economic Policy (CIEP) whose staff was headed by an assistant to the president for international economic affairs, Peter G. Peterson. Nixon thereby created an organizational analogue to the National Security Council (NSC) under whose umbrella Henry Kissinger was dominating political-military foreign policy. Neither CIEP nor Peterson ever achieved anything approaching comparable authority, but they did help remedy the inattention to broad international economic strategy which had marked the first two Nixon years.

Most important for trade policymaking, however, was the rebuilding of the Office of the Special Representative for Trade Negotiations. In September 1971, William D. Eberle (already designated the U.S. representative on the Rey group) was named special trade representative, with a clear mandate to work toward a new round of multilateral negotiations. He soon recruited two strong deputies (his predecessor had not been allowed even one): William R. Pearce, of Cargill, to work with the Congress and affected interest groups; and Harald B. Malmgren, who had served previously in STR at a lower level, to take the lead in the international consultations aimed at inaugurating the new trade round.

19. *Policy Perspectives for International Trade and Economic Relations*, Report by the High-Level Group on Trade and Related Problems to the Secretary-General of OECD (Paris: Organisation for Economic Co-operation and Development, 1972), p. 110.

20. Harald B. Malmgren, "The United States," in Wilfrid L. Kohl, ed., *Economic Foreign Policies of Industrial States* (Lexington Books, 1977), p. 39.

The formal U.S. commitment to engage in a new multilateral round of trade negotiations derived from events set in motion on August 15, 1971, when President Nixon shook America's trading partners by suspending the convertibility of the dollar and imposing a 10 percent surcharge on imports. In the weeks thereafter Secretary of the Treasury John B. Connally set forth very demanding terms for an international economic settlement, including major unilateral trade concessions by the European Community and Japan. A softening of the stance led to the Smithsonian Agreement of December 1971, in which the United States lifted the surcharge in exchange for substantial exchange rate realignment. Following up on that agreement in February 1972, the United States reached agreements with both the European Community and Japan that provided for limited unilateral trade concessions by these trading partners and the inauguration of comprehensive new multilateral negotiations based on "mutual advantage and mutual commitment with overall reciprocity."[21]

Participation in such negotiations required new statutory authority, and the executive branch began its efforts to prepare a draft bill to submit to Congress through interagency task forces coordinated by the staff of CIEP. These included a group on adjustment assistance led by the Labor Department and a committee on export promotion led by the Commerce Department.

In mid-1972, two broader-purpose interagency committees were formed.[22] One, chaired by Malmgren, was charged with surveying international options and, even before the trade bill was submitted to Congress, international agreement was reached to open the new negotiations formally with a Tokyo meeting in September 1973. Another, the Trade Legislation Committee, was initially headed by a relatively junior CIEP official. This proved the more important because the legislation to be proposed was the main matter at issue, and Pearce had joined STR in the expectation that he would chair such a group. But there had been a change at CIEP. In February Peterson had been succeeded as assistant to the president by Peter M. Flanigan, who, unlike Peterson, sought operational control of trade issues and viewed STR as an arm of CIEP. (He was, in fact, to press for formal incorporation of STR under CIEP the following year.)

21. Testimony of William D. Eberle, *Trade Reform,* Hearings, pt. 2, pp. 343–44.

22. Richard S. Frank, "Trade Report: Administration Torn between Domestic, Overseas Interests in Drafting Trade Bill," *National Journal,* January 13, 1973, p. 46.

The question of who chaired the committee had substantive significance, for the executive branch contained a range of trade policy views.
Most important was the tension between the neomercantilist and free
trade perspectives. Neomercantilists saw the United States, in the words
of Flanigan, as "more sinned against than sinning."[23] And they tended
to see international trade as a competition among nations, with the
United States needing to recoup losses in its relative position. Connally
epitomized this attitude; and at the working level the Treasury staff—
concerned with improving the balance of payments but also with protecting the value of the currency—was predisposed toward pushing for
trade concessions as a means of achieving the first end without sacrificing
the second.[24] Trade negotiations were seen not just as a means of protecting or extending international liberalization—thus expanding the
volume of trade—but of also improving the U.S. position vis-à-vis other
countries—the *balance* of trade. By contrast, those with a free trade
orientation—in STR, the State Department, and the Council of Economic
Advisers, and to some extent in the Agriculture and Labor departments
—looked primarily for reciprocal reduction of import barriers and did
not expect or press for one-sided U.S. gains. They saw trade as the international extension of competition among producers; and they saw the
gains of trade in terms of either classical economics—enhanced efficiency and welfare, worldwide—or postwar politics—reinforced relations with allies.

Thus in the drafting process, free traders argued mainly for liberalization, with safeguards for industries truly injured by competition. Neomercantilists argued for a tough bargaining posture, because other countries would need to make larger concessions if the trade balance were to
be set right. They called for "sticks," provisions allowing the president
to raise barriers against specific products and against countries whose
external accounts were out of balance.

There was also a difference in political perspective. Neomercantilists
read the public and congressional mood as tough-minded, skeptical.
They believed that only tough provisions and stern rhetoric could get a
bill through the treacherous congressional waters, and saw the Mills
bill of 1970 as evidence of this mood. Free traders had a different reading

23. Ibid., p. 45.
24. For a good, concise summary of Connally's stance and attitudes, see Robert
Solomon, *The International Monetary System, 1945–1976: An Insider's View*
(Harper and Row, 1977), pp. 190–91.

of the Mills bill experience. To them, the problem with trade liberalization is that the costs are concentrated and the benefits diffuse. Congressmen tend to hear from the interests most affected; thus a vote for freer trade was, as Pearce later put it, "an 'unnatural act' unless it [could] be identified with an overriding national interest."[25] The Nixon administration, therefore, had invited the Mills bill phenomenon in 1969–70 by submitting a minor, "housekeeping" trade bill and then breaching the no-quotas principle by endorsing them for textiles. A more ambitious bill, however, could be effective *if* it were linked to a major trade negotiating initiative, and *if* it scrupulously avoided giving particular prizes to particular industries that others could demand for themselves on equity grounds.

Compared to these two perspectives, the protectionist or orderly marketing view was less prominent in the executive branch. There was some support in Commerce for general safeguards against market disruption from imports and particular protection for textiles, shoes, and steel. The leading proponents were Stans, while he was secretary, Stanley Nehmer, the deputy assistant secretary for resources, and Seth Bodner, head of the Office of Import Programs. These last two officials had had lead Commerce responsibility in the textile negotiations, very important to Stans, and were therefore in a strong position vis-à-vis the deputy assistant secretary for international economic policy, Lawrence A. Fox, who took a more liberal stance. Their views, however, seldom won administration-wide endorsement.

The drafting of the legislation in 1972 and early 1973 took place in a curious vacuum of leadership. George Shultz had become secretary of the treasury in 1972 but as the year ended was only beginning to move into the position of economic policy czar. In December 1972, Nixon made Shultz head of a new cabinet-level Council on Economic Policy (CEP), to which CIEP gradually was subordinated, and Shultz was to become, in practice, a deputy president for economic matters. But he had stronger views on domestic than on foreign economic issues, and in trade he played a less active role than he did in the monetary sphere. Thus he was more a general overseer, court of appeal, and link to the president than a force for controlling substance. His general support of the trade negotiations initiative was indispensable. His inclination to take at least a moderately tough line, partly because it might strengthen the U.S. hand in monetary negotiations, was also influential. Further-

25. Pearce, "Outline for Remarks," p. 6.

more, he saw unilateral U.S. trade actions as a means of pressing countries with chronic balance-of-payments surpluses to take corrective action—a means of ensuring that the United States got a fair shake in trade. "You cannot expect the exchange rate system to carry the full load of adjustment," he said in March.[26]

President Nixon's role was even more limited. He was personally uninvolved and relatively inaccessible until the final stages, and the signals the White House sent were not encouraging to advocates of trade liberalization. When the White House took a protectionist action, it announced it with fanfare, whereas decisions against domestic industries were left to the special trade representative to announce. White House fears that leaks would damage Nixon with particular industries limited what could be done before the election. Nixon did, however, give considerable emphasis to free trade values when it came time to send the message to Congress.

The combination of intergovernmental divisions, limited leadership from the cabinet and above, and the election constraint meant that the initial drafting progressed slowly. But things improved when the chairmanship of the drafting committee was assumed by Deane R. Hinton, a strong, effective bureaucrat on detail to CIEP from the State Department. After the election the pace quickened when Flanigan agreed that Pearce's office could draft issues and options papers drawing on the themes of the *Williams Commission Report*. This procedure structured the issues and began to resolve differences, with Hinton ruling on disagreements and Shultz available for appeals.

The 100-page bill that resulted was a far-reaching proposal, a melange reflecting both free trade and neomercantilist perspectives but with few out-and-out protectionist elements. In sending it to Capitol Hill, Nixon reiterated "his central assumption that what really matters about trade is its effect, potential or actual, on foreign policy."[27] Thus he gave emphasis to the foreign policy goals of trade policy, which had been largely implicit in a drafting committee dominated by trade and eco-

26. Richard S. Frank, "Economic Report: Shultz Takes Charge as United States Presses for Monetary, Trade Reforms," *National Journal*, March 10, 1973, pp. 352, 353. For an analysis of the dominance of senior bureaucrats in the drafting process see Wilfrid L. Kohl, "The Nixon-Kissinger Foreign Policy System and U.S.-European Relations: Patterns of Policy Making," *World Politics*, vol. 28 (October 1975), pp. 33–35. See also Anne H. Rightor-Thornton, "An Analysis of the Office of the Special Representative for Trade Negotiations: The Evolving Role, 1962–1974," in *Murphy Commission Report*, vol. 3, pp. 98–99. See chapter 1, note 1, for full reference.

27. *Economist*, April 14, 1973, p. 51.

nomic policy specialists. But the bill he sent forward was nonetheless a two-edged sword, usable for erecting trade barriers as well as dismantling them.

The Nixon Trade Proposal[28]

Theoretically, the administration could have sought from Congress only the authority it needed to engage in trade negotiations. But there were in the business community long-standing complaints about other trade issues. The Tariff Commission had to apply rather stringent criteria in determining whether an industry was injured by imports before it could recommend relief; similarly stringent provisions existed for adjustment assistance to help trade-affected firms and workers move to other lines of endeavor. The long-standing law on countervailing duties, in form a protection against subsidies given by foreign governments to products entering the U.S. market, was in practice seldom applied. There were also outstanding U.S. promises to grant tariff preferences to developing countries in the American market and to extend most-favored-nation treatment to the Soviet Union and other Eastern bloc countries. The political and policy case was strong for including all of these (except perhaps Soviet MFN status) in one bill, and so the bill submitted to Congress dealt with four broad areas: (1) the authority to negotiate changes in tariffs and nontariff barriers, (2) relief for import-impacted industries, (3) preferences for developing countries, and (4) most-favored-nation status for the Soviet Union.

Negotiating Authority

One of the most important provisions of the new trade bill was the renewal of presidential negotiating authority on tariffs, which had expired in 1967. The drafters resolved the problem of how much to seek by asking for the maximum: unlimited authority to raise or lower tariffs. This gave the administration the strongest carrots and sticks for international bargaining; it also nicely papered over interdepartmental differences by postponing the choice of how liberal or how tough to be. And in practice, it was a way of allowing Congress to develop—and take credit for—whatever limitations in negotiating authority were imposed.

28. The proposed bill, a summary, and the president's message are included in *Trade Reform*, Hearings, pt. 1, pp. 4–152.

A more difficult problem was nontariff barriers (NTBs). Since the Kennedy Round's success in dealing with tariffs, increasing attention had been drawn to the growing problem of buy-national laws, quotas, customs valuation procedures, environmental regulations, industrial standards, governmental aids to industry, and so on—all of which could directly affect the volume or composition of trade. Nontariff barriers in the United States were rooted in domestic laws, often laws with major nontrade objectives. Changing them would normally require action by both houses of Congress. How then could the executive branch negotiate credibly on such issues? Here the Kennedy Round experience was sobering, for Congress had never implemented an agreement to change the American selling price (ASP) system of calculating duties on certain chemicals and other products. Other nations, fearing similar future failures in implementation, might refuse to negotiate seriously on NTBs.

Executive officials, particularly in State and CIEP, would have liked blanket advance authority to negotiate NTB reductions.[29] This would not only strengthen U.S. diplomatic leverage but would reduce political problems at home, since organized interests hurt by particular NTB changes negotiated at Geneva could not overturn them by appealing to Congress. But Congress seemed unlikely to grant such blanket authority. And it might well have been unconstitutional. So the bill ultimately included a compromise developed by STR general counsel, John H. Jackson: for certain specified NTBs relating to customs procedures (including ASP), advance presidential authority to take implementing action; for other NTBs, authority to implement them unless either house of Congress voted to override within ninety days. This proposal was put forward despite concern among administration lawyers about the precedent such a "legislative veto" might establish. (And as noted in chapter 12, President Ford would later challenge the constitutionality of *other* legislative vetoes which Congress added to the Trade Act.)

Relief from Import Competition

Under the Trade Expansion Act of 1962, an industry could obtain relief from imports (a) if the Tariff Commission found that it had suf-

29. Robert A. Pastor, "Legislative-Executive Relations and U.S. Foreign Trade Policy: The Case of the Trade Act of 1974," paper prepared for the 1976 annual meeting of the American Political Science Association, p. 13. Pastor's full analysis of the Trade Act experience appears in "Legislative-Executive Relations and the Politics of United States Foreign Economic Policy, 1929–1976" (Ph.D. dissertation, Harvard University, 1977), pp. 213–79.

fered serious injury, the major cause of which was the increase in imports due to U.S. tariff concessions, and (b) if the president then acted on this finding by restricting imports in one of three ways: raising tariffs, imposing quotas, or negotiating orderly marketing arrangements with foreign exporters. Such relief was internationally sanctioned under the GATT escape clause. As it turned out, the eligibility requirements proved difficult to meet, and the law was rarely invoked. With these procedures unfruitful, industries increasingly sought special statutory protection.

To counter this trend, Nixon's 1969 trade proposal had dropped the link between increased imports and prior tariff concessions and required only that increased imports be the "primary" cause of serious injury. ("Major cause" meant larger than all other factors combined; "primary cause" was defined as the largest single cause.) Commerce officials proposed going further in 1973, requiring determination only that imports were causing "material injury," and that "market disruption" was present.[30] But the administration essentially repeated its 1969 request and maintained presidential discretion in responding to Tariff Commission findings of injury. Relief could be supplied for up to five years, with a two-year extension for exceptional cases. The proposal did add, however, market disruption as prima facie evidence that increased imports were the major cause of injury. And the more generous Commerce standard was in fact incorporated in the title dealing with imports from the Soviet Union and other countries not then receiving MFN treatment.

A more constructive long-term means of compensating for injury caused by imports is to help workers and firms move to other productive endeavors. The Trade Expansion Act of 1962 had therefore inaugurated a program of adjustment assistance, including loans, tax breaks, and technical aid for firms; and jobless benefits, retraining, and relocation aid for workers. This program had been important in winning labor support for the act. But it had gone largely unimplemented, one important reason being that the eligibility requirements were essentially the same as those for import relief. Many free traders felt that to encourage adjustment, it should be easier to qualify for this kind of aid than for tariff or quota protection. Moreover, there was evidence that the pace of change in world trade was accelerating, increasing the domestic economic impact and the need for programs to cope with it. Since 1962,

30. "Market disruption" was defined as a situation where imports of a product were increasing rapidly, both absolutely and as a proportion of domestic consumption, and were being offered at prices substantially below those of comparable domestic articles.

organized labor had become disillusioned with adjustment assistance as part of its turn away from support of trade liberalization, but there was nevertheless reason to believe that a stronger program would increase the bill's attractiveness on the Hill.

For substantive and political reasons, State, Labor, and STR favored liberalization of eligibility criteria and benefits and some restructuring to improve the program's effectiveness. But Shultz was highly skeptical of trade adjustment aid and was joined in the skepticism by OMB, Commerce, and CIEP. They argued for a more intensive effort to improve regular unemployment benefits, to guarantee pension rights, and to establish new retraining programs for all workers, not just those affected by trade. Shultz was particularly strong in believing that categorical programs responding to trade-induced (but not other) industry and labor adjustment problems were economically unsound and of limited political use.[31]

Shultz prevailed, and the adjustment assistance provisions were weak. Although the administration bill liberalized the eligibility criteria for workers' adjustment assistance (imports needed only to have "contributed substantially" to loss of work), the level and duration of benefits were substantially reduced. Instead, Nixon called for increases in state unemployment benefits for all workers. In separate legislation, he proposed adoption of minimum federal standards for weekly jobless benefits, recommending that federal adjustment assistance meeting those projected standards be provided only until the new standards could be phased in. The program of adjustment assistance for firms established in 1962 was to be terminated.

The bill devoted a separate title to "relief from unfair trade practices." The most general provision to this end gave the president sweeping authority to retaliate against any country that maintained "unjustifiable or unreasonable tariff or other import restrictions" against the United States, or pursued other discriminatory or subsidy policies that damaged the U.S. trade position.[32] He could, if unable to obtain elimi-

31. For a careful exposition of his views, see George P. Shultz and Kenneth W. Dam, *Economic Policy Beyond the Headlines* (Stanford Alumni Association, 1977; W. W. Norton, 1978), pp. 139–45.

32. Under current law, the president could strike back at discrimination against U.S. manufactured goods abroad by withdrawing tariff concessions and thus returning to pre-1934 levels. Only if the discrimination were against U.S. agricultural products could he otherwise raise tariffs or impose quotas in retaliation. The 1973 bill eliminated the agricultural/manufactured distinction.

nation of such practices, impose duties or quotas at any level "on a most-favored-nation basis or otherwise, and for such time as he deems appropriate."

To cope with unfair competitive practices in U.S. markets, the administration proposed to tighten existing countervailing duty and anti-dumping laws. Existing laws allowed the Treasury Department to respond to export subsidies and dumping with offsetting duties. However, in most cases, no duties were assessed, in part because the laws stipulated no time limits for investigation or action. The administration sought to modernize them by setting strict time limits but retaining the treasury secretary's discretion in action.

Generalized System of Preferences

Duty-free treatment for the manufactured and semimanufactured goods of developing countries was first proposed in the early 1960s. The initial U.S. reaction had been cool. But by the 1970s, the generalized system of preferences (GSP) had become "a rallying point for developing-country action—its political importance far transcending its possible trade impact."[33]

President Lyndon B. Johnson had agreed in 1967 to consider preferences; a 1969 Nixon proposal to extend preferences was rejected by Congress. Meanwhile, eighteen other industrialized nations had made tariff preferences available to developing countries.

The Nixon administration remained committed to preferences but had deferred presenting further legislation on the matter because of opposition by organized labor and its supporters in Congress. In the drafting committee, the State Department argued strongly for GSP on the ground that the United States had an international commitment on which it had to deliver. Their argument prevailed, but this left open the question of the form preferences would take. State wanted to allow zero duties for ten years, but this idea was rejected because it was felt to be unworkable in Congress as long as Canada, Japan, and the European Community provided more limited preferences in the form of tariff quotas. Ultimately Hinton came up with the compromise idea, a $25 million ceiling. When a country's exports of a particular article to the United States reached this level, or if they were 50 percent of the total

33. Guy F. Erb and Charles R. Frank, Jr. "U.S. Trade Reform and the Third World," *Challenge*, vol. 17 (May–June 1974), p. 64.

U.S. imports of that product, preferences would not be applied. This compromise is what the administration proposed.

Soviet Most-Favored-Nation Status

On October 18, 1972, the United States had signed a trade agreement with the Soviet Union calling for providing that country most-favored-nation status.[34] Its implementation required congressional action, which could come either as part of the omnibus trade bill or in a separate piece of legislation. The question of which course to propose was "strongly debated within the Administration,"[35] for the issue was heating up rapidly on Capitol Hill—linked to Soviet restrictions on emigration of Jews to Israel.

On October 4, resolutions denying MFN status to countries that barred emigration had been introduced in both houses of Congress. Henry Jackson sponsored the Senate resolution, with seventy-two cosponsors. Charles A. Vanik sponsored the House version; by early 1973 a majority of House members, including Wilbur Mills, had joined in this cause. Inclusion of MFN in the trade bill thus could jeopardize the entire bill, for this proposal was unacceptable to the administration, and Jackson had sworn to attach it to any request for MFN status.

But the signals were mixed. Mills had indicated that a comprehensive bill would be best, and staff specialists Harry Lamar of the House Ways and Means Committee and Robert Best of the Senate Finance Committee both felt that Congress could not effectively handle two major trade bills in one session.[36]

Within the executive branch, Pearce wanted to remove MFN from the omnibus trade bill and send two bills to Congress simultaneously, moving the Soviet bill first. Flanigan and Hinton were strongly in favor of a combined bill, arguing that MFN, being part of the popular détente policy, would actually strengthen the trade bill's chances. Kissinger and Shultz also apparently favored a combined bill.[37] And this view prevailed. Title 5 of the bill therefore authorized the president to extend, for a renewable period of three years, most-favored-nation treatment to

34. The texts are in *State Department Bulletin*, vol. 67 (November 20, 1972), pp. 595–604.

35. Pearce, "Outline for Remarks," p. 11.

36. For a detailed, illuminating account of the entire Jackson amendment controversy, see Paula Stern, *Water's Edge: Domestic Politics and the Making of American Foreign Policy* (Greenwood Press, 1979).

37. Ibid., pp. 60–61.

any country currently barred from receiving it (as most Communist countries were). The inclusion of Soviet MFN in the bill was to have major political consequences.

Special Duties and Quantitative Limits

To provide a clearer authority for actions like those undertaken on August 15, 1971, the bill gave the president explicit power to impose temporary duties or quantitative limits on imports to combat a serious U.S. balance-of-payments deficit; it also provided converse authority—to reduce or suspend tariffs or quotas in the event of a persistent balance-of-payments surplus. This provision was opposed by some drafters, such as Pearce, who felt that exchange rate adjustment was the proper cure for payments imbalances. But Shultz disagreed, as noted earlier; he wanted to link trade and monetary reform for international bargaining purposes.

Finally, the bill authorized the president to reduce duties or ease quantitative restrictions temporarily as a means of restraining inflation.

And Off to Congress

The Trade Expansion Act of 1962 had been sent to Capitol Hill in January; both Houses had acted by September. Nixon administration officials hoped for similar dispatch in 1973, allowing the international negotiations to begin in earnest the following year. They were not to be so fortunate. Instead of eight months, twenty passed—longer than anyone expected. Nor could anyone have foreseen the political and institutional complications that those twenty months would bring.

CHAPTER TEN

The Trade Bill in the House, 1973

ON APRIL 10 the proposed Trade Reform Act of 1973 was formally transmitted to Capitol Hill. The time seemed particularly inauspicious.[1] The trade balance reflected a deficit of $6.4 billion in the preceding year, the worst to date in the twentieth century. To many this seemed an indictment of previous U.S. trade bargaining. There was a "raw atmosphere of confrontation between the White House and Congress," exacerbated by the unprecedented scope of President Richard Nixon's impoundment of appropriated funds and by the Watergate scandal. And the means by which the administration papered over internal differences —by asking broad discretionary authority for the president—not only aroused Hill opposition but alarmed others as well. George Ball, former under secretary of state, saw "serious danger in giving the executive the very broad powers that this bill contemplates," fearing it "would make it very difficult for any president to resist the very intense and highly focused pressures that can be generated by special interests."[2]

Yet notwithstanding the much-touted threat of protectionism, the bill emerged from the House Ways and Means Committee in October and from the full House in December at least as liberal, on balance, as it was when it emerged from the White House. One reason was that U.S. international trade statistics, in the interim, took a sharp turn for the better. Another was that the administration's lobbying for the bill was as constructive, coordinated, and effective in 1973 as it had been malcoordinated and ineffective in the 1970 fiasco.

1. See Marilyn Berger, "Nixon Trade Bill: Worst Time to Seek Authority From Hill," *Washington Post*, April 30, 1973.
2. Ibid.

Background

Before the bill was sent to the House, consultation with Congress had been more formal than substantive. Special trade representative William D. Eberle, his deputy, William R. Pearce, and presidential assistant Peter M. Flanigan had briefed several dozen congressmen and senators (particularly ranking members of the Ways and Means and Finance committees) in very general terms. As Robert A. Pastor notes, the purpose was basically to "give them a chance to know what was going on and let them make some comments."[3] No major substantive changes resulted.

Particular effort was devoted to the congressman believed to be the key to enactment of the bill, House Ways and Means Committee chairman Wilbur D. Mills. Flanigan flew to Arkansas in February when Mills was recuperating from a bad back; Harry Lamar, trade specialist on the staff of the Ways and Means Committee, was shown drafts of the pending legislation. So also was an important senior trade consultant to Mills, Anthony Solomon, a former assistant secretary of state for economic affairs. On March 21, Mills made a statement on the House floor designed both to indicate general support for the forthcoming trade initiative and to prod the administration to resolve its remaining differences. Mills endorsed in general terms a number of the bill's anticipated provisions, concluding: "I trust [it] will reflect the need for urgent action to which I am confident the Ways and Means Committee will desire to respond."[4] And on the day the bill was submitted, Mills said, "I'm for it,"[5] though he did not mean to predict any departure from the usual practice of the committee's redrafting such bills itself.

Considerable administration attention was also lavished on organized labor. No one expected labor to support the bill, but there was hope that its opposition might be softened. President Nixon met with the AFL-CIO executive council in Bal Harbour, Florida, on February 19, presenting what George Meany cautiously labeled "a very practical approach

3. "Legislative-Executive Relations and U.S. Foreign Trade Policy: The Case of the Trade Act of 1974," paper prepared for the 1976 annual meeting of the American Political Science Association, pp. 14–15.

4. Congressional Record, March 21, 1973, pp. 8886–88.

5. Washington Post, April 30, 1973.

to the trade question." According to Meany, "he wants to negotiate with these countries with authority from Congress to apply differ-ent methods of negotiation—to block them off if they are blocking us off. . . . From the point of view of a trade unionist, who likes to go to the bargaining table with your options open and with authority to give and take, I think that the idea itself is attractive."[6] Treasury Secretary George P. Shultz also cultivated Meany, playing golf with him at Bal Harbour and keeping him briefed on the bill's contents.

On April 10, the administration proposed other bills along with the Trade Reform Act, in an effort to influence labor's trade stance. One bill liberalized pension benefits, another called on states to raise un-employment compensation. In addition, the president's trade message to Congress included proposals to tighten the laws governing taxes paid by multinational corporations on foreign earned income.[7]

Despite this broad effort, the package was spurned by labor. Meany found the tax, pension, and unemployment compensation proposals wanting, and declared that the trade bill "would open the door to further deterioration of America's position in the world economy and to the further export of American jobs."[8] He reiterated his support for the Burke-Hartke bill.

In the hearings on May 17, I. W. Abel formally stated labor's position: "The AFL-CIO doesn't believe we are being alarmist—or protectionist —when we say: The Congress must move quickly and decisively to slow the massive flood of imports into the U.S. market which are sweep-ing away jobs and industries in wholesale lots."[9] But labor's opposition in the end was not to prove very effective. And the administration benefited from three other factors: the improved economic climate, a shift of leadership within the Ways and Means Committee, and a strong, effective lobbying effort led by Pearce.

In April, the U.S. trade deficit for 1973 was already $800 million for

6. Philip Shabecoff, *New York Times*, February 20, 1973; Charles Culhane, "Trade Report: Labor Shifts Tactics on Administration Bill, Seeks Concessions on Imports, Multinationals," *National Journal*, July 28, 1973, p. 1091.

7. Culhane, "Trade Report: Labor Shifts Tactics," p. 1093.

8. Ibid., pp. 1091, 1094.

9. *Trade Reform*, Hearings before the House Committee on Ways and Means, 93 Cong. 1 sess. (Government Printing Office, 1973), pt. 4, pp. 1209–10. Some unions took more moderate positions. See testimony of Communication Workers of America and United Auto Workers, ibid., pt. 7, pp. 2013–15 and pt. 3, pp. 849–914.

the first quarter, and a repeat of 1972 seemed likely.[10] But the exchange rate adjustments in 1971–73 had improved U.S. competitiveness about 25 percent on a trade-weighted basis, and during the hearings of May and June and the formal drafting (markup) sessions from then through October, the trade balance took a sharp turn for the better. The surplus of $873 million in September was the largest for a single month since March 1965, and it wiped out the $720 million deficit incurred in the previous eight months.[11] Along with a drop in unemployment from 5 percent to 4.5 percent (lowest in several years), these improving statistics weakened labor's argument that the rising tide of imports was taking jobs away from U.S. workers.[12] It allowed the administration to argue that monetary adjustment was resolving the trade balance problem, limiting congressional efforts to seek one-sided foreign concessions.

Over the same period, new congressional developments rendered the Ways and Means Committee particularly responsive to administration leadership. The first was the absence of Mills during most of the markup period. He was hospitalized after the second week and "did not return to Washington until early November, a full month after the Committee reported the bill to the House."[13] His absence was particularly significant because committee members had come to depend heavily on Mills's political leadership and substantive expertise. His departure left responsibility to acting chairman Al Ullman, an able, conscientious nine-term veteran who, like most other committee members, knew relatively little about the details of trade law and practice. Ullman had a difficult task—he needed to lead the committee but, with the time of Mills's return uncertain, he could only gradually establish the authority to do so.

Secondly, a House effort to reform the committee system put pressure on the Ways and Means Committee to demonstrate it could act constructively and effectively on trade. A select committee, headed by Richard Bolling, saw the Ways and Means Committee as a principal target. (Eventually, citing the committee's slowness in moving on key issues, the Bolling committee recommended stripping it of much of its

10. Richard S. Frank, "Trade Report: Administration's Reform Bill Threatened by Dispute over Relations with Russia," *National Journal,* November 24, 1973, p. 1742.

11. *Economist,* November 3, 1973, p. 38.

12. Frank, "Trade Report: Administration's Reform Bill Threatened," p. 1742.

13. Ibid.

jurisdiction—moving trade, for example, to the International Relations Committee. This proposal was never implemented.)

If the committee was to meet these challenges, it needed more expertise than its members and their one-man professional trade staff could muster; hence it was particularly dependent upon executive branch resources. Its decision to continue its past practice of holding closed markup sessions, despite new House reform rules encouraging the opposite, strengthened the potential influence of administration spokesmen, since they were, by tradition, allowed to participate in such sessions.

The improved economic climate and the weakened position of Ways and Means gave the administration an opportunity, which it exploited with an effectiveness it had seldom shown on legislative matters. Central to this accomplishment, by all accounts, was the role played by Pearce. A year earlier, he had been denied chairmanship of the drafting committee. But there was, he later reported, "little competition for the job of representing the Administration" once the bill went to the Hill, partly because it apparently seemed a thankless task.[14]

In policy convictions, Pearce and STR were clearly at the free-trade end of the administration spectrum. But he nonetheless had good relations with Flanigan and Hinton of CIEP, attending Flanigan's staff meetings regularly and moving at Flanigan's behest into an Executive Office Building suite while the bill was before the House. Pearce also had Shultz's confidence, and he soon gained the confidence of the Ways and Means Committee as well. As another key trade official put it, "When Bill took over responsibility, conflict seemed to die down." Moreover, he achieved this even though Flanigan was seeking to have STR formally incorporated under CIEP (President Nixon notified Congress in April that he would take this action once CIEP's statutory life was extended). This struggle, ultimately resolved when the administration (with Shultz as arbiter) backed down before congressional pressure, consumed considerable staff time in that spring and summer, with Eberle, Pearce, and Harald B. Malmgren of STR joining in the fight.[15]

14. William R. Pearce, "Outline for Remarks by William R. Pearce before the Committee on Foreign Relations," December 11, 1974, p. 9.

15. When Nixon first endorsed, in 1970, the proposal of his Advisory Council on Executive Organization to establish CIEP, it was part of a broader proposal to incorporate STR in a White House office of foreign economic policy, but this larger step was not taken when CIEP was created in 1971. However, the Williams commission had "assumed" that the special trade representative would "operate under

The Ways and Means Committee Markup

The Ways and Means Committee concluded hearings on the trade bill on Friday, June 15; the next Monday it moved immediately into its deliberations on the bill's substance. The committee and the administration representatives agreed to limit executive branch attendance at markup sessions to ten officials, only two of whom would be allowed to speak. The ten varied according to subject matter, but the two active participants were generally Pearce and STR general counsel John H. Jackson, a trade law expert on leave from the University of Michigan. And the two decided they would play distinct roles, with Pearce acting as administration advocate and Jackson serving as analyst and expert. In these roles they thus supplemented, and sometimes supplanted, the support role played by the committee's staff.

During the nearly four-month markup period, they spent day after day with the committee, producing paper after paper, analyzing issues, and arraying alternatives. And Pearce repeated, time after time, his major themes—that the way to improve the trade *balance* was through exchange rate adjustment, as the latest monthly data illustrated; and that to maintain a good, liberal bill it was necessary that no industry

---

the direction of" CIEP (*Williams Commission Report*, p. 285; see chapter 1, note 11, for full reference), and Nixon was interested in consolidating them within the Executive Office of the President. Moreover, the STR was in fact working under the general direction of CIEP in 1972 and early 1973, and CIEP in turn had emphasized trade much more than other foreign economic issues.

Arguments against the merger, however, were strong. STR was an operating, line unit, placed anomalously in EOP because there was no acceptable neutral home in a cabinet department. CIEP was a staff unit and was to coordinate but not itself conduct operations. Moreover, whereas STR was seen on Capitol Hill as a professional, relatively objective office responsible to the Congress as well as the president, Flanigan's previous service as a senior political assistant to the president meant that CIEP was viewed as political, unaccountable to the Congress, and likely to act as "fixer," juggling interests for political ends.

STR fought the merger; Pearce, for example, made it clear he would resign if it were implemented. Called to testify on the merger to the Senate Foreign Relations Committee, he presented a decidedly cool Eberle statement giving a rationale for the merger; when Chairman William Fulbright asked for "your own view," Pearce responded that "as a representative of the administration" he supported the merger decision made. *International Economic Policy Act Amendments*, Hearings before the Senate Committee on Foreign Relations, 93 Cong. 1 sess. (GPO, 1973), pp. 26–28. Ultimately, the House Ways and Means Committee helped resolve the matter by adding to the trade bill a provision establishing STR as a separate statutory office.

be granted statutory favors and that all have access to relief through equitable procedures. The committee, as always, rewrote the bill the administration submitted; but what resulted served the administration's purposes almost equally well.[16]

Negotiating Authority

TARIFFS. The committee (as widely expected) rejected the request for unlimited authority almost from the outset, and the administration offered its fallback proposal, patterned after the 1962 act: the president would be allowed to eliminate tariffs of 5 percent and under, cut other rates by 50 percent, and cut without limit the duties on products for which OECD countries account for 80 percent or more of world exports. Textile and chemical industry representatives opposed the OECD exemption, since it would permit tariff eliminations on their products, and the committee responded sympathetically. Pearce and committee member Phil M. Landrum, a textile industry advocate, worked out a compromise: the president was authorized to eliminate tariffs of 5 percent and under, reduce by up to 60 percent the tariffs on items with present duties of 5 percent to 25 percent, and reduce by 75 percent the tariffs on items with duties greater than 25 percent (but to a level of no less than 10 percent).[17]

The committee report explained that the modifications were necessary "to ensure that the authority will not be exercised to the detriment of domestic interests."[18] Pearce said of the compromise, "It is workable, and it's probably all the authority we can use in this negotiation."[19]

The administration request for unlimited authority to raise tariffs met with a similar response, and a similar modification was worked out along the lines of the fallback proposal. The president could increase duties as high as 50 percent above the 1934 level or 20 percent above the level of 1973. The committee report recorded the understanding that this authority "would not be used to raise tariffs across the board."[20]

NONTARIFF BARRIERS. In the crucial area of nontariff barriers, the president was given the "mandate to negotiate" and also the requested

16. The following summary draws particularly on *Trade Reform Act of 1973*, H. Rept. 93-571, 93 Cong. 1 sess. (GPO, 1973); Frank, "Administration's Reform Bill Threatened," pp. 1741–52; and Pastor, "Legislative-Executive Relations."

17. Frank, "Trade Report: Administration's Reform Bill Threatened," p. 1743.

18. *Trade Reform Act of 1973*, H. Rept. 93-571, p. 20.

19. Frank, "Trade Report: Administration's Reform Bill Threatened," p. 1743.

20. Ibid.; *Trade Reform Act of 1973*, H. Rept. 93-571, p. 20.

authority to implement nontariff barrier (NTB) agreements not vetoed by one house of Congress within ninety days. Advance consultation was required, however, and the advance authority to eliminate American selling price (ASP) and other NTBs related to customs procedures was not adopted. Instead, they were made subject to the congressional veto procedure. Winning the committee's approval of the procedure at all was a considerable achievement; staff aide Lamar believed it could be unconstitutional. The committee did, however, respond to industry concerns by tightening a generalized provision regarding consultation with affected parties. On both tariffs and NTBs, it required the president to "seek information and advice from representative elements of the private sector" on U.S. negotiating objectives and bargaining positions.

SECTORS. The administration was less successful on an issue pressed by Congressman Joseph E. Karth—negotiation by sectors. Representatives from the electrical manufacturing industry, the electronics industry, the chemical industry, and others asked that concessions made in one industry group or sector be balanced by gains in that same sector rather than in another. One of their fears was that industrial concessions might be made to win major breakthroughs in agriculture. Spokesmen for agricultural export interests, by contrast, felt that they had more to gain if negotiations were not conducted by separate sectors. And the administration argued against such a requirement since it would clearly limit both the scope for bargaining and the potential overall gains.

Nevertheless, the committee responded to industry pleas and adopted the Karth amendment, which provided that NTB trade agreements "shall be negotiated, to the extent feasible, on the basis of each product sector of manufacturing and on the basis of the agricultural sector." The phrase "to the extent feasible" was Pearce's effort to maintain administrative flexibility. He felt the committee had in fact recognized the limits of a sectoral approach, and that the committee report would reflect this, thereby limiting the requirement's significance. But instead the report, drafted by Lamar, actually reinforced the Karth amendment.[21]

Finally, the committee—responding directly to the CIEP merger proposal—added a provision to title 1 of the bill giving statutory existence to the *office* of the special trade representative. (The 1962 act had created only the *position.*) The committee's report stressed that "a strong and independent office, headed by a government official reporting directly to the President and responsible to the Congress, is the

21. *Trade Reform Act of 1973*, H. Rept. 93-571, p. 22.

best means of assuring that in trade policy matters the United States is speaking with one strong voice on behalf of the executive branch and that positions taken accurately reflect the intent of the Congress."[22]

Relief from Import Competition

IMPORT RELIEF. The administration proposed to make escape clause relief easier to obtain by requiring imports to be only the "primary" (greatest single) cause of serious injury and to make relief available from all imports, not just those resulting from U.S. tariff concessions. The committee agreed to the latter and further liberalized the former, substituting "substantial" (important and not less than any other) for "primary." On the other hand, the committee dropped the proposed "market disruption" test after testimony from business groups that the clause made relief too easy to obtain. As Daniel L. Goldy of the U.S. Chamber of Commerce said, "After too long a period of tilting the scales against providing relief, we must now be very careful that we do not go too far in tilting them the other way."[23] Donald M. Kendall of the antiquota Emergency Committee on American Trade (ECAT) agreed: "It is highly likely that there will be a multitude of instances when domestic producers are in bad economic straits and market disruption under this formulation would be found to exist but when, in fact, there is no relationship whatsoever between the two. Were import restrictions provided in these instances, it would be the absolutely wrong cure."[24]

At the behest of Congressman Sam M. Gibbons, the committee incorporated into the bill a list of remedies for injury, giving priority to the least trade-restrictive. The president would first evaluate whether adjustment assistance had been or could be made available. If he found import relief necessary, the order of preference was (1) tariff increases by up to 50 percent; (2) tariff-rate quotas; (3) quantitative restrictions; and (4) orderly marketing agreements. The committee accepted the administration's five-year time limit (with two-year extensions) on import relief actions. But it provided for a ninety-day, one-house veto procedure by which either the House or the Senate could disallow the most restrictive of these remedies (3 and 4 above).

ADJUSTMENT ASSISTANCE. The committee emphasized adjustment assistance as much as the administration had neglected it, despite the AFL-

22. Ibid., p. 40.
23. *Trade Reform*, Hearings, pt. 5, p. 1381.
24. Ibid., pt. 3, p. 661.

CIO's unconcern over this issue. It rejected Shultz's proposal to phase out adjustment assistance as a separate relief program for trade-displaced workers and firms (a proposal that proved impractical when state unemployment insurance commissioners blocked Shultz's plan to strengthen protection for workers against all unemployment-generating economic changes). Instead the committee strengthened the trade-related program. "It was the overwhelming sentiment of the Committee," said Ullman, "not knowing exactly where we were going to wind up but knowing that we had to produce something good."[25] Pearce, who had lost to Shultz on this issue in the drafting process, was therefore asked by the committee to help develop a much-expanded program. After Ullman (at Pearce's behest) spoke directly with Shultz, the treasury secretary yielded: he agreed reluctantly to an expanded adjustment assistance program if the cost were held below $500 million. (The plan worked out by Pearce, other administration officials, and the committee involved an estimated $350 million.)

Furthermore, whereas the administration proposed relaxing eligibility criteria and *reducing* benefits, the committee relaxed the eligibility criteria further and *increased* benefits. The committee also added adjustment assistance to firms harmed by import competition.

"UNFAIR" TRADE PRACTICES. The committee welcomed and reinforced the administration emphasis on combating "unfair" trade practices. It granted the president's request for authority to impose tariffs or quotas on the products of any country enforcing unjustified or unreasonable restrictions against U.S. goods. It also granted the requested authority to retaliate when foreign export subsidies created discrimination against U.S. goods in third-country markets but added a power that the administration opposed—the authority (beyond that in the countervailing duty law) to retaliate against countries that subsidize goods shipped to the U.S. market. Congressman Joe D. Waggonner, Jr., introduced this amendment with the strong support of the steel industry, which was concerned with the implicit subsidies involved in exports by nationalized steel industries. Unlike the countervailing duty law, Waggonner's amendment authorized higher tariffs or quotas on the products of the subsidizing nation than required to offset the subsidy. The amendment's fate was not settled until October 3, 1973, when the committee met to vote on the final version of the bill. But opponents of the provision suc-

---

25. Frank, "Trade Report: Administration's Reform Bill Threatened," p. 1728. See also Pastor, "Legislative-Executive Relations," p. 16.

ceeded in rendering it, as Richard S. Frank put it, "so fenced in by restrictions that it is likely to prove meaningless."[26]

COUNTERVAILING DUTIES. The administration goal had been to tighten up the existing laws in this area but leave considerable discretion in implementation—allowing the secretary of the treasury to waive imposition of countervailing duties (imposed to offset foreign government export subsidies) if he determined they would cause "significant detriment" to overall U.S. economic interests. In particular, the administration wanted to be able to waive countervailing duties throughout the Multilateral Trade Negotiations (MTN), or for up to five years, to facilitate negotiations limiting export subsidies.

However, the administration made a tactical error early in the committee's deliberations: a Treasury official put forward the view that his department had not been enforcing the existing law, which naturally inclined the committee toward removing the secretary's discretion. Administration officials then sought to get the committee to define "bounty or grant" in a way which would at least update the ancient statute and permit to other countries practices that were now used by the United States, such as government export credits. But the committee preferred to leave such issues to the MTN. Instead it granted the secretary discretionary authority not to impose duties for four years (one year in cases in which the subsidized products are produced by government-owned or controlled factories in developed countries) in cases where he determined that their imposition would "seriously jeopardize" completion of the MTN. The committee also allowed U.S. producers of competing products judicial appeal of negative determinations on their countervailing duty petitions.[27]

ANTIDUMPING. The committee added a provision on antidumping procedures little noticed at the time but destined to generate major controversy four years later. Under the rules of the General Agreement on Tariffs and Trade (GATT)—and in customary practice—dumping was defined as selling goods in export markets at prices below those charged at home. But the new provision required that if some or all of an indus-

26. Frank, "Trade Report: Administration's Reform Bill Threatened," pp. 1747–48; *Trade Reform Act of 1973*, H. Rept. 93-571, pp. 64–67. The president would be allowed to retaliate against subsidized sales in the U.S. market, but only if the Tariff Commission found that such sales were reducing the sales of U.S. products in the domestic market and if the president found that neither countervailing duties nor antidumping duties provided relief.

27. *Trade Reform Act of 1973*, H. Rept. 93-571, pp. 73–77.

try's home market sales were, for an extended period, at below the full cost of producing the article, the Treasury Department had to disregard these sales in assessing whether the industry was dumping. It would rely instead on "constructed value," a procedure (already in the law) for estimating the full cost of producing an article, including an 8 percent profit. This new procedure made it easier for U.S. firms to prove dumping, and in some circumstances it could lead to such a finding even when home market and export prices were the same![28]

Generalized System of Preferences

Rather surprisingly, the committee adopted title 5, preferences for developing countries, with no important substantive changes. This occurred despite the very limited involvement of senior State Department officials. Preferences did have significant congressional support. Dante B. Fascell's Subcommittee on Inter-American Affairs of the House Foreign Affairs Committee had held hearings on trade preferences for Latin America and the Caribbean, and Fascell testified in favor before the Ways and Means Committee.[29]

Most-Favored-Nation Status

The committee adopted the administration's proposal for discretionary authority to grant most-favored-nation (MFN) status to communist countries, with one crucial qualification: it adopted the Jackson-Vanik proposal that MFN status be conditioned on a presidential determination that the country did not deny its citizens freedom to emigrate.[30] Congress could veto this determination within ninety days. The target was restrictions imposed by the Soviet Union on emigration of Jews (mainly to Israel).

The politics of this issue were particularly hot.[31] And its handling by the administration was particularly maladroit. Pearce, who was close to the scene, had no mandate to bargain on MFN. The administration position was controlled by Kissinger and (to a lesser degree) Flanigan,

28. For a retrospective critique, see Robert J. Samuelson, "The Anti-Dumping Laws—Rx for the Steel Industry?," *National Journal*, November 22, 1977, pp. 1636–40.

29. *Trade Reform*, Hearings, pt. 14, pp. 4911–28. Fascell was to introduce and explain this title on the House floor.

30. The proposal was sponsored by Senator Henry Jackson and Congressman Charles A. Vanik. See chapter 9.

31. For a full account, see Paula Stern, *Water's Edge: Domestic Politics and the Making of American Foreign Policy* (Greenwood Press, 1979).

who grossly underestimated the force of the Jackson-Vanik coalition. As Congressman Barber Conable put it, "The President and Mr. Kissinger have not kept track of what was going on here. They did not realize that MFN was being opposed not just by the American Jewish community, but by a very impressive coalition."[32] This coalition included the AFL-CIO, which saw the amendment as a means of rendering the trade bill unacceptable to the administration, and antidétente and human rights forces generally.

The Ways and Means Committee delayed final consideration of the MFN title in hopes of having Kissinger (now in the process of becoming secretary of state) testify. Pearce won his reluctant assent at a meeting with the president, but this agreement was never consummated. Nor could Pearce get the administration to back a compromise. So he was forced to defend a position that had become politically irrelevant: for granting MFN and against the Jackson-Vanik proposal.

Congressmen James C. Corman and Jerry L. Pettis proposed to grant MFN status with an annual congressional opportunity to cancel if the Soviets were not easing emigration restrictions. The administration left this opportunity unexploited. But Henry Jackson, as Corman described it later, "took the Senate floor and called it a sellout, and the Jewish community got terribly upset." Ways and Means was "inundated with phone calls and telegrams," and the proposal was dropped.[33] A subsequent loss-cutting initiative by Conable suffered a similar fate. The only administration victory on MFN was the defeat (by 12–12) of Vanik's proposal to also deny credits to countries restricting emigration. Opponents argued that the issue was under the jurisdiction of the House Banking and Currency Committee. The proposal was a special threat to U.S.-Soviet trade, since credits were economically far more important to the Russians than the largely symbolic matter (for a state-trading nation) of most-favored-nation status. But Vanik vowed to seek a rule allowing him to offer this amendment again on the floor.

The Bill as a Whole

On October 3, the committee completed action on the bill and voted, 20–5, to report it. On balance, the product was impressive. The proposed

32. Frank, "Trade Report: Administration's Reform Bill Threatened," p. 1750.
33. Ibid.

Trade Act of 1973 granted the president the general authority he requested on most issues, though with restraints, guidelines, and in some instances, congressional veto procedures.

Reasonable limits were placed on reductions (and increases) in tariffs, although potentially troublesome language on conducting negotiations by product sectors was included. The president was granted authority to implement nontariff-barrier agreements subject only to congressional veto, albeit with stricter procedural requirements for keeping Congress informed. The escape clause standard for import relief was further relaxed, from primary to substantial cause, but the market disruption test was deleted and priority was given to the least restrictive forms of relief. Adjustment assistance was maintained and strengthened. Authority to retaliate against foreign trade restrictions was granted but subjected to guidelines and congressional veto; antidumping and countervailing duty laws were tightened, but some discretion was retained. Preferences survived substantively intact; authority to adjust trade barriers to meet balance-of-payments or inflation problems also was granted, again with limits and guidelines. Only on Soviet MFN status did the bill veer sharply from administration wishes.

Ullman summarized the committee's approach: "To withhold the needed Presidential authorities would weaken the capacity of the United States to defend its economic interest in trade negotiations; to grant such authorities without developing effective Congressional controls over their use would be irresponsible. The Committee has attempted to respond to both challenges."[34] Herman T. Schneebeli, the committee's ranking Republican, said the bill "is a little unusual because it probably gives the White House more authority than it ever had before and at the same time it gives the Congress more oversight and more veto power than it ever had before. It says, 'you go out and negotiate, but if we think you haven't made a good deal, we want the power to veto.' So we've given them latitude to negotiate, but with a proper leash."[35] As the committee report put it, the new authorities "envisage a degree of consultations and oversight activity not previously considered under past extension of trade agreements authority."[36] One of these provisions called for the appointment of accredited congressional advisers to the Multilateral Trade Negotiations.

34. Ibid., p. 1741.
35. Ibid.
36. *Trade Reform Act of 1973*, H. Rept. 93-571, p. 42.

The bill was an impressive achievement in executive–congressional relations. Acting chairman Ullman had responded to the challenge of Mills's disablement by engaging the broad, constructive participation of his committee colleagues in the drafting, and by working closely with the executive branch. On the executive side, Pearce and his colleagues were at once persistent in their substantive goals, responsive to the committee's concerns, competent, politically sensitive, and personally congenial. In a tribute to their efforts, the committee rose and gave them a standing ovation at the close of the final markup session.

And the protectionist challenge to the bill had proved far weaker than anticipated. The AFL-CIO had made only one concrete effort to change the bill: on July 16, James A. Burke, third-ranking democrat on the committee and cosponsor of the Burke-Hartke bill, offered two quota provisions based on that bill. One would have triggered quotas when imports exceeded current levels; the other would have related quotas to the foreign-owned share of the U.S. market for each product. Each was rejected by a 7–17 vote.[37]

After this failure, labor apparently decided that its only strategy was to kill the bill altogether. The AFL-CIO convention in August adopted a resolution calling the committee bill "worse than no bill at all."[38] Labor may thus have lost a chance to influence its contents, at least marginally. When Karth and several other labor-oriented members of the committee met with AFL-CIO legislative director Andrew J. Biemiller on June 12, they offered to consider any amendments to improve the bill from labor's point of view. And Karth voted for Burke's amendment the next month. But they heard nothing further until the day the bill was voted out of the committee, when Biemiller asked them to vote against the entire bill.[39] Karth, for one, did not.

Pearce had achieved what he had by remaining within the international trade policy framework: resolving as many issues as possible at his level, consulting with Shultz and Flanigan, but retaining day-to-day operational control of the lobbying effort. But staying within this framework had its costs, for the issue that continued to disrupt the progress of the bill was outside the trade policy mainstream: the proposed linkage of MFN status and trade credits to Soviet emigration policies. In

37. Frank, "Trade Report: Administration's Reform Bill Threatened," p. 1752; *Congressional Quarterly Almanac*, vol. 29 (1973), p. 841.
38. Frank, "Trade Report: Administration's Reform Bill Threatened," p. 1752.
39. Ibid.

foreign policy terms, the broad questions were how much U.S. leverage should be directed to changing Soviet emigration practices and whether a visible, statutory linking of U.S. trade concessions to sensitive Soviet domestic practices would be productive or counterproductive. Once some form of linkage was apparently inescapable, the problem was to choose among foreign policy priorities. Should the administration risk the demise of the trade bill, and thus a major setback in relations with Europe and Japan, to avoid a dramatic public rebuff to the Soviet Union? Or should it move ahead on the trade bill, while seeking the least damaging resolution possible on the Soviet question? Within the administration, Kissinger and Flanigan gave priority to détente; STR, Commerce, USDA, Labor, and Treasury wanted above all to move the trade bill forward.

To the House Floor

The House Rules Committee quickly cleared the bill for floor consideration, under a modified closed rule, which would permit votes on three amendments: Vanik's Soviet credit restriction, a Conable proposal to delete the most-favored-nation title entirely, and an amendment deleting preferences for developing countries. Floor action was scheduled for October 17 or 18.

But on October 6, the Yom Kippur War broke out, and Kissinger immediately engaged in an intensive, personal Middle East mediation effort. Arguing that the Vanik amendment would undercut his efforts to work with Moscow for a cease-fire, he engineered the first of several delays. Flanigan also supported delay, partly as a matter of legislative strategy, for the Senate was certain to pass the Jackson amendment, and House enactment would thus weaken possibilities for compromise. Through the end of November, House floor action was repeatedly postponed at presidential request, to the immense frustration of Ullman and Pearce. Ullman saw the coalition supporting the bill as fragile and vulnerable to assault, particularly from organized labor. "We have the votes now, and the longer we delay, the more difficult our problem becomes," he said.[40] Pearce agreed, and feared that further delay "would push final [Senate and conference] consideration of the bill into the preelection period. . . . not a good climate for legislation of this kind."[41]

40. Ibid.
41. *Congressional Quarterly Almanac*, vol. 29 (1973), p. 844.

By now Kissinger and Flanigan took the position that the entire title on trade with the Soviet Union should be dropped, as Conable had proposed. But the prospect of achieving this was now very slim, as was that of defeating Vanik's proposal to add restrictions on Soviet credits. So at Kissinger's behest, the president warned he might veto the bill if the Jackson-Vanik amendment was included. For Pearce, this threat was a "disaster," since it joined the coalition of Jewish groups and anti-détente forces to labor, which saw Jackson-Vanik as a means of sinking the trade bill as a whole.[42]

Thus on Saturday, December 1, Pearce went to Shultz to persuade him to go to the president. The STR official stressed the dangers of losing "a major tool for rapprochement with Western Europe on economic issues," and for no gain, since the Jackson-Vanik amendment was bound to be attached to the Export-Import Bank legislation coming up shortly. Shultz at first resisted, then agreed to try. On that same day, Ullman was at the White House for a dinner and made a strong argument to Nixon that political support for the bill would erode unless it was passed by Christmas. Responding to these arguments, Nixon reversed himself and agreed to support a House vote.

But, though Ullman and Pearce won this round, Kissinger won the next. The Nixon letter of December 3 to Speaker of the House Carl Albert, asking him to move on the bill, was drafted initially by Pearce. But Kissinger rewrote it, deleting the strong support for the core of the bill and emphasizing the president's opposition to the Vanik amendment. This the letter called "unacceptable," thus threatening a veto if it were included.[43] To Ullman, the letter was a monstrosity, and he interpreted it as Kissinger's effort to kill the bill. And it alienated the Democratic leadership in the House, which began to doubt whether they had the votes to pass the bill. Concern was also expressed by lobbying groups like the Emergency Committee for American Trade, which proponents were counting on to mobilize support of the legislation. But Ullman and Pearce were convinced the votes were there, and were able to persuade the leadership—and ECAT—to push it forward.

The bill came to the House floor on December 10, 1973. The first vote was on the modified closed rule limiting amendments. Labor lobbied against the rule, and its defeat would likely have caused the Ways and

42. Pearce, "Outline for Remarks," p. 12.
43. *Congressional Quarterly Almanac,* vol. 29 (1973), p. 844; Edwin L. Dale, Jr., *New York Times,* December 4 and December 15, 1973.

Means Committee to withdraw the bill. And although the vote to sustain the rule was not close, 230–147, it is notable that the northern Democrats, closely attuned to labor, voted 39–103 against.[44] The remaining votes went as generally expected. On December 11, after seven hours of debate, the House adopted the Vanik amendment by a margin of 319–80 and rejected the administration-backed Conable amendment to delete the MFN title by 106–298.[45] Then it passed the entire bill by a 272–140 vote. Northern Democrats—strong supporters of free trade in the sixties —voted for Vanik's amendment, 130–16, and against the entire bill, 52–101, but, ironically, the Vanik amendment apparently prevented even more liberals from defecting.[46] In committee drafting sessions, members who voted for provisions opposed by labor were able to point to their strong support of the MFN amendment, which was championed by Meany. And on final passage, an STR official estimated that the bill "picked up 50 to 60 extra votes because the Vanik amendment was in it."[47]

The bill was coherent and liberal—a tribute to effective administration lobbying and to Ullman's playing a difficult role well. The next step, however, was the Senate, traditionally more responsive to special interests on trade matters. Moreover, the international economic environment was undergoing profound change. As a Senate staff analysis of the trade bill would state, less than two months after the House voted, "It's a totally new ball game, which was not envisaged in the planning and conception of the Trade Reform Act."[48]

44. *Congressional Quarterly Almanac*, vol. 29 (1973), p. 148-H.
45. *Congressional Record* (December 11, 1973), pp. 40769–813.
46. *Congressional Quarterly Almanac*, vol. 29 (1973), p. 148-H.
47. Ibid., p. 844.
48. *Summary and Analysis of H.R. 10710—The Trade Reform Act of 1973*, prepared for the Senate Committee on Finance, 93 Cong. 2 sess. (GPO, 1974), p. 2.

CHAPTER ELEVEN

The Trade Bill in the Senate, 1974

THE SENATE PREPARED to consider the trade bill in early 1974, a particularly difficult period for the world economy. The oil embargo triggered by the Yom Kippur War was followed by a fourfold increase in oil prices; higher prices for energy and other commodities were contributing to double-digit inflation and threatening recession and unemployment in all major industrial countries. A Senate Finance Committee staff report captured the prevailing mood:

In the two or more years that have transpired since the Trade Reform Act was conceived by the Executive and considered, amended, and passed by the House of Representatives, the world economy had suffered severe shocks.

Traditional trade problems have usually been associated with rising imports and their effect on industries, firms and jobs. . . . Current trade problems are more typically due to shortages—food and fiber, energy, metals and many others. We have moved into an era of resource scarcity and accelerated inflation—an era in which producing countries are increasingly tempted to withhold supplies for economic or political reasons. It's a totally new ball game, which was not envisaged in the planning and conception of the Trade Reform Act."[1]

When this committee began hearings on March 4, 1974, the embargo was still in effect. Committee members Abraham Ribicoff and Walter F. Mondale had prepared amendments to authorize U.S. export embargoes and quotas, and to "retaliate against countries which wage economic warfare against us."[2] Special trade representative William D. Eberle

1. *Summary and Analysis of H.R. 10710—The Trade Reform Act of 1973*, prepared for the Senate Committee on Finance, 93 Cong. 2 sess. (Government Printing Office, 1974), p. 2.

2. Ribicoff, *Trade Reform Act of 1973*, Hearings before the Senate Committee on Finance, 93 Cong. 2 sess. (GPO, 1974), p. 3; see also p. 179; *National Journal*, March 9, 1974, p. 371.

was sympathetic, though claiming that the retaliation provision in the House bill "clearly provides sufficiently broad authority . . . against unfair foreign export controls on essential raw materials."[3] But the "new ball game" placed him and the administration under pressure to establish the relevance of legislation that was prepared to deal with older problems.

As things turned out, the effect of the "era of resource scarcity and accelerated inflation" on the trade bill proved modest—mainly changes in nuances, relating trade authorities more explicitly to export controls and other scarcity-induced actions by national governments. More important was the new institutional environment the administration faced as the bill moved to the north side of Capitol Hill.

Background

Al Ullman was an acting chairman with limited trade background and flexible views. Russell Long, by contrast, had chaired the Finance Committee since 1966 and was regarded as one of the Senate's most astute and powerful members. He also had some strong ideas he did not hesitate to express.

In opening the hearings, Long declared himself "tired of the United States being the 'least favored nation' in a world which is full of discrimination. We can no longer expose our markets, while the rest of the world hides behind variable levies, export subsidies, import equalization fees, border taxes, cartels, government procurement practices, dumping, import quotas, and a host of other practices which effectively bar our products."[4] And while deputy special trade representative William R. Pearce had argued persuasively before the House committee that the trade balance should not be considered a function of trade negotiations or trade policy, in senators' minds the two were linked from start to finish. Long tied the U.S. position of least-favored-nation to the decline in the trade balance and insisted, "it must be demonstrated that the next decade of our trading relations will be different from the last."[5] His committee report argued, moreover, that the United States consistently inflated its trade accounts by including aid-financed exports and measur-

3. Quoted in *National Journal*, March 9, 1974, p. 371.
4. *Trade Reform Act of 1973*, Hearings, p. 2.
5. Ibid.

ing imports free-on-board (FOB) rather than by cost, insurance, and freight (CIF).[6] And even on an FOB basis, U.S. trade statistics in 1974 proved as congenial to the committee's mercantilist view as those of 1973 had to Pearce's view. In fact, mainly because of much higher oil prices, 1974 trade statistics were mirror images of 1973's: surpluses the *first* four months, sharp (and, for August, record) deficits through the summer, ending the year in the red by $3.07 billion overall, then the second largest deficit of the twentieth century.[7]

To Long and the Finance Committee staff, the deficits reflected the fact that "U.S. trade policy has been the orphan of U.S. foreign policy."[8] The executive branch had "granted trade concessions to accomplish political objectives," and its "soft trade policy" had "actually fostered the proliferation of barriers to international commerce." There was considerable sympathy for this view among Long's colleagues. As Raymond Garcia of the liberal Emergency Committee for American Trade (ECAT) put it, "when you attend the committee hearings, you certainly come away with the impression that the Senators on that committee felt generally that U.S. negotiators have done a fairly poor job in the past in gaining for the United States the benefits of trade negotiations."[9] This was one reason the committee felt that the House had granted the administration too much power. Another was the view, held particularly by Herman Talmadge, second-ranking member of the committee, that the provision granting authority to change nontariff barriers (NTBs) was unconstitutional. In the judgment of the Senate committee, the House bill "represented the largest delegation of trade negotiating authority to the Executive in history"; thus the Finance Committee needed "to establish appropriate and constitutionally sound guidelines and criteria to govern the exercise of the authority."[10]

The reason that the bill took a full year to pass the Senate, however, was neither the change in the international economic environment nor the different institutional one. Rather, it was what had delayed the bill

6. Thus, the committee found that "although the U.S. Government reported to the American people and to the world a healthy balance of trade surplus of $2.6 billion for the period 1966–74, the country in reality experienced a deficit totaling $42.8 billion." *Trade Reform Act of 1974*, S. Rept. 93-1298, 93 Cong. 2 sess. (GPO, 1974), p. 12.

7. Edwin L. Dale, Jr., *New York Times,* January 28, 1975.

8. *Trade Reform Act of 1974*, S. Rept. 93-1298, p. 11.

9. Quoted in Richard S. Frank, "Trade Report: Distrust Leads Congress to Tie Strings to New Authority," *National Journal*, October 5, 1974, p. 1483.

10. *Trade Reform Act of 1974*, S. Rept. 93-1298, p. 14.

for two months in the House—the Jewish emigration issue. Senator Henry Jackson was determined to use the most-favored-nation (MFN) issue as a lever to change Soviet emigration policy; Secretary of State Henry Kissinger was equally determined to avoid damage to détente. And Long was determined not to be caught, as Ullman had been caught, with *his* bill hostage to an extraneous dispute outside of his control. Thus he carefully linked the committee's work on the bill to progress on negotiations outside his committee aimed at resolving the MFN issue.

After the bill had passed the House, Pearce resigned to return to the Cargill Corporation. His position as deputy special trade representative remained unfilled throughout 1974, and responsibility for lobbying thus rested with Eberle and his other deputy, Harald B Malmgren. When Peter M. Flanigan left the government in June, Eberle also became executive director of the Council on International Economic Policy (CIEP).[11] Thereafter, Malmgren was the only presidential appointee giving full time to STR, and as the year progressed, he increasingly took on a major share of the lobbying responsibility.

One important international effort early in that year was to negotiate concessions from the European Economic Community to compensate for losses to U.S. trade caused by the entry into the EEC of Denmark, Ireland, and the United Kingdom. STR leadership sought to show the Finance Committee that "accomplishment of the impossible was possible through diligence,"[12] that they could be tough and successful bargainers, and the concessions they won did apparently make the committee more receptive to the trade bill. Another important event in trade diplomacy was the trade pledge of June, in which the twenty-four countries of the Organisation for Economic Co-operation and Development (OECD) declared their intention to avoid for one year unilateral measures which would shift the burden of their oil-induced current account deficit to their trading partners.

But Eberle and Malmgren found the Soviet MFN issue largely beyond their influence, just as Pearce had the preceding fall. Kissinger

11. This appointment fueled renewed speculation of an STR/CIEP merger. On August 1, Eberle answered, "Let me be very positive in saying that there is no merger. It just happens that you have one man that is holding two titles. It is my intent to see that the STR remains an independent organization because it does have a rather special function to carry out, quite different from that of CIEP. The people there will remain professional, civil servants."

12. Malmgren's characterization of congressional perceptions in "Sources of Instability in the World Trading System," *Journal of International Affairs*, vol. 30 (Spring/Summer, 1976), p. 14.

took active personal control of the issue; by March, he had begun serious negotiations with Jackson to find a solution. STR fed Kissinger formulas for resolving the issue, but this communication was one way: sometimes there was no response from Kissinger; at other times, particularly when STR explored alternatives with Senators Long or Ribicoff, Kissinger aide Helmut Sonnenfeldt would respond with a "blast" by telephone, demanding that it stay out of the issue. Thus, as winter gave way to spring and spring to summer, frustration at STR grew. Its construction was hostage to an issue beyond its reach, and precious time was being lost. Kissinger was no longer acting, as in 1973, as if he would be just as happy to see the trade bill die. He now saw that the threat to his détente policy was strong and required positive, constructive response on his part. But there was still no reason to believe that enactment of the bill and inauguration of serious multilateral trade negotiations were anywhere near the top of his list of priorities. And Long was playing a very careful game, generating doubts as to whether *he* wanted a trade bill enacted in 1974.

The Finance Committee Markup

The Finance Committee's formal hearings on the bill began March 4 and concluded on April 10. Kissinger had taken care to testify in that forum, in what he characterized, remarkably enough, as "the first public testimony in which I have engaged since I have been Secretary of State."[13] (He had become secretary almost six months before.) He devoted most of his formal statement to "one particularly vexing aspect of our trade strategy: The normalization of commercial relations with the Soviet Union." And he stated that if the bill reached the president's desk in its present form, "today I would be inclined to recommend a veto." But he acted to resolve the most-favored-nation issue almost entirely outside the committee, operating as an intermediary between Jackson and the Soviet government.[14]

In the spring he made only limited progress, and Long bided his time. He scheduled no markup sessions in April and none in May. At President Richard Nixon's request, he finally convened the first formal markup

13. *Trade Reform Act of 1973*, Hearings, pp. 453, 463, 472.
14. For the story of these negotiations, see Paula Stern, *Water's Edge: Domestic Politics and the Making of American Foreign Policy* (Greenwood Press, 1979).

session on June 3,[15] but the second was not held until July 29 (by which time the House Judiciary Committee had overwhelmingly recommended Nixon's impeachment). Long did predict after that meeting that the trade bill would be passed in 1974 unless the Senate was occupied with a long presidential impeachment trial.[16] And the committee met on the bill for five days that week, then "recessed subject to call."[17]

Then at noon on August 9, Nixon's sudden resignation took effect and Gerald R. Ford became president; an isolated and frequently inflexible chief executive was replaced by an accessible politician who could see the need for compromise. President Ford, at Eberle's behest, quickly moved to break the MFN impasse. On August 14, he met for half an hour with Long, who commented after the meeting, "The President is anxious to move along the trade bill. I personally hope that negotiations to reach a compromise on the Jackson amendment will be productive."[18] The next morning Ford had breakfast at the White House with Kissinger, Jackson, Ribicoff, and Senator Jacob Javits, after which the senators praised Ford's initiative and announced that a compromise was near.[19] But Long continued to move cautiously. The committee met just three more times on the bill in August, on the twentieth through the twenty-second, then recessed "to meet again September 5."[20]

Committee markup did resume on September 10, with six other meetings that month.[21] Before September ended, George Meany had denounced the move toward MFN compromise, but Jackson nonetheless persevered. The Russians were getting skittish, but Kissinger also continued his efforts. On October 18, the Kissinger-Jackson compromise was made public: the president could grant MFN status to the Soviet Union for eighteen months if he received Soviet assurances that Soviet practice would lead "substantially" to free emigration. Thereafter, the president could recommend renewal for an additional twelve-month period and could implement this recommendation unless Congress vetoed it. Crucial to winning Jackson's agreement was an exchange of letters with Kissinger in which each set forth his expectations as to the emigration

15. Edwin L. Dale, Jr., *New York Times*, May 24, 1974; *Congressional Record, Daily Digest*, June 3, 1974, p. D378.

16. *New York Times*, July 30, 1974.

17. *Congressional Record, Daily Digest*, August 2, 1974, p. D578.

18. Marjorie L. Hunter, *New York Times*, August 15, 1974.

19. *New York Times*, August 16, 1974.

20. *Congressional Record, Daily Digest*, August 22, 1974, p. D642.

21. *Congressional Record, Daily Digest*, September 1974.

policies Russia would pursue. Presumably reflecting his direct discussions with Soviet leaders, Kissinger conveyed "our assumption" that "the rate of emigration . . . would begin to rise promptly from the 1973 level."[22] Jackson stated—much less conditionally—his understanding that emigration would rise to a "benchmark" level of some "60,000 per annum," a very substantial number whose use Kissinger had acquiesced in without endorsing. Jackson claimed victory (over Russia) at a White House news conference the same day.

By this time, the Finance Committee had nearly completed its markup of the bill, meeting six days of the first ten in October. Long continued to defer final action. One reason was his conviction that the bill could be handled more easily in the postelection congressional session, when senators would not be so vulnerable to particular interests. Another (discussed in greater detail subsequently) was his apparent determination not to publicly expose the committee's final decisions until close to the time the Senate voted. Of continuing importance, however, was the fact that Long and his committee wanted the emigration issue resolved and wanted Henry Kissinger to discuss the resolution formally before them. So when the Finance Committee voted on November 20 to report the bill, it was "with the understanding that the bill will not be taken up on the floor of the Senate until Secretary of State Henry A. Kissinger appears before the Committee to answer questions."[23] Kissinger was scheduled to appear on December 3.

The publicity on the trade bill went to Kissinger, Jackson, and the emigration issue, but the committee had been addressing the details of other trade bill titles since late July—and intensively since the Senate's return from recess in September. It did so far less formally than its House counterpart. Attendance was sparse. Long was usually there but sometimes only one or two others out of seventeen members. Administration lobbyists played a less dominant role, and the committee's trade staff, larger than that of Ways and Means, had somewhat greater impact. And unlike Ullman, Long needed the bill far less than it needed him. He dominated the process and played a close hand. His committee, as noted, was more inclined than Ways and Means to be critical of past U.S. trade negotiating performance. And it was also more oriented

22. *New York Times*, October 19, 1978. For text of letters, see ibid., and *Trade Reform Act of 1974*, S. Rept. 93-1298, pp. 203–05.

23. *Congressional Record, Daily Digest*, November 20, 1974, p. D781.

toward agricultural interests, with nearly half of its members representing farm states.

Nevertheless, Eberle and Malmgren were astute in finding ways to lobby effectively on the Senate side. The seven-month prelude to the markup, frustrating at the time, proved a blessing—they were able to spend enough time informally with Long and other committee members to establish productive working relationships. Long would not be party to a formal arrangement on their role at executive sessions, but he generally invited them, sometimes suggesting they not bring other agency representatives, sometimes leaving this up to them. As Malmgren later noted, STR "made every effort to handle the legislation itself, avoiding the use of Presidential legislative staff, so that the bill was insulated against *tradeoffs* in relation to other Presidential issues"[24]—except of course on Soviet MFN status. But the fact that STR officials usually operated independently of the White House and the secretaries of state and the treasury limited their leverage also; they were dependent on the committee, and above all on Long, to respond constructively to their arguments.

Organized labor again expressed strong general opposition to the bill but made no more effort than in 1973 to change its specifics; to the AFL-CIO's Ray Denison, "That would be like putting ten patches on a rubber raft that has 100 holes."[25] Instead, labor continued to hope that the Jackson amendment would bring either Senate stalemate or a presidential veto. In his testimony, Meany urged the committee "to give the House-passed bill a quick burial, and turn its time and attention to the writing of new trade legislation which will be comprehensive, flexible, and realistic, and which will meet the complex needs demanded by today's world."[26] Leonard Woodcock of the United Auto Workers opposed the bill "because of what we consider willfully inadequate provisions for adjustment."[27] He said the House bill was "somewhat better than that proposed by the Administration but still, in our opinion, extremely inadequate." He also called for temporary quotas on imported automobiles.

But if labor spurned active lobbying on specifics, industrial and agri-

24. Harald B. Malmgren, "The United States," in Wilfrid L. Kohl, ed., *Economic Foreign Policies of Industrial States* (D. C. Heath, 1977), p. 40.
25. Frank, "Trade Report: Distrust Leads Congress to Tie Strings," p. 1484.
26. *Trade Reform Act of 1973*, Hearings, p. 1136.
27. Ibid., pp. 857–59.

cultural interests did not, and their stands and proposals had important impact on the committee's treatment of specific titles.

Negotiating Authority

TARIFFS. Tariff-cutting authority was never a key issue. The committee authorized deeper cuts at the bottom of the tariff scale and lesser reductions at the top than the House bill had. Existing tariffs of 10 percent or less could be eliminated and all others cut by as much as 50 percent. While the administration found this acceptable, it preferred the House version because it would make bargaining at the Multilateral Trade Negotiations in Geneva easier, since U.S. trading partners wanted certain high U.S. tariffs drastically reduced. A comparison of tariff rates by the General Agreement on Tariffs and Trade (GATT) had concluded that while the United States and the European Community had comparable average tariffs of 6 percent to 7 percent, 12 percent of U.S. tariffs were 20 percent or more, compared with only 0.4 percent of EEC tariffs.[28]

NONTARIFF BARRIERS. A much bigger issue was the administration's request for authority to implement NTB agreements involving changes in U.S. law, subject to veto by either house of Congress.

Livestock and dairy interests feared the administration would use its NTB authority to bargain away their protection. Patrick B. Healy, secretary of the National Milk Producers Federation, called it a formula for the "studied destruction of the American dairy industry."[29] He cited the "Flanigan report," actually a study prepared for Flanigan by the Department of Agriculture in 1972, which recommended liberalizing agricultural trade to take advantage of the tremendous U.S. comparative advantage: projected expansion of dairy imports by nearly a billion dollars would be more than offset by a $10 billion export increase, particularly in wheat, feed grains, and soybeans.[30] Administration spokesmen repeatedly insisted that this was only a tentative proposal; however, Secretary of Agriculture Earl L. Butz had said publicly and frequently that the United States intended to put the issue of U.S. import quotas on the bargaining table in Geneva, though always adding that nothing

28. *Summary and Analysis of H.R. 10710*, pp. 68–71.

29. *Trade Reform Act of 1973*, Hearings, p. 965.

30. U.S. Foreign Agricultural Service, *Agricultural Trade and the Proposed Round of Multilateral Trade Negotiations*, Committee Print, Senate Committee on Agriculture and Forestry, 93 Cong. 1 sess. (GPO, 1973), especially pp. 10–28.

would be bargained away without substantial return.[31] Healy urged Congress to "retain the power to determine national policy in areas so important as food production" by requiring all NTB agreements to return to Congress for positive, rather than negative, action. The National Farmers Union, the National Farmers Organization, and the Midcontinent Farmers Association proposed identical changes in a joint memorandum to the committee in August. The American Farm Bureau Federation, however, strongly endorsed the House NTB provisions.[32]

The Finance Committee was responsive to dairy industry pleas. Even more important, it judged the House-passed NTB procedures to be unconstitutional. In the words of second-ranking majority member, Herman Talmadge, this was just "not the way we make laws." He argued that reorganization plans, through which Congress had previously allowed the president to change domestic law subject to congressional veto, were different from NTB agreements, which involve not organizational structure but the substance of policies and programs imbedded in domestic law.

The first STR reaction was dismay, for Eberle and Malmgren felt they could not live with Talmadge's initial alternative—that the president should simply submit NTB agreements to Congress, to be acted upon (or not acted upon) in the traditional manner. For to bargain effectively on NTBs, negotiators needed at minimum the assurance that the agreements they reached would receive expeditious congressional action. However, staff work by committee aides Richard Rivers and Mark Sandstrom led to a suggestion that Congress might handle NTB-implementing legislation "with a discharge procedure to assure timely consideration." STR pressed further: could a floor vote in each house be guaranteed within a limited time, without amendment? The answer was *yes and no*—Congress could not bind itself absolutely, but the law could be written so as to make it very hard for a member to use con-

---

31. On March 6, Butz told the Finance Committee, "I have taken the position that when we go into negotiations here we are prepared to put our section 22 import restrictions on the negotiating table, that we are not going to give them away for free." *Trade Reform Act of 1973*, Hearings, p. 377.

Section 22 of the Agricultural Adjustment Act (7 USC 624) authorizes the president to raise tariffs or impose quotas on agricultural imports if he concludes that they would render ineffective any of the domestic price supports for farm products. The provision has been frequently used, especially for dairy products.

32. *Trade Reform Act of 1973*, Hearings, pp. 966, 1014; *National Journal*, October 5, 1974, p. 1486.

gressional procedures to prevent Congress from acting on NTB-implementing bills *as submitted by the president.*

This solution won general acceptance; the Finance Committee agreed to incorporate in the law procedural rules offering "virtual assurance" of a vote on implementing NTB agreements within ninety legislative days (sixty for nonrevenue bills).[33] Committee member William Roth said he didn't think Congress would reject many agreements under such a system. " 'I think the important difference is that the chief executive and the negotiators realize that there is that power in the Congress,' and that it must be taken into account by the Administration while it is negotiating trade agreements."[34]

Having worked out this procedure on NTB agreements, the committee acted to strengthen congressional influence on other executive decisions, particularly involving retaliation, import relief, and countervailing duties, by allowing them to be overridden by one or both Houses.

SECTORS. The House amendment added by Joseph E. Karth, which called for sector-by-sector negotiations "to the extent feasible," proved to be a difficult problem for the Finance Committee and required it to call for additional testimony as late as September 26. On one side were the chemical, iron and steel, electrical, aluminum, electronics, and dairy industries, who wanted to negotiate substantially within sectors. On the other side were agricultural export interests, who wanted to use industrial concessions to win major breakthroughs on agriculture.

Bill H. Jones of the National Livestock Feeders Association expressed the widely held view that agriculture had been "sold down the river" during the Kennedy Round by separating agricultural and industrial negotiations. William J. Kuhfuss, president of the American Farm Bureau Federation, said sector negotiations "could be disastrous for agriculture" and urged the committee to "add a provision that explicitly would direct the President and the U.S. negotiators to conduct joint negotiations on agriculture and industrial products." He called it "inescapable that our negotiators must be prepared to make concessions with regard to removing or reducing restrictions on imports of certain industrial products produced in Japan and the EEC," in order to expand U.S. agricultural exports to those countries. Predictably, Healy of the National Milk Producers Federation took the opposite stance, urging

33. *Trade Reform Act of 1974*, S. Rept. 93-1298, p. 107.
34. *National Journal*, October 5, 1974, pp. 1486–87.

"inclusion of specific sector areas along commodity lines for agriculture."[35] He was joined in this proposal by the National Farmers Union and the National Farmers Organization.[36]

The administration, unhappy with the Karth amendment, asked the Finance Committee to drop it. Eberle said the administration was afraid that the clause "could be interpreted as requiring us to use [a sector approach] throughout the negotiations and not have the opportunity to look at the overall benefits and reciprocity."[37]

With product interests thus divided, the committee and STR officials worked out a compromise providing most of the flexibility the administration sought. The Karth amendment was qualified by the phrase, "to the extent consistent with the objective of maximizing overall economic benefit to the United States." Moreover, a phrase was added requiring that "to the maximum extent feasible," agricultural trade liberalization "shall be undertaken *in conjunction with*" industrial trade liberalization; however, this was "not a directive for cross-sectorial trade-offs between agriculture and industry." Finally, the committee report singled out steel, aluminum, electronics, chemicals, and electrical machinery as sectors which "lend themselves to a sector negotiating technique." The implication was that Congress would hold the negotiators accountable at least for trying, even if not for succeeding.[38]

ADVISORY COMMITTEES. The Finance Committee bill created advisory committees representing labor, industry, agriculture, consumers, and the general public, to increase participation in trade negotiations. For senators, such committees were particularly useful because they absorbed political pressure: as long as there were such established forums for considering these special interests, the legislators could refer petitioners there, deflecting any proposals for immediate legislative action.

TARIFF COMMISSION AND SPECIAL TRADE REPRESENTATIVE. The Senate committee added a provision renaming the Tariff Commission the United States International Trade Commission (USITC), "because tariffs are no longer the major impediments to trade." It also provided for expanding the commission from six to seven members, lengthening members' terms gradually to fourteen years, and strengthening its legal power—

35. Quotations in paragraph from *Trade Reform Act of 1973*, Hearings, pp. 948–49, 966, 1004, 1013–14.
36. *National Journal*, October 5, 1974, p. 1488.
37. *Trade Reform Act of 1973*, Hearings, p. 248.
38. *Trade Reform Act of 1974*, S. Rept. 93-1298, pp. 78–79.

all to "enhance the Commissioners' independence from Executive domination."[39]

The committee adopted the House provision to make STR a statutory office, adding the explicit requirement that it be located in the Executive Office of the President.

Relief from Import Competition

Like the House, the Finance Committee liberalized the eligibility requirements for temporary industry protection from imports and for workers to receive unemployment benefits, retraining, and relocation aid. However, the committee bill went well beyond the House bill in making escape clause relief available to industry. It also further expanded and liberalized adjustment assistance but gave the administration a modest victory on its financing.

IMPORT RELIEF. The Finance Committee adopted the House criterion for injury determination ("substantial cause"), but it *required* the president to provide some form of relief when the International Trade Commission found the criterion was met. Moreover, the committee not only deleted the House "order of preference" of forms of relief but also provided that if the president did not follow the ITC's specific relief recommendation, Congress could override his decision by a concurrent resolution, thereby requiring him to implement that recommendation.[40]

This move reflected a belief that the executive had not adequately followed the intent of the 1962 act. In hearings on March 5, Senator Ribicoff had asked why President Nixon had not yet acted on a Tariff Commission finding, made the previous July, that the ball bearing industry (concentrated in Ribicoff's state of Connecticut) was being injured by imports from Japan and elsewhere and was thus eligible for relief under the escape clause provisions of the Trade Expansion Act. He asked, "What is the use of seeking liberalization of this clause if you have been so reluctant to apply even a stricter clause?"[41]

The administration preferred the more liberal House version. Alan Wolff of STR said the Finance Committee provision ignored the fact that the president must take more into account than the commission finding—such as the broad domestic and international consequences of

39. Ibid., p. 25.
40. Ibid., pp. 119–26.
41. *Trade Reform Act of 1973*, Hearings, p. 233.

providing relief. Eberle, however, concluded that "we can certainly live with it," though he was "not wildly enthusiastic about it."[42]

ADJUSTMENT ASSISTANCE. The committee liberalized eligibility for adjustment assistance by basing the injury test on an absolute, rather than a relative, increase in imports. Benefits were raised to 70 percent of a worker's average weekly earnings for up to fifty-two weeks; the House bill reduced benefits to 65 percent after the first twenty-six weeks. But unlike the House, the Finance Committee agreed to the administration's proposal that the federal government pay only the difference between state unemployment benefits and the higher adjustment assistance levels. Because the states would thus absorb an estimated $100 million a year, the more generous plan would cost the federal government $335 million a year, approximately what the lesser benefits would cost it. Senator Roth was instrumental in winning committee acceptance of this package, working in particular with Senators Mondale, Gaylord Nelson, and Lloyd Bentsen.[43]

The bill kept the House provisions for adjustment assistance to firms and added a new program of community adjustment assistance which would provide loans and technical assistance to "trade impacted areas."[44]

"UNFAIR" TRADE PRACTICES. The committee agreed with most of the House provisions for combating foreign import restrictions or export subsidies but added that presidential retaliatory actions "should generally be on a selective basis, that is, only against those countries found to discriminate against U.S. commerce," rather than against all producers of similar products.[45] If the president chose to act against "innocent countries," the Congress could overrule him by concurrent resolution.

COUNTERVAILING DUTIES. These generated more committee action than other relief items. Organized agriculture made a strong case that, despite clear evidence of European export subsidies for dairy products, the Treasury Department had shown great reluctance to respond with countervailing duties (CVDs). Farm representatives asked the committee to delete the House-granted waiver of countervailing duties during the period of the trade negotiations and to make CVD applica-

---

42. *National Journal*, October 5, 1974, p. 1491.
43. Ibid., p. 1492.
44. *Trade Reform Act of 1974*, S. Rept. 93-1298, p. 28.
45. Ibid., pp. 31, 168; *National Journal*, October 5, 1974, p. 1490.

tion mandatory.[46] Manufacturing representatives like E. Douglas Kenna of the National Association of Manufacturers also called for a further tightening of the executive's discretionary power with CVDs, "to assure that valid cases receive prompt and justified attention."[47]

On September 12, dairy representatives met with Mondale, Nelson, and STR representatives to discuss their complaints. They apparently convinced the senators that the moratorium during the multilateral trade negotiations should be deleted and that countervailing duties should be mandatory upon a finding of export subsidy, but Malmgren called their demands unreasonable and politically unrealistic; in the light of Watergate revelations about the dairy industry's contributions to Nixon, no one was going to give them that much. Finally, the administration agreed to drop its request for the moratorium (which thus removed the unwanted distinction between private and nationalized industries) in exchange for discretionary authority to waive CVD application for two years if three rather stringent conditions were met: (1) the foreign government had taken steps to "reduce substantially or eliminate the adverse effect of the bounty or grant"; (2) there was "a reasonable prospect" that an NTB agreement would be negotiated; and (3) imposition of duties "would be likely to seriously jeopardize the satisfactory completion of such negotiations."[48] Unlike the House, the Finance Committee provided that either house of Congress could override such a waiver.

ANTIDUMPING. To the House changes in the law, the Finance Committee added the right of judicial review of negative findings on dumping. Importers and foreign producers already had the right to appeal positive findings. This paralleled the provision added by the House allowing such review of negative CVD decisions.

Generalized System of Preferences

The House had approved trade preferences for developing countries, but then came the oil embargo imposed by the Organization of Petro-

46. *Trade Reform Act of 1973*, Hearings: Patrick B. Healy of the National Milk Producers Federation, pp. 987–88; William J. Kuhfuss of the American Farm Bureau Federation, p. 1005; and Bill H. Jones of the National Livestock Feeders Association, p. 963.

47. Ibid., p. 744.

48. *Trade Reform Act of 1974*, S. Rept. 93-1298, pp. 34, 186–87. See also Robert A. Pastor, "Legislative-Executive Relations and U.S. Foreign Trade Policy: The Case of the Trade Act of 1974," paper prepared for the 1976 annual meeting of the American Political Science Association, p. 18.

leum Exporting Countries. Mondale expressed a common congressional feeling at the hearings: "What OPEC stands for, it seems to me, is an outrageous, uncivilized, extorting, monopolistic strategy to take a critical world commodity, increase the price out of any economic proportion, not only to generate revenues but to extort political concessions as well, to the point that the oil prices are doing more to break up NATO and the Common Market than the Russians ever could do."[49]

Responding to the oil crisis, the committee voted to exclude from eligibility *all* OPEC countries. The administration objected: Malmgren argued that exclusion put the United States in the position of being unable to help those in OPEC who hadn't embargoed oil to the United States. But because Mondale and other committee liberals dissented vigorously from the administration's position, Long found little substantive or political reason to respond. And the committee went further, excluding from preferences all Communist countries, all members of other cartels which seek to "disrupt prices and supplies," all countries which do not take adequate steps to prevent narcotics from illegally entering the United States, all countries expropriating property of U.S. nationals without adequate compensation, and all countries granting preferential treatment to third countries resulting in an adverse effect on U.S. commerce.[50]

The State Department was upset by these provisions. In the opinion of many diplomats, preferences brought only limited economic gains to developing countries, anyway; their real value was political and symbolic. The Senate's exclusions destroyed this political value, as would be illustrated in January 1975 when Latin American nations unanimously condemned the OPEC exclusion as "discriminatory."[51] But Kissinger did not enter this dispute, apparently, until after the bill was reported; and while STR shared State's view, it did not give this issue a high priority.

Most-Favored-Nation Status

The Finance Committee bill retained the House language on freedom of emigration, pending the final testimony of Kissinger; it reserved the right "to recommend . . . such amendment as may be necessary" thereafter. It changed the House bill to require affirmative congressional action (under expedited procedures) on future bilateral commercial

49. *Trade Reform Act of 1973*, Hearings, p. 180.
50. *Trade Reform Act of 1974*, S. Rept. 93-1298, p. 65.
51. Pastor, "Legislative-Executive Relations," p. 25.

agreements under the title but did not apply this retroactively to the Soviet Union. And it excluded Czechoslovakia from its provisions unless that country met its obligations to U.S. citizens in full; the committee disapproved of the State Department's agreement to settle Czech debts to U.S. citizens at only a fraction of their principal amount, despite the fact that Czech assets held by the U.S. government more than equaled the total principal.[52]

A More Restrictive Bill

With these changes, the Finance Committee reported the bill favorably to the Senate by a 17–0 vote on November 20, with the proviso that it would not receive floor consideration until Kissinger testified on MFN status. On balance, it was more restrictive than the House version. The administration won greater flexibility on negotiation by sectors, but this and other gains were more than counterbalanced by requirement of affirmative action on NTB agreements, restrictions on preferences, and sharp limitations on executive discretion—of the president on relieving injured industries, of the secretary of the treasury on countervailing duties. The committee also dropped the provision allowing trade barrier relaxation to combat inflation, and whereas the House had only *authorized* the president to take specific actions to correct payments imbalances, the Finance Committee bill *required* the president to follow these actions in deficit situations or explain to Congress why he should not. Moreover, Senator Long would not so subtly signal his view of the bill's limitations by successfully proposing, on the Senate floor, that its name be changed from Trade Reform Act to Trade Act, since he did not want to claim too much for it.[53]

Strategy for the Senate Floor

What worried supporters at this point, however, was not so much the substance of the Finance Committee bill as the timing of its report. The

52. *Trade Reform Act of 1974*, S. Rept. 93-1298, pp. 214–17; see also Pastor, "Legislative-Executive Relations," pp. 22–23.

53. *Congressional Record, Daily Digest*, December 13, 1974, p. D480.

administration had won the negotiating authority it needed in a bill that was unanimously approved by a relatively conservative congressional committee. But the hour was late. Four years before, a trade bill had reached the Senate floor in December, only to become entangled in parliamentary maneuvering and to die without coming to a vote. This bill could meet the same fate. A number of senators indicated they would offer nongermane amendments on issues such as natural gas deregulation and taxation of overseas earnings of multinational firms; even should this kind of hurdle be surmounted, the substantial differences between the House and Senate versions would have to be resolved in conference.

A lot depended upon whether Russell Long really wanted the trade bill enacted, and about that there were differing views. The chairman had maintained control of the bill, while its most controversial title was negotiated elsewhere, by slowing the pace of committee deliberations; unlike Ullman, he was not going to complete action until the emigration matter was resolved. The question was whether he now had a strategy for moving the bill rapidly to enactment. Some believed that he did not, that he was going to hold the bill hostage to other objectives, such as a costly oil cargo preference bill strongly supported by the U.S. maritime industry.[54]

In fact, Long did have a strategy, part of which was to make others believe that he did not. As the chairman explained it to STR lobbyists, he would turn the late hour (and others' doubts about his intentions) to the trade bill's advantage. He would push suddenly for quick action, catching opponents off balance and thus limiting their ability to mobilize counterpressure on senators. Working to the advantage of Long and the administration was the fact that with majority leader Mike Mansfield visiting China, Robert Byrd of West Virginia was acting in his place. Byrd, who aimed to be Mansfield's successor, wanted to demonstrate that he could steer a major bill through the chamber. Once he was convinced that the bill had enough support, he was ready to cooperate.

54. This bill was also brought to the Senate floor that December, and approved there. Reports circulated that Long had extracted a promise from President Ford to sign the oil bill if Long moved the trade bill to enactment. In a December 20, 1974, editorial, the *Washington Post* reported and condemned this "squalid deal," which "evidently cannot be undone." In fact, Long's deal with Ford was apparently more limited—the president only agreed not to oppose the cargo preference bill coming to a vote in the Senate, and in fact killed that bill by pocket veto two weeks later.

And Eberle and Malmgren worked hard to demonstrate that the votes were there, with the 17–0 Finance Committee ballot a nice piece of evidence. They worked closely with a coalition of supporters, mainly from private industry and free-trade groups; they made sure individual senators heard from interests who saw gains in the legislation as well as those who saw problems. When Byrd reportedly asked them where the United Mine Workers stood, they could reply that he would "be receiving a telegram from them tomorrow morning" basically in favor of the bill, but that they would just as soon not have it publicized because "they don't want to fight with the AFL-CIO." Byrd was impressed: "You guys think of everything." So when he saw (and presumably double-checked) their vote count, he assured them of his support, adding that he would remain publicly undecided a while longer in order to maneuver for more votes.

With the way thus smoothed by adroit STR lobbying, Long put his blitzkreig strategy into operation. On December 3, Kissinger gave his promised testimony to the Finance Committee, declaring that "a satisfactory compromise was achieved on an unprecedented and extraordinarily sensitive set of issues" but emphasizing that the Soviet Union would repudiate any statement that a formal agreement on emigration had been reached.[55] The secretary was walking a tightrope, trying to salvage MFN status for Russia and the 1972 U.S.-Soviet commercial agreement. Also, unlike in 1973, he was acting to salvage the trade bill. One apparent reason was that, spurred by the oil embargo, he had grown more sensitive to problems of international economic interdependence and the importance of effective cooperation among the advanced industrial economies. A second was that, unlike Nixon, Ford had signaled clearly that he wanted the emigration issue compromised and the trade bill enacted.

On December 5, the bill reached the Senate floor. On December 11, only the second day of its active consideration, Senator Byrd presented a cloture petition to limit debate. This was unusual, for cloture was normally proposed only for bills which opponents were seeking to kill through protracted debate, and debate on the trade bill had hardly begun. But its use in this case made it possible for nongermane amendments to be ruled out of order.[56] On December 13, the cloture petition was passed 71–19, eleven votes over the two-thirds majority required.

55. *Emigration Amendment to the Trade Reform Act of 1974*, Hearings before the Senate Committee on Finance, 93 Cong. 2 sess. (GPO, 1974), pp. 54, 53.

56. *Congressional Quarterly Almanac*, vol. 30 (1974), p. 558.

The Senate then proceeded to adopt twenty-nine floor amendments, including the Jackson amendment embodying his compromise with Kissinger by a vote of 88–0, before passing the bill that same day by the lopsided margin of 77–4. All of the amendments were accepted by Long; none altered the bill fundamentally. One, sponsored by the chairman, provided cabinet-level status to the special trade representative; another, by Mondale, made Rumania and Yugoslavia eligible for preferences. And though Long observed on the floor, "We had footwear protected five different ways in this bill when we reported it,"[57] he accepted three further changes put forward by New England senators concerned about the industry: by Thomas J. McIntyre, authorizing the president to negotiate a multilateral agreement on footwear like the existing textile accord; by John O. Pastore, excluding certain footwear and other product categories from preferences (thus writing into law an informal administration commitment); and by William D. Hathaway, providing that the treasury secretary's waiver authority on countervailing duties not apply to "import sensitive items, including, but not limited to, footwear."[58] These amendments helped assure unanimous support of the bill from that oft-protectionist region. The Senate did reject by 35–49 a McIntyre amendment, also drafted with footwear in mind, prohibiting the president from lowering import restrictions on articles where imports exceeded one-third of U.S. consumption. But as part of the effort to defeat the amendment, Eberle wrote McIntyre what amounted to a promise that the administration would approve import relief for the shoe industry if the question came before it. "The escape clause provisions of the Trade Reform Act are ideally suited for use by the American non-rubber footwear industry," he declared, and if the industry sought such relief, and "if the procedures suggested" the need for it, "you can be assured the Administration would move expeditiously to provide it."[59]

On final passage, only one senator strongly identified with labor, Vance Hartke, voted nay. He was joined by Lee Metcalf, James Abourezk, and James McClure. Several other prolabor senators privately told administration officials they were happy for an opportunity to vote against the AFL-CIO as long as the tally was sufficiently one-sided to protect them from reprisals. Moreover, they had learned that particular unions did not always share George Meany's position.

57. *Congressional Record* (December 13, 1974), p. 39815.

58. *Congressional Quarterly Almanac*, vol. 30 (1974), p. 559.

59. Letter of December 11, 1974, reprinted in *Congressional Record* (December 13, 1974), p. 39813. As noted in chapter 12, this promise was not kept.

The Trade Act of 1974

House and Senate conferees met on December 18 and 19, then filed their report. The senators generally prevailed; commented Long, "I do not think there has been a case in the consideration of a major piece of legislation when the House has been as considerate of the Senate position as it has on this bill."[60] One reason was that STR officials had prepared the way on the House side, being anxious for final enactment and convinced that major revisions in the Senate language were impossible in the short time remaining. In addition, the senators came to the conference better informed about the legislation because they had dealt with it more recently. And Wilbur Mills, who had dominated many conferences with the Finance Committee in the past, was retiring from the Ways and Means chairmanship, no longer a force to be reckoned with.

The conferees authorized the president to eliminate tariffs on goods carrying duties of 5 percent or less, and to reduce higher tariffs by up to 60 percent. (The Senate had allowed only 50 percent on tariffs of over 10 percent.) On nontariff barriers, Talmadge's views prevailed.[61] Nontariff barrier agreements negotiated at Geneva would not enter into force unless implementing legislation was adopted by Congress under expedited procedures. The various congressional approval procedures and overrides established by the Senate were generally adopted by the conferees, as were the Senate's provisions allowing greater negotiating flexibility among sectors. The renaming of the Tariff Commission was approved, but the membership stayed at six, with each serving nine years (up from the current six). The office of the special trade representative was placed by statute where it has previously been by presidential order, in the Executive Office of the President. And Long's amendment providing cabinet-level salary for the STR passed, despite what he labeled "vigorous opposition" from Eberle and the administration.[62]

The Senate also had its way generally in the areas of industry import relief and worker adjustment assistance, but the conferees toned down some of its provisions. The Senate had unconditionally required the

60. *Congressional Record* (December 20, 1974), p. 41637.
61. Ibid.
62. Ibid.

president to provide relief if the ITC recommended that he do so; the conference committee allowed the president to reject an ITC recommendation if he found that it was not in the national economic interest; however, the Congress could override the president's decision by concurrent resolution, forcing the implementation of the ITC recommendation. And the committee deleted the House language establishing an "order of preference" in the forms of relief to be provided. The level of adjustment assistance benefits in the Finance Committee bill was retained. The Senate's financing scheme, favored by the administration, was also accepted. So was adjustment assistance to firms and much of the Senate's provision for adjustment assistance to "trade impacted areas." The conferees generally adopted the Senate's retaliation and antidumping provisions almost verbatim. But the amendment prohibiting the secretary of the treasury from waiving countervailing duties on "import-sensitive items" was limited strictly to nonrubber footwear. The Senate's more stringent criteria for a CVD waiver during trade negotiations were adopted, but for the longer period provided by the House —four years. On the employment of import restrictions to combat payments deficits, the House version prevailed—permitting but not requiring such action. The House provisions on liberalizing imports to combat inflation were dropped.

On preferences, the restrictive Senate provisions were generally retained, although the president was given discretion to extend preferences in certain cases (countries nationalizing U.S. property without compensation, those not taking adequate steps to prevent illegal narcotics from entering the United States, and those failing to recognize international arbitration settlements) if he found it "in the national economic interest of the United States." Mondale's amendment permitting preferences to Rumania and Yugoslavia was also accepted. So—as everyone expected—was the compromise amendment on Soviet MFN status that Jackson had worked out with Kissinger, even though the Soviet Union was denouncing it as unacceptable the day the conference met.[63]

63. On December 18, in a highly unusual action, the Soviet government released a sharply critical letter dated October 26 from Andrei Gromyko to Kissinger. It stated that the Kissinger-Jackson correspondence had created "a distorted picture of our position, as well as of what we told the American side" on emigration prospects. The Gromyko letter in fact declared that the figures his government did convey illustrated "the present tendencies toward a decrease in the number of persons wishing to leave the USSR and seek permanent residence in other countries." A *Tass* statement of December 18 declared that "leading circles" in the Soviet Union " 'flatly reject as unacceptable' any attempt to attach conditions to the reduc-

On December 20, adjournment day, Congress approved the conference report. The Senate vote was 72–4, the House vote was 323–36.[64]
Ullman called the bill a monumental piece of legislation affecting "not
only the economy of the United States but of the whole world, the free
world, the developing countries, and the Communist world."[65] Congressman Charles A. Vanik, now a supporter, called it "unprecedented"; it
was the first time economic legislation took into account "some regard
for the liberty and happiness of people."[66] Senator Hartke and Congressman James A. Burke were among the few remaining opponents. Hartke,
noting Long's amendment changing the name to the Trade Act, said, "I
wholeheartedly share with Senator Long his concern for the quality of
the bill," and offered "an even more appropriate title, The Unemployment Act of 1974."[67] He did not make this a formal proposal, however,
and on January 3, 1975, President Ford signed the Trade Act of 1974 into
law.

---

tion of tariffs on imports from the Soviet Union." Christopher S. Wren, *New York
Times,* December 19, 1974.

This action had no impact on the Trade Act. But on January 10, unhappy also
over a congressionally imposed ceiling on Export-Import Bank credits, the Soviet
government informed Kissinger that it would not implement the 1972 agreement.
Leslie H. Gelb, *New York Times,* January 15, 1975.

64. The roll call votes are in *Congressional Quarterly Almanac,* vol. 30 (1974),
pp. 83-S, 162-H.

65. Ibid., p. 562.

66. Ibid.

67. *Congressional Record* (December 20, 1974), p. 41639.

CHAPTER TWELVE

Trade Policymaking: Politics and Organization

WHY WAS THE TRADE BILL finally enacted? What explains why 1974 was different from 1970, when Congress had nearly passed a far more protectionist measure?

One reason is that the currency realignment set in motion on August 15, 1971, brought improvement in U.S. trade accounts. During House deliberations, their steady improvement buttressed the argument that the trade balance problem was best addressed by monetary adjustment rather than trade legislation. It also made some difference on the Senate side (given the Finance Committee's more mercantilist approach) that the United States could boast a substantial nonoil trade surplus in 1974, despite the deterioration in the overall trade account. Thus the "system-shaking" action of President Nixon in 1971 helped to strengthen the international trade system in 1973 and 1974 by making it easier for the administration to win the authority to enter a new round of trade negotiations.

Another important reason for the bill's enactment, however, was effective executive branch lobbying. In 1970, the administration had been deeply divided on trade policy: the special trade representative's office (STR) had formal lead responsibility, but less liberal Commerce Department officials often preempted it on key issues. In 1973 and 1974, STR had the lead in fact as well as form. Moreover, William D. Eberle, William R. Pearce, and Harald B. Malmgren dealt adroitly within two very different legislative frameworks. They worked closely with key legislators, spending a large portion of their time on the Hill, dealing with the Congress purposively and yet with respect. They developed an understanding of what congressmen and senators needed and what they didn't need—they needed to have their interests and convictions taken seriously; they didn't need—or want—to yield to special interests if ways could be found to do something about their legitimate concerns. In a two-year period of unprecedented turmoil in executive–legislative relations and of substantial turnover in senior executive economic policy officials, the STR effort made possible an unprecedented grant of authority to U.S. trade negotiators and innovative provisions for executive–congressional collaboration in future trade policymaking.

Administration dealings with Congress were far less effective on those issues outside the trilateral trade and foreign policy concerns to which STR gave priority. On the issue of most-favored-nation status (MFN) it lost control, as did its congressional allies; in consequence, administration policymaking on this issue was both more fractious and less astute. On preferences, STR kept control of the lobbying but lost control of the substance, in part perhaps because trade with developing countries was marginal to its priorities. Also outside of STR's central concern were the constitutional issues raised by the plethora of congressional override provisions. This issue came belatedly to a head in August 1976, when President Ford decided not to give relief to U.S. honey producers, despite a 3–2 International Trade Commission recommendation for quotas. Acting on the advice of lawyers in the Justice Department and the White House, and against the strong objections of trade advisers, Ford stated in his decision announcement the view that congressional vetoes were unconstitutional and implied that any such veto might be ignored. For the trade policy community, this posed for a time the threat that the whole structure of executive–legislative cooperation, so painstakingly constructed in 1973 and 1974, might unravel.[1] And in 1978, Jimmy Carter sent a message to Congress contesting the constitutionality of "unnecessary and unwarranted legislative veto procedures," though with no specific reference to trade.[2]

If trade policy coordination was less effective on issues outside the central trade policy framework, it was probably facilitated by the absence of strong voices for one concern: overall industrial policy. This lack is sometimes deplored by free-trade advocates: it was Pearce who gave his name to the Williams commission comment cited in chapter 9, underscoring the need for a "national industrial and manpower policy."[3]

1. For a cogent summary, see United States–Japan Trade Council, "Trade Roundup No. 53," October 14, 1976.

2. See "Legislative Vetoes," Message to the Congress, June 21, 1978, *Weekly Compilation of Presidential Documents*, vol. 14 (June 26, 1978), p. 1146.

3. *Williams Commission Report* (Government Printing Office, 1971), p. 9. See chapter 1, note 11, for full reference.

He apparently saw this as a way of supporting industries whose international competitiveness was greatest, but it would likely lead also to institutionalized advocacy of the interests of particular industries in cases where they sought insulation from the international marketplace. It would thus link their protectionism to a broader national policy interest. This happens now in agriculture policy: section 22 of the Agricultural Adjustment Act authorizes tariffs and quotas to control agricultural imports if they would render particular domestic price support programs ineffective. And industrial policy institutions like Japan's Ministry of International Trade and Industry (MITI), though concerned about strengthening international competitiveness, often argue in practice for protection of import-threatened industries, whatever their future competitive potential.

The Immediate Aftermath

During the final years of the Ford administration, the Trade Act did not lead to major trade liberalization; instead it buttressed a holding action against protectionism. The Multilateral Trade Negotiations (MTN) in Geneva moved slowly; not until 1977 did the negotiators agree on a timetable for their completion, and actual agreement on tariff reductions and codes governing nontariff barriers did not come until April 1979.

The primary reason the Geneva talks moved slowly was the unfavorable world economic climate. In 1973 and early 1974 the predominant economic problem of the Organisation for Economic Co-operation and Development (OECD) countries was inflation, and to counter this "country after country unilaterally cut its import barriers."[4] But as the trade bill moved to final enactment, the advanced industrial countries plunged into the worst recession in forty years, and the old pressure to limit imports and thus "export unemployment" returned. Aware that such policies could generate retaliation and thus deepen the economic crisis, the OECD countries renewed in 1975 and 1976 their June 1974 pledge to avoid unilateral import-restricting steps to improve their trade balance at one another's expense. Their commitment to an open world economic order was dramatically underscored at the economic summit

---

4. C. Fred Bergsten, "The International Economy and World Politics in the Post-Postwar Era," in Wilfrid L. Kohl, *Economic Foreign Policies of Industrial States* (D. C. Heath, 1977), p. 9.

meetings in Rambouillet in November 1975, Puerto Rico in June 1976, London in May 1977, Bonn in July 1978, and Tokyo in May 1979. But through the Ford administration, progress at the MTN was very limited, in part because 1976 was an election year in Germany and Japan as well as the United States.

One area of trade policy in which the Ford administration was unusually active in 1975 and 1976 was relations with the Third World. The developing countries were increasingly united and militant in their demands for a New International Economic Order (NIEO), which would give them a larger share of world income. A central demand was for arrangements to raise and stabilize world market prices for primary commodities. Secretary of State Henry A. Kissinger, long criticized for his ignorance of economic matters, was impressed by the impact of the oil cartel and the difficulty of mobilizing effective international counteraction. He came to believe that "economic issues are turning into central political issues."[5] He had concluded that U.S. opposition to NIEO demands had strengthened an artificial alliance between OPEC and the oil-importing developing countries, who suffered most from OPEC's pricing policy. Continuation of a rigid U.S. stance would mean North–South polarization, which would damage U.S.–Japanese and U.S.–European relations as well, since the latter were unlikely to take stands as adamant as the U.S. stand. The alternative, as Kissinger saw it, was for the United States to move into a position of leadership in order to ameliorate North–South tensions. In May 1975 the secretary declared at Kansas City a willingness on the part of the United States "to discuss new arrangements in individual commodities on a case-by-case basis."[6] And on September 1, a major Kissinger address presented comprehensive proposals addressing the trade and development problems of Third World countries.[7]

These initiatives involved top State Department leadership more actively and aggressively in international economic issues than had been the case for some years. They also generated very sharp conflict within

5. "Statement Before the Ministerial Council of the OECD, May 28," *Department of State Bulletin*, vol. 72 (June 23, 1975), p. 852.

6. "Strengthening the World Economic Structure," *Department of State Bulletin*, vol. 72 (June 2, 1975), p. 717.

7. The speech was delivered by UN representative Daniel Patrick Moynihan because Kissinger was in the Middle East; for text, see "Global Consensus and Economic Development," *Department of State Bulletin*, vol. 73 (September 22, 1975), pp. 425–41.

the U.S. government between State Department officials anxious to improve the political posture of the United States and economic policy officials, especially those in the Treasury Department, doctrinally opposed to the substance of NIEO demands—particularly market-sharing and price-fixing arrangements. The Kansas City speech was the opening shot in this internal battle. It was drafted late and was cleared with economic officials only at the eleventh hour. One reason was that Kissinger had originally planned to devote this address mainly to food issues, broadening the subject only after declaring he found initial drafts boring. But another reason was that Assistant Secretary Thomas O. Enders saw such tactics as necessary if such a speech was to be given at all. Economic officials fought back, protesting to the press[8] and working to ensure that future Kissinger economic speeches were carefully reviewed and received the president's personal attention. The September 1 speech in fact was the product of thorough interagency consultation, first at the staff level and then, under Kissinger's chairmanship, at the State Department and the White House. The president personally resolved the remaining differences, mostly in favor of State. And one of the key proposals—creation of a development security fund in the International Monetary Fund to make loans compensating poor countries for shortfalls in export earnings—was apparently proposed by the Treasury Department, though perhaps because it was seen there as less objectionable than other possible solutions.[9]

But the conflict between State and Treasury continued through 1976, over both trade in specific commodities like tin and coffee and broader issues such as the U.S. attitude toward the common fund the developing countries wanted for financing buffer stocks of a range of commodities. When Kissinger traveled to Nairobi in May to present a proposal for a new international resource bank to the fourth session of the UN Conference on Trade and Development (UNCTAD), the haggling with Treasury over the text continued by cable, and these internal differences

8. William Safire referred to the "Enders run," the assistant secretary's "technique of getting far-reaching decisions made with a minimum of consideration." "Brother, Can You Spare a Paradigm," *New York Times*, June 2, 1975. See also James Reston, "A New Economic Order," *New York Times*, May 30, 1975, and Bernard Gwertzman, "Kissinger's New Role: His Speeches on Economic Policy Irk Officials Who Prefer More Research," *New York Times*, June 4, 1975.

9. This account relies primarily on interviews with officials involved. For an extensive contemporary account, see Richard S. Frank, "Economic Report: U.S. Takes Steps to Meet Demand of Third World Nations," *National Journal*, October 25, 1975, pp. 1480–89.

were a factor in the conference's 33–31 rejection of that proposal.[10] This conflict subsided, however, when the Carter administration came to power. The new State leadership was not as aggressive on the issue; Treasury leaders were more sympathetic to the Third World countries, and less inclined toward ideological formulations, than were their predecessors.

Also in these final two years of the Ford administration, the liberalized Trade Act procedures for import-affected industries went into effect. Relief petitions multiplied: the number of countervailing-duty investigations initiated by the Treasury Department in response to industry complaints rose from one in 1973 to thirty-eight in 1975; escape-clause investigations undertaken by the ITC increased from two to thirteen.[11] There was also a particularly dramatic case, the United Auto Workers' charge that twenty-eight foreign automobile manufacturers in eight countries were guilty of dumping in the American market.[12]

Inevitably this increased activity generated concerns abroad that the

10. Six days before the conference opened, but after Kissinger had left for Africa, Assistant Secretary of the Treasury Gerald L. Parsky sharply criticized the Third World's program in testimony before several subcommittees of the House International Relations Committee. *United States Commodity Policies,* Joint Hearings before the Subcommittee on International Resources, Food, and Energy; International Economic Policy; International Organizations; and International Trade and Commerce of the House Committee on International Relations, 94 Cong. 2 sess. (GPO, 1976), pp. 106–53. Jeremiah Novak, in a *Washington Post* article (May 31, 1976) concluded that this "surprised the State Department [and] derailed Kissinger's planned presentation," leading to a hasty redrafting of the entire speech and undercutting the effort to sell the proposal to the Third World. This was an exaggeration. Parsky apparently did not clear his testimony with State, and it certainly didn't help U.S. diplomats make their case to suspicious developing countries. But Kissinger's international resources bank proposal was agreed to before he left Washington and was presented essentially as agreed to; subsequent haggling with Treasury was over relatively trivial details. And an important impediment to selling it proved to be Kissinger himself— he wanted to keep the proposal secret until he delivered it, in order to achieve maximum impact. Thereafter he wanted to line up support from the developed countries before bargaining with the Third World. This meant that consultations were delayed and were, ultimately, insufficient.

Nevertheless, interagency conflict did hurt, not the least because the U.S. government was *perceived* by others as deeply divided. Said Senator Abraham Ribicoff eight months later: "Last spring, I [accompanied] Secretary Kissinger to Nairobi at the UNCTAD Conference. There I watched with dismay the cables back and forth and conversations between Treasury and State to allow the Secretary of State to speak for the United States." Quoted in Robert J. Samuelson, "Carter's Economic Team Playing Together in the Middle of the Road," *National Journal,* January 29, 1977, p. 168.

11. *International Economic Report of the President, March 1976,* p. 45.

12. Richard S. Frank, "Trade Report: Growth of Imported Car Sales Triggers Charges of Dumping," *National Journal,* September 20, 1975, pp. 1337–38.

United States was being swept by a new protectionist wave. Officials rightly insisted that the volume of complaints and investigations was something the administration could not control. But the trade bill had encouraged them by relaxing the criteria for granting relief, and the sum total of these complaints and investigations inevitably sent protectionist signals abroad.[13] Throughout the Ford administration, as noted in the March 1976 *International Economic Report of the President*, "the actual results were small."[14] On May 4, 1976, the Department of the Treasury dropped the UAW-generated antidumping investigation in return for assurances of corrective action by foreign manufacturers.[15] And though the ITC found injury or the threat thereof in seven cases in 1975–76, President Ford took restrictive action on only one, specialty steel. Faced with the threat of a congressional override if he took no action, he negotiated an orderly marketing agreement (OMA) with Japan and imposed quotas on other exporters. He expedited adjustment assistance in four cases, including nonrubber footwear, and decided against any action in two others. And the Congress did not exercise its power to override these decisions.[16]

The Carter Administration

However, the Trade Act clearly had one important, if unintended, political effect. If, by substituting general procedures for industry-specific remedies, members of Congress were able to deflect lobbying pres-

13. See, for example, Robert J. Samuelson, "Protecting the Shoe and Steel People: Trade War Ahead?" *The New Republic*, April 24, 1976, pp. 13–15; and Paul Lewis, "Protecting the Talks and the Trade: A Hard Act to Follow," *National Journal*, April 17, 1976, pp. 502–11.

14. p. 44.

15. Paul Lewis, "Cancel One Trade War," *National Journal*, May 22, 1976, p. 717. U.S. auto manufacturers did not support the complaint, reflecting the fact that about 40 percent of the cars imported in 1974 were produced by their subsidiaries, particularly in Canada. Frank, "Trade Report: Growth of Imported Car Sales," p. 1337.

16. *International Economic Report of the President, January 1977*, p. 47; Lewis, "Protecting the Talks and the Trade," p. 505. On footwear, Eberle had in fact promised more sympathetic action during administration lobbying for the Trade Act (see chapter 11). But a congressional override was impossible here for a technical reason—a majority of the ITC did not favor any particular form of relief. The Trade Act was quickly amended to make overrides in most similar cases possible in the future. The Ford footwear decision is analyzed at length in Roger B. Porter, "Presidential Decisionmaking: The Economic Policy Board" (Ph.D. dissertation, Harvard University, August 1978), chap. 6. Porter was executive secretary of the EPB in the Ford administration.

sure from themselves, they placed the president more squarely before the firing line than ever before. As long as pre-1974 criteria made Tariff Commission injury determinations unlikely, a chief executive could finesse product-specific issues. Lyndon Johnson, for example, had instructed his aides to "keep the pot boiling" on the question of textile quotas, meaning to maintain enough activity to offer some hope of relief to the industry but to prevent the issue from coming directly and unambiguously to *him* for decision. This course was not open to Jimmy Carter when he entered the White House in 1977. Already, on January 6, the ITC had found serious injury to the nonrubber footwear industry and on February 8 it formally recommended a stringent five-year tariff-rate quota for relief. On March 25, the ITC found similarly on imports of color television sets and recommended a sharp increase in tariffs.

In both cases, the president had to decide within sixty days whether to accept the ITC proposal and, if not, what relief, if any, to provide. If he chose not to follow the specific ITC recommendation, the Congress could override him. Thus, even before his special trade representative had been selected and confirmed by the Senate Carter faced two very difficult, domestic–international trade-off issues on which the industry arguments of injury from imports were particularly strong and on which his senior advisers offered sharply divided counsel.[17] He resolved each by compromise, rejecting the ITC remedies but ordering negotiation of OMAs: with Taiwan and Korea on shoes, and with Japan on color TVs.

Before the year was out, the Carter administration faced a larger trade policy challenge. Rising steel imports, coupled with depressed conditions in that industry both in the United States and worldwide, led to sharply increased pressure for import restrictions, particularly from the newly formed steel caucus on Capitol Hill. The president's first response was to promise vigorous enforcement of the antidumping laws; at a White House meeting on October 13 he apologized for previous government "derogation of duty" in this regard.[18] This response was

17. For a step-by-step summary of decisionmaking in the former case, see David S. Broder, "The Case of the Missing Shoe-Import Option," *Washington Post,* July 23, 1977. The article is based on a decision analysis conducted inside the government as part of the reorganization study of the Executive Office of the President. The author of this book participated in the decision analysis project, though he was not responsible for that specific case.

18. Robert J. Samuelson, "Trade Report: The Anti-Dumping Laws: Rx for the Steel Industry?" *National Journal,* October 22, 1977, pp. 1636–40; Matthew J. Marks, "Remedies to 'Unfair' Trade: American Action against Steel Imports," *World Economy,* vol. 2 (January 1978), pp. 223–37.

consistent with the basic Trade Act reliance on procedural remedies for import relief claims, particularly in cases where "unfair" trade practices were involved. The industry had several such cases pending and had already had some success. But on further examination, officials found the antidumping approach less attractive. Its actual trade impact was hard to predict in advance, and important U.S. trading partners—particularly the Japanese—found the Trade Act's antidumping provisions unfair to them and inconsistent with the General Agreement on Tariffs and Trade.[19] And American steel producers were uneasy with the antidumping route because they weren't sure it would provide enough protection.

Therefore, with their support, the administration instituted a reference price system for steel developed by a task force headed by Under Secretary of the Treasury Anthony Solomon. Reference prices were based on the estimated production costs of the world's most efficient producers, the Japanese; if imports came into the United States at prices below them the Treasury Department would inaugurate antidumping investigations against the supplier. This proved an effective short-term political expedient. But it underscored broader problems with the Trade Act's emphasis on combating "unfair" trade practices. No one could quarrel with this in principle, but in practice procedures that assured fairness to American producers were almost bound to seem unfair to foreign competitors, given the enormous complexity in determining whether a firm was in fact selling below cost in a foreign market or whether a foreign government was providing a trade-distorting subsidy.

The Carter administration was also greeted with a burgeoning of the U.S. trade deficit. The American economy was recovering more rapidly than the economies of its trading partners, thus attracting more imports, particularly of oil. The result was an excess of imports over exports of $26.7 billion in 1977, more than four times the previous high. And 1978 brought another record deficit—$28.5 billion—though by midyear the figures began showing improvement and continued to improve in 1979.

As in 1972, this deficit strengthened those who argued that the United States could not afford a liberal trade policy or that the United States was victimized by an unfair international trading system in which other countries—especially its Japanese and European trading partners—subsidized exports and impeded imports. Of particular concern was the trade deficit with Japan, which reached $8.1 billion in 1977, twice the level that had generated widespread alarm in 1972. Japan was running

19. See chapter 10.

a large worldwide current account surplus, which U.S. officials saw as a drag on world economic recovery, and the Carter administration first used multilateral consultations to press Japan to eliminate this surplus. When, despite Japanese projections to the contrary, the surplus increased, stronger pressure was applied, producing the predictable political uproar in Tokyo.

By the end of 1977, matters had reached the point where a formal agreement was necessary to avert a serious crisis in bilateral relations that threatened to undercut the shaky economic recovery in Tokyo and to strengthen protectionism in Washington. So the Japanese government made some concessions, Washington scaled back its demands, and an accord was reached in January 1978, announced in a joint communique issued by Carter's special trade representative, Robert Strauss, and the new Japanese minister for external economic affairs, Nobuhiko Ushiba. The United States won Japanese recognition that "in the present international economic situation, the accumulation of a large current account surplus was not appropriate," and a commitment to seek its "marked diminution" immediately and a further reduction "aiming at equilibrium" later.[20] It also won modest tariff reductions, quota liberalization, specific import promotion measures, and a commitment to more stimulative Japanese economic policies. Nonetheless, the bilateral Japanese trade surplus with the United States grew further, to $11.6 billion in 1978, and the Japanese worldwide current account surplus remained at its record level. In the first half of 1979, however, the bilateral imbalance declined and Japan's current account surplus disappeared entirely.[21]

Completion of the MTN

But by no means all of the Carter administration's trade policy energy went to countering trade-restrictive pressure. Through a strong personal effort, Strauss succeeded in breathing life into the Multilateral Trade Negotiations. He was able to get serious bargaining under way on tariffs and nontariff matters, including the thorny questions of agricultural

20. The joint statement is reprinted in the New York Times, January 14, 1978. For an analysis of this negotiation, see I. M. Destler, "U.S.–Japanese Relations and the American Trade Initiative of 1977: Was This Trip Necessary?" in William J. Barnds, ed., Japan and the United States: Challenges and Opportunities (New York University Press for the Council on Foreign Relations, 1979), pp. 190–230.

21. The bilateral improvement reflected—after the normal lag—the remarkable total appreciation of about 50 percent in the dollar value of the yen between December 1976 and November 1978. In the months thereafter, this trend was reversed, with the yen losing much of this gain.

trade barriers and government subsidies. Using the Bonn economic summit as an action-forcing deadline, the United States, the European Community, Japan and other major developed countries reached agreement in July 1978 on a "framework of understanding on the Tokyo Round." The talks suffered a setback that fall, when the Ninety-fifth Congress failed to extend the four-year period during which the secretary of the treasury could waive imposition of countervailing duties. (This authority expired on January 3, 1979.) Moreover, that same Congress also passed a bill, vetoed by President Carter, which would have forced withdrawal of the textile tariff concessions the United States had already made in the MTN. Europeans refused to complete the negotiations unless Congress extended the waiver retroactively in early 1979. However, the U.S. textile industry was threatening to block any waiver bill or to get its tariff proposal added as an amendment.

For a while it seemed possible that both the international and the domestic political base for the MTN might unravel. But Strauss negotiated an agreement with the textile industry giving it most of what it wanted, committing the administration to tightened enforcement of existing quota restrictions and imposition of new ones as needed.[22] With this under his belt, he succeeded in winning congressional enactment of the waiver in March, and on April 12, 1979, the major work of the MTN was formally completed. Tariff reductions averaged about 30 percent from current levels. More important in their potential impact was a series of codes established to regulate nontariff distortions to trade. The most important concerned subsidies and countervailing duties, antidumping, customs valuation procedures, and government procurement.[23]

Thereafter, congressional implementation of the nontariff barrier agreements proved remarkably smooth, a tribute to the innovative procedures provided for in section 151 of the Trade Act. On January 4, President Carter gave the required notification to Congress of his intention to enter into trade agreements on NTBs. Thereafter, he was required to consult with the Ways and Means and Finance committees concerning

22. The text of this agreement was released by the White House on March 22, 1979; it is reprinted in the *Congressional Record*, daily edition (May 21, 1979), p. E2412.

23. For the text of the codes, see *Multilateral Trade Negotiations: International Codes Agreed to in Geneva, Switzerland, April 12, 1979*, Joint Committee Print, House Committee on Ways and Means and Senate Committee on Finance, 96 Cong. 1 sess. (GPO, 1979). For analysis of the MTN results and the implementing legislation, see *Trade Agreements Act of 1979*, H. Rept. 96-317, 96 Cong. 1 sess. (GPO, 1979) and *Trade Agreements Act of 1979*, S. Rept. 96-249, 96 Cong. 1 sess. (GPO, 1979).

the substance of these agreements and the necessary implementing legislation, in preparation for the expeditious congressional consideration of this legislation, with amendments prohibited. In practice, the two committees insisted on recommending to the executive branch a complete draft implementing bill. By March, they were holding what participants labeled "nonmarkups" to prepare legislative proposals in collaboration with STR and other executive branch representatives. In May, the two committees held a "nonconference" to reconcile their differences. Not every issue was resolved, and the administration refused to accept a few minor congressional recommendations. Moreover, the substance was necessarily constrained by what had been agreed to at Geneva. But the implementing legislation the administration submitted in June was, in all major respects, the product of this committee-based drafting process. The Trade Agreements Act of 1979 was approved overwhelmingly in July: 395 to 7 by the House of Representatives; 90 to 4 by the Senate. Interestingly, no less than five of the eleven opposing legislators were from the state of Wisconsin, whose dairy industry was unhappy about concessions allowing an increase in U.S. cheese imports.

Substantively, the main reason for the overwhelming approval was that STR had bargained very carefully with major industry interests before the MTN was completed and had generally come to terms with them. Moreover, the implementing legislation included expedited timetables for decisions on countervailing duty and antidumping petitions, which some experts felt would result in more determinations favorable to complainant industries. But the section 151 procedures clearly fulfilled their function, enabling the United States to negotiate significant, ratifiable NTB agreements. The implementing bill in fact extended these procedures for eight more years, to cover agreements negotiated by the president through January 3, 1988.

The Role of Strauss and STR

Dominating the public trade stage until the summer of 1979 was the personality of Robert Strauss. Never had a special trade representative been so visible a public figure and so important a presidential adviser; never had one had comparable independent political stature; never had one displayed such dramatic political virtuosity. Strauss was serving congressional masters as well as the president. When Carter, after finding several other candidates unacceptable to labor or other interests, offered the job to the former chairman of the Democratic Party (whose pacification of that party's warring elements had won him a formidable political reputation), Strauss went to a long-time friend, Russell Long, to consult before giving his reply. As one report recounted their conversation:

Long told Strauss a man should be aware of his options, then outlined the two he thought Strauss faced: either he could take the job, make a success of it and be a hero; or he could turn the President down, in which case, Long promised, "we'll run you out of town."

"Russell," Strauss replied, "you've explained it even clearer than the President did."[24]

Strauss is, of course, sui generis, but he also represents the culmination of a trend: the movement of the special trade representative into the position of overall trade policy broker. Before he came to the post, the experience of lobbying the trade bill through Congress had inclined the office toward sympathizing with import relief petitions when the industry had a good case. In interagency debates during the drafting of the trade bill in 1972–73, STR had been very much at the liberal end of the spectrum. On President Ford's 1976 decision on imports of shoes, STR was reportedly the strongest administration advocate for relief, while Kissinger and William E. Simon, adversaries on other economic issues, wrote a joint memo in opposition. An important reason was Eberle's December 1974 promise that the administration would "move expeditiously to provide" escape clause relief for shoes "if the procedures suggested" the need.[25] In preparation for Carter's shoe decision ten months later, STR first joined with Commerce, Labor, and the Office of Management and Budget in support of tariff-rate quotas (which apply an additional tariff on all imports above a base level [quota]), while State, Treasury, and the Council of Economic Advisers wanted relief limited to adjustment assistance. Then Strauss took the lead in sponsoring a middle option, negotiation of an orderly marketing agreement with key exporters, which Carter accepted.[26] On color TVs, the OMA that Strauss brought back from Tokyo was so stringent that three of the president's senior ad-

24. Robert G. Kaiser, "Politics of Trade Post: How Strauss Ended Up as Negotiator," *Washington Post*, March 13, 1977.

25. Letter to Thomas J. McIntyre from Eberle, December 11, 1974, reprinted in *Congressional Record* (December 13, 1974), p. 39813.

26. Broder, "Case of the Missing Shoe-Import Option." State argued, however, that an OMA could actually be more restrictive than a tariff rate quota, since it imposed an absolute limit on imports.

visers formally urged Carter to order its renegotiation to allow greater imports in its second year.

Finally, it was significant that STR was now handling such product-specific negotiations with particular exporters. In the sixties, its role centered on major multilateral negotiations; on issues involving special products like textiles and steel its involvement was limited.[27] By 1977, STR had extended its scope, and while interagency teams continued to be the norm for trade negotiations, STR's congressional clients left no doubt at Strauss's confirmation hearings about who they wanted to *lead* the negotiations—and on all issues, not just the MTN. Long even suggested "it might be a good idea for us to ask" the secretaries of state and treasury to meet with Finance Committee members, "so that there can be no misunderstanding" about STR's primacy.[28]

And congressional trade leaders particularly needed a strong STR now, because their ability to control trade action on the Hill had declined. When Wilbur Mills presided over the Ways and Means Committee, it served as a firebreak against protectionist pressure. Mills and his colleagues listened sympathetically to industry pleas for relief and frequently encouraged the executive to make some accommodation, but Mills was basically a free trader who resisted statutory proposals to protect particular products. He could use his power—and a closed rule (limiting debate and amendments)—to keep such proposals from reaching the House floor, where one-sided pressure might make it difficult for members to say no. And on occasions when the more open Senate had said yes, Finance chairman Long had generally yielded to Mills in conference. This pattern was changing in the Trade Act period, when Ullman replaced Mills at Ways and Means. By 1975, House procedural reforms had reduced a chairman's ability to control his committee and the committee's ability to control action on the House floor—making closed rules, for example, very hard to obtain. By that time Long had replaced Mills as the most important congressional figure in trade policy. But in the relatively free-wheeling Senate he lacked the power Mills had had to control the floor agenda. Thus he and his Senate and House colleagues badly needed a Robert Strauss, who would cope adroitly with

27. For example, until 1965 STR was not even made a member of the interagency committee which oversaw textile trade policy, and STR did not have the lead in any of the bilateral or multilateral negotiations leading to the conclusion of the multifiber agreement (MFA) in December 1973.

28. *Nominations,* Hearing before the Senate Committee on Finance, 95 Cong. 1 sess. (GPO, 1977), p. 4.

trade pressures, giving legislators ample credit for toughness (for example, in insisting on fair treatment of American products overseas), but keeping the action in his own court—and out of theirs.

Like the ITC, the Congress now absorbed fewer trade pressures. When the president, contrary to Strauss's recommendation, decided against the commission's recommendation for relief for the nuts and bolts industry in February 1978, Ways and Means trade subcommittee chairman Charles A. Vanik pressed for an override. He won a majority of his subcommittee before losing narrowly in the full committee. Then, rather than seeking to sustain this outcome on the House floor, the committee asked (at Vanik's urging and with Strauss's acquiescence) that the ITC undertake a new investigation. The commission again recommended relief, and in December, Carter went along. Similarly, once the Senate passed the previously mentioned proposal prohibiting any reductions of U.S. textile tariffs at the MTN—a step which Senate trade subcommittee chairman Abraham Ribicoff said could "insure the failure of the negotiation"[29]—Ways and Means couldn't block the proposal in the old Mills manner, for the committee could not keep it from the House floor once the Senate had enacted it. The only thing left to do was to attach it to an insignificant measure, a bill authorizing the sale of Carson City silver dollars, so the president could veto it and take the heat himself.

The central role of STR and its current effectiveness raises questions about its relations to institutions responsible for broader foreign economic policy coordination. In urging import relief for the shoe industry and the nuts and bolts industry and in negotiating a stringent OMA on color TVs, STR gave priority to the politics of trade policy. But economic policy officials and analysts argued that those shoe firms that had been injured by imports would not receive most of the benefit from import restraint. It would, however, bring windfalls to the prosperous segments of the shoe industry, be a burden on consumers, and contribute to inflation. The OMA on color TVs would also have an inflationary impact, economic officials felt, particularly in its second year, after inventories of imported TVs had been depleted. And both OMAs burdened U.S. relations with the countries affected.

These *economic* and *foreign policy* concerns were marginal to STR's central purpose of coordinating *trade* policy and maintaining its domestic political base. But should trade policy be the predominant frame-

29. *Congressional Quarterly Almanac*, vol. 34 (1978), pp. 279–80.

work within which these issues are coordinated and staffed for presidential decisions? In many cases, the answer will surely be no. Yet recent experience shows recurrent tension between the need for effective trade brokering and the need for broader foreign and economic policy coordination.

In the mid-sixties, STR apparently worked well within the lightly staffed foreign economic policy coordinating system based in the National Security Council. But, as noted in chapter 9, conflict arose between STR and the Council on International Economic Policy in 1972 and 1973. At that time, STR was in practice reporting to Nixon through Peter M. Flanigan (though also through George P. Shultz). And CIEP—a young staff institution searching for opportunities to establish its role—naturally fastened on trade as the very sort of interagency issue suitable to EOP staff brokering and leadership. STR survived the threat of merger, largely because it had better congressional allies. But were a formal EOP international economic policy coordinating staff to be reestablished at some future time, such a conflict would almost certainly recur.

Under Ford, STR operated relatively smoothly within the broader Economic Policy Board system. Where possible, interagency trade differences were resolved by subcabinet committees chaired by STR officials. On issues that needed cabinet-level discussion or a presidential decision, the EPB became the primary forum and its staff the coordinatoi of presidential decision papers, but STR acted as the lead agency. The fact that the EPB staff was small and sought smooth process management rather than substantive policy leadership helped make this a workable arrangement. So, of course, did Ford's strong personal commitment to the EPB system. But the Carter administration's EPG did not play a comparable role in managing presidential trade decisions, for reasons described in chapter 13.

Trade Reorganization?

Finally, the Carter period brought renewed debate about existing U.S. trade policy organization. The massive trade deficits of 1977 and 1978 generated demands for a stronger export promotion effort. Industry complaints multiplied about the Treasury Department's enforcement (or, some said, nonenforcement) of countervailing duty and antidumping laws. There was also growing criticism of general fragmentation in trade policymaking. As the Senate Finance Committee put it, "major trade functions are spread throughout the Executive branch making formulation of trade policy and implementation of trade policy haphazard and in some cases contradictory."[30] In particular, the committee worried, as did others, that the existing structure might not be up to the job of asserting U.S. rights under the new NTB codes. The most comprehensive remedy was put forward in August 1977 by Senator William Roth and Senator Ribicoff. They proposed to create a new department of international trade and investment, consolidating STR, the Export-Import Bank, the Overseas Private Investment Corporation, the international commercial and investment offices of State, the trade and investment offices of Commerce, the Treasury offices responsible for administering the customs and the antidumping and countervailing duty laws, and certain functions of the ITC.[31] They put forward a similar proposal in February 1979.[32]

This initiative was particularly significant because Ribicoff and Roth were the chairman and ranking minority member, respectively, of Finance's trade subcommittee. Ribicoff was also chairman of the Committee on Governmental Affairs, which had direct jurisdiction over executive reorganization. When the Finance Committee began to meet on the trade-implementing legislation in March 1979, it voted to recommend that such a department be established by that legislation! Ways and Means members were cool to the idea, and the administration resisted—though it had difficulty reaching agreement on a counterproposal. Finally a compromise was reached: the draft Trade Agreements Act of 1979 required that the administration consider various options, including a department of trade, and submit its specific restructuring proposal not later than July 10. When this date passed without such a proposal, the Finance Committee held up final floor action on the trade-implementing legislation.

On July 19, the administration did present a proposal, which it called "a major reorganization."[33] After further administration consultation with Capitol Hill, the proposal, in modified form, was formally submitted as a reorganization plan, meaning that it would go into effect unless

---

30. *Trade Agreements Act of 1979*, H. Rept. 96-317, p. 268.

31. Senate bill 1990 is summarized in *Congressional Record*, daily edition (August 3, 1977), pp. S13443-44. A similar proposal is put forward in Stephen D. Cohen, *The Making of United States International Economic Policy: Principles, Problems, and Proposals for Reform* (Praeger, 1977), pp. 167-73.

32. Senate bill 377 is summarized in *Congressional Record*, daily edition (February 7, 1979), pp. S1261-66.

33. White House fact sheet of July 19, 1979.

vetoed by either house within ninety days. STR would be renamed the Office of the United States Trade Representative (USTR), with "international trade policy development, coordination and negotiation functions" centralized within it.[34] The Department of Commerce would "become the focus of nonagricultural operational trade responsibilities." Specifically, the plan would strengthen the trade representative's authority to coordinate trade policy and give him certain responsibilities traditionally exercised by State, such as commodity and East-West trade negotiations and representation to the GATT. It would transfer to Commerce State's responsibility for commercial attachés stationed overseas and Treasury's responsibility for enforcement of antidumping and countervailing duty laws (though USTR would have policy oversight over such enforcement).

Overall, the reorganization is modest and reasonable, building on STR's record of accomplishment.[35] As of the fall of 1979, it appeared very likely that Congress would acquiesce and that these changes would go into effect.

This outcome would be fortunate, for the risks of creating a new trade department seem clearly to outweigh the potential gains. A cabinet trade department would consolidate a number of related trade functions. But by this very achievement it would tend to insulate trade policymaking from economic and foreign policy interests, which it so deeply affects. The administration's reform, by contrast, would maintain trade policy as an interagency process led by USTR but deeply engaging Treasury, State, and other departments with important and legitimate stakes. And senior trade officials *need* to have these perspectives engaged to balance the pressure from import-affected industries which might otherwise become dominant.

---

34. Message to the Congress Transmitting Reorganization Plan No. 3 of 1979, September 25, 1979, *Weekly Compilation of Presidential Documents*, vol. 15 (October 1, 1979), pp. 1729-30.

35. As noted earlier in this chapter, STR's accomplishment is primarily in two broad areas: multilateral negotiations in the GATT framework and managing domestic trade politics. The reorganization makes sense because it builds on these strengths. However, following this logic, USTR, not Commerce, should be assigned the responsibility for enforcing countervailing duty and antidumping laws, since this requires balancing competing policy concerns. On the other hand, East-West and commodity (primarily North-South) negotiations are not well-linked to the trilateral, GATT framework, which STR quite properly emphasized. Thus it seems unwise to move them operationally from State, though they should be included in USTR's oversight of trade policy.

The case for a new department does have a certain organizational logic. STR is, of course, an organizational anomaly, carrying out predominantly operational functions of the sort normally conducted by a cabinet department. Trade promotion and regulation do involve a range of discrete activities, separable for organizational purposes. And with total U.S. imports and exports now exceeding $250 billion, trade is undeniably important enough to justify cabinet department status.

But the key question is how such a department would perform in practice. Second- or third-order gains from consolidating certain functions are not worth the broader loss if consolidation were to separate trade policymaking from economic and foreign policy. Moreover, it might end up producing a weak senior U.S. trade official, the secretarial title notwithstanding. Stephen D. Cohen, a trade department advocate, argues that "as head of a new cabinet-level department," the special trade representative "becomes a man with a new title and wider power over all U.S. foreign trade policy."[36] This he might be in form, but he might become a very isolated, vulnerable official in practice. The secretary would have difficulty competing with his counterparts at Treasury and State for presidential attention and confidence, since his responsibility—from the president's vantage point—would be far narrower than theirs. Yet his status as cabinet-level rival would make it harder to develop necessary alliances with these counterparts, as Eberle and Pearce did with Shultz in 1973. Instead, the secretary of trade might have to draw his leverage from the industries with which he deals, a common weakness of regulating institutions. Rather than balancing industry interests against other—often broader—interests, he might become their captive. The special trade representative also has difficulty maintaining leverage in periods when no major legislative or negotiating initiative is under way.[37] But the fact that trade is an interagency process allows other senior officials to carry, when necessary, more of the trade policy

36. *The Making of United States International Economic Policy*, p. 203.

37. One important study argues that STR should be abolished two years after a major multilateral trade negotiation is completed. STR's weakness in 1969–71 certainly lends weight to such a recommendation. However, the Tokyo Round is likely to require far more follow-up work than the Kennedy Round did, given the need to develop and enforce the new nontariff barrier codes. Also, the volume of import relief cases has grown substantially since 1969–71. For the recommendation, see Edward K. Hamilton, "Summary Report: Principal Lessons of the Past Decade and Thoughts on the Next," in Griffenhagen-Kroeger, "Cases on a Decade of U.S. Foreign Economic Policy: 1965–74," *Murphy Commission Report*, vol. 3, app. H, p. 16. See chapter 1, note 1, for full reference.

burden. Putting everything into a department of trade would remove this flexibility from the system.

Prediction of how any new department will perform is inevitably speculative. But this is probably the most powerful argument against major change, particularly if the existing system works tolerably well. Government reorganization should build on institutions and arrangements of proven strength rather than casting them aside in a quest for paper perfection. And in the seventies, STR has demonstrated strength. The office led in negotiating the MTN agreement. It worked effectively with the Congress in the enactment of major trade bills in 1974 and 1979. In the achievement of these goals, it worked with other departments and agencies to accommodate competing concerns, without policy becoming captive to any one. On balance, it is a record of considerable success, of achievements that appeared anything but certain when the Nixon administration began drafting its trade bill in 1972.

CHAPTER THIRTEEN

Coordinating Foreign Economic Policy

C HAPTER 1 INTRODUCED two general organizational choices. The first involved the degree of *centralization:* how much should foreign economic policy be managed or coordinated by a single organizational entity? The second concerned the *substantive orientation* of coordinating institutions: should they be linked to *foreign* policy or *economic* policy, or be independent of either and seek to *bridge* the two? This chapter returns to these questions, drawing on the experience treated in the body of the book but developing also an analysis of the international economic policymaking systems of recent presidents and their advisers.

The Limits of Centralization

Should foreign economic policymaking be centralized? Certainly the preceding pages illustrate that the opposite is current practice. On food aid, for example, at least five agencies had major roles—Agriculture, State, Treasury, the Office of Management and Budget, and the Agency for International Development—and none had a clear lead role. On trade policy, there was a lead agency after early 1973 in fact as well as form: the Office of the Special Representative for Trade Negotiations (STR). But State, Treasury, Commerce, and Agriculture continued as major departmental actors. And on trade with developing countries or with communist bloc countries during this period, leadership came not from STR but rather several other places, particularly the National Security Council in 1972 and 1973 and the State Department thereafter.

A superficial response to this decentralization would be radical reorganization of the entire executive branch to pull everything involving foreign economics together. This would mean, presumably, establishing a department of foreign economic policy incorporating STR, the economic offices of State, and the international offices of Treasury, Commerce, Agriculture, Labor, and others. But this makes little practical sense. As food and trade experience demonstrates, the reason that bits and pieces of foreign economic policy responsibility are scattered throughout the federal establishment is that they are linked to other important governmental responsibilities: to farm commodity management at Agriculture, to overall relations with particular countries and regions at State. To put everything foreign-economic in one place would sever such linkages. Indeed, existing departments would then find it necessary to reestablish economic and trade offices. A secretary of state needs expertise within his department to develop a diplomatic position on food (or to direct food aid to political clients); a secretary of agriculture could not forgo active involvement in sales to Russia without undercutting his ability to carry out his primary responsibility for U.S. commodity markets and the welfare of American producers.

In some cases, the intertwining of foreign-economic with related policy concerns is so close that one cannot even distinguish on technical grounds between what is a foreign economic policy action and what is not. The decision on food reserves is one such case, tied to an international negotiation but integral also to domestic policy on stock accumulation and management. And even when the boundary is formally clear, actions taken on one side of the divide can have major impact on the other. International acts like selling wheat to Russia, embargoing soybean exports to Japan, and limiting Japan's color TV sales to the United States, may have important influence on the U.S. economy. And domestic decisions spill over to affect others. One illustration is the famous decision by Lyndon Johnson *not* to raise taxes in 1966. Because it fueled inflation at home and weakened the dollar abroad, this decision "probably did more to shape both the context and the substance of American foreign economic policy in the ensuing five years than any other single action."[1] Another example is the failure to lift acreage restrictions in time for the planting of the 1973 winter wheat crop. A third is any action that raises or lowers U.S. interest rates, which is bound to affect international capital movements.

---

1. Matthew J. Golden, "The 'No-Tax Decision' of 1966," in Griffenhagen-Kroeger, "Cases on a Decade of U.S. Foreign Policy: 1965–74," *Murphy Commission Report*, vol. 3, app. H, p. 185. See chapter 1, note 1, for full references.

One clearly cannot pull all or most of these responsibilities into one department without making its size approach that of the current executive branch in its entirety. Though some specific consolidations may be possible, decentralization of operating responsibilities and of policy concern and influence will remain the basic fact of governmental life. The goal must therefore be not the impossible (and probably undesirable) one of burying international economic policy conflict and trade-offs within some large organizational machine, but of building institutions and processes for surfacing these conflicts and resolving them.

This raises the question of policy leadership and coordination. For while it is not practical to consolidate all or most government activities affecting the international economy in a single department, it may still be possible to establish a single locus of coordination and leadership. Is this possible and desirable? Can a single department or office be assigned responsibility for leadership and direction of foreign economic policy, including not only food and trade issues but other issues, like energy and international money?

In fact, the Council on International Economic Policy (CIEP) was established for this ostensible purpose at the beginning of the period covered by this study. As stated in the presidential memorandum of January 1971 and subsequent legislation, CIEP's mission was to provide "a clear top-level focus for the full range of international economic policy issues," and to "deal with international economic policies (including trade, investment, balance of payments, and finance) as a coherent whole."[2] And since (as recognized at the time by the Williams commission) the cabinet-level council, chaired initially by the president, was "unlikely [to] meet as a whole" very often, its effectiveness would "depend to a very large extent on the Executive Director and his supporting staff."[3] In this it paralleled, of course, the National Security Council, serving as an umbrella for a staff of substantive aides reporting directly to the president. And at its peak, the CIEP staff totaled twenty-odd substantive officers.

How well did this staff perform its functions on the issues examined in this study? On food, it was certainly not effective in forcing considera-

2. International Economic Policy Act of 1972 (86 Stat. 646); Dominic Del Guidice, "Creation and Evolution of the Council on International Economic Policy," in National Academy of Public Administration, "Making Organizational Change Effective: Case Studies of Attempted Reforms in Foreign Affairs," *Murphy Commission Report*, vol. 6, app. O, p. 112.

3. *Williams Commission Report*, p. 278. See chapter 1, note 11, for full reference.

tion of competing policy perspectives when such was most needed. CIEP played a minimal role on the Russian sales. It played a larger role in decisionmaking on soybeans, chairing one important interagency task force and participating in others, but in general it did not—and perhaps could not—act forcefully to ensure that foreign and trade policy concerns received the attention they deserved. In developing the trade bill, CIEP did exercise strong interagency leadership in 1972 and early 1973. But it did so largely by supplanting STR, though CIEP executive director, Peter M. Flanigan, was sometimes able to bring a broader political perspective to bear, because he stood closer than the special trade representative to the president and his immediate entourage.

Nor did CIEP's contribution in other policy areas approach even remotely its sweeping statutory responsibilities. The first executive director, Peter G. Peterson, played an important role in 1971 in persuading President Nixon and senior policy officials that the international economic environment had changed. In subsequent years, the staff exercised leadership on issues like technology transfer and international aviation policy, which fell between existing agency jurisdictions. But otherwise, the CIEP staff became, as a number of officials describe it, not so much a coordinator as a competitor for a piece of the policy action, which itself needed to be coordinated. Or else it served as a resource drawn on intermittently by those who did have strong actual policy coordination roles: George P. Shultz under Nixon and the Economic Policy Board under Gerald Ford. The Murphy commission reflected the prevailing consensus in 1975 when it came out against "the simplicity of a single centralized structure" for foreign economic policy coordination and urged that CIEP be abolished.[4] The Carter administration allowed the council to expire two years later.

The CIEP experience suggests that a relatively large staff in the Executive Office of the President (EOP) with a very broad mandate is not sufficient to achieve effective coordination. In fact, these very attributes can complicate the coordination problem. There is ample evidence in the organizational literature that large staffs tend to "go into business for themselves," to carve out particular roles and empires which bear limited relationship to the purposes for which they were established. Even if the head of such a staff could achieve what no CIEP executive director ever did—a position as one of the president's primary day-to-

4. *Murphy Commission Report,* chap. 5, pp. 61, 63.

day issues managers—staff officials one to three layers below him would be unlikely to be sufficiently sensitive to presidential priorities, or possess sufficient delegated authority, to play broad coordinating roles effectively.[5]

It follows therefore that decentralization is inevitable, not only of operational responsibility but of leadership and coordination responsibility as well. For particular policy areas, moreover, the appropriate lead agencies are relatively easy to name: STR certainly for most trade issues, USDA for food, the Energy Department for issues within its sphere, Treasury for monetary matters, State for foreign assistance and some other Third World issues. But it is much harder, of course, to assure that they will keep their parochialism in check. And no single department or cabinet member can exercise effective oversight of overall foreign economic policy. Occasionally a strong personality like George Shultz can combine a cabinet portfolio with a broad personal mandate. But continuing foreign economic predominance for any department seems improbable and undesirable.

The State Department was long the best candidate, and in the Douglas Dillon period it did coordinate effectively across a rather broad range of issues. But its leverage was built primarily around trade and aid policy. Since then STR and the Agency for International Development have been established, taking the responsibility for these two areas. And aid has declined in its impact on U.S. international economic relations and is increasingly given through international institutions, for which State shares responsibility with Treasury. Another problem with State is that it tends to subordinate economic to political/strategic issues at both the leadership and working levels. The Treasury Department, by contrast, is in a relatively stronger position today. But though its international staff has grown in size and responsibility, its orientation remains too specialized—too much toward protecting traditional Treasury interests, like the current value of the dollar—to be accepted as a leader and arbiter for reconciling foreign economic concerns.

Thus far the message of this chapter is predominantly negative. All

5. This is despite the fact that the first two CIEP directors, Peter G. Peterson and Peter M. Flanigan, also held the title of Assistant to the President for International Economic Affairs. For fuller discussion of the problems of staff size and effectiveness in policy coordination, see I. M. Destler, *Presidents, Bureaucrats, and Foreign Policy: The Politics of Organizational Reform* (Princeton University Press, 1972), pp. 233–45.

foreign economic policymaking cannot be brought into a single entity. Even overall leadership and coordination cannot be centralized effectively in a foreign economic policy staff, or by a single cabinet member or department. It must be delegated to particular senior advisers and their departments and agencies according to issue area.

Yet some central oversight is badly needed. It is needed to counterbalance the biases of particular agencies on issues where they have the lead—Treasury on monetary policy, STR on trade, USDA on food. It is needed to bring issues into interagency forums where all important policy concerns can be both voiced and scrutinized. It is needed to raise issues to the presidential level when his personal decision is desirable, and to assure that the president and his senior advisers receive solid information and analysis on all reasonable options. It is needed also to assure that the president hears the views of those senior advisers whose responsibilities are most relevant. It is needed to see that presidential decisions are implemented in ways consistent with the substance and spirit of those decisions, striking the desired balance among competing concerns. Within a relatively open, decentralized overall process there must be some central staff management capacity, some group of people able, in Francis M. Bator's words, to "identify situations where decentralization is likely to cause serious trouble," as when issues on one track have major implications for issues on another, and then to bring these issues, with "strategic choices formulated . . . to high-level decision" and, where necessary, continued central monitoring and coordination.[6]

These functions must be performed within the president's executive office by a staff group that specializes in international economic policy and combines professional economic competence, skill in brokering issues, and the ability to "translate" frequently technical questions for the president and other nonspecialized senior policy advisers.[7] Such a group must work closely with subcabinet foreign economic officials in the departments and agencies, particularly the under secretary of state and the assistant secretary of state for economic affairs, the under secre-

6. *U.S. Foreign Economic Policy: Implications for the Organization of the Executive Branch,* Hearings before the Subcommittee on Foreign Economic Policy of the House Committee on Foreign Affairs, 92 Cong. 2 sess. (Government Printing Office, 1972), p. 111.

7. See the recommendations of Bator, ibid., and Edward K. Hamilton, "Summary Report: Principal Lessons of the Past Decade and Thoughts on the Next," in Griffenhagen-Kroeger, "Cases on a Decade of U.S. Foreign Economic Policy: 1965–74," pp. 12–13.

tary of the treasury for monetary affairs, and the assistant secretary of the treasury for international affairs.

The staff should be small. Edward K. Hamilton argues that the senior staff person playing this role should be supported by "probably no more than two professionals."[8] This was the size of the Bator staff on which Hamilton served in the mid-sixties. It may be that, with the increased number of issues marked by difficult trade-offs between domestic and international interests, today's workload requires a slightly larger staff—but it should still operate as the Bator staff operated.

Location of a Coordinating Staff

This brings us to the second major organizational question. *Where, within the executive office, should this staff be located?* Should it be part of the president's national security staff, part of an economic policy staff like that serving Ford's Economic Policy Board, or an independent unit that bridges the foreign and economic policy communities?

CIEP was an experiment in the last approach. The primary argument in its favor is that linking foreign economic staffing to either the foreign or the economic policy community imparts a bias against the other.[9] Unfortunately, there is also reason to believe that this neutral, between-two-stools position is a formula for ineffectiveness. CIEP might well have achieved greater leverage had its executive director established himself as one of the president's principal substantive policy aides, but it was much harder for him to do so than for Henry A. Kissinger, national security adviser under Nixon, or for L. William Seidman, Ford's assistant for economic affairs. For these advisers, unlike Peterson or Flanigan of CIEP, staffed issues of greater priority to the president: international relations, war and peace, and the nation's economic welfare.[10] But *foreign economic* policy has not been given continuing priority by any

8. Ibid.

9. See Stephen D. Cohen, *The Making of United States International Economic Policy: Principles, Problems, and Proposals for Reform* (Praeger, 1977), especially pp. 163–64.

10. The Employment Act of 1946 mandates that the president give priority to the country's economic health; and it is generally accepted that he will do so, given the power of voters—and historians—to reward or punish leaders according to economic indexes. Thomas E. Cronin, *The State of the Presidency* (Little, Brown, 1975), pp. 12–19, argues that postwar presidential priorities have been, in descending order, foreign policy, economic policy, and domestic policy.

postwar president, and even the annual economic summits since 1975 have not made it so. As C. Fred Bergsten put it:

The CIEP effort has demonstrated once more that powerful forces inherently pull the locus of decisionmaking back to where real power lies: with those who manage the domestic economy, those who manage overall foreign policy . . . and ultimately the president himself. There is little room for real power to reside in a hybrid intermediary standing somewhere among these three poles of power.[11]

But if a separate international economic staff unit does not seem a promising approach, there is another way of bridging foreign and economic policy concerns. As CIEP was fading into obscurity, several analysts came forward with proposals arguing essentially that the increased intertwining of foreign and domestic issues rendered separate EOP substantive staffs obsolete. There should be instead, as one of them put it, "a single, unified staff replacing the currently autonomous staffs of the NSC, the Domestic Council, and the Economic Policy Board."[12] Conceptually, this is appealing. If the foreign economic policy problems analyzed in this study are characteristic of a broader policy world where the boundary between foreign and domestic matters has faded, then certainly presidential staff organization should reflect this change. And the problem of where to locate foreign economic staff responsibility is seemingly resolved by creation of such a unified staff.

Yet it is only the form of the problem which changes. The questions become how the unified staff will be organized and where foreign economic responsibility will be placed within it. Should the staff report to the president through a single chief? Then theoretically this individual integrates all perspectives; in practice everyone, including the president, is dependent on his sense of priorities and is vulnerable to his policy biases. Such an arrangement also gives this person enormous power. This and other dangers of overcentralization have led proponents to propose a staff headed jointly by several substantive aides who are co-

11. *Extension of the Council on International Economic Policy*, Hearings before the Subcommittee on International Finance of the Senate Committee on Banking, Housing, and Urban Affairs, 93 Cong. 1 sess. (GPO, 1973), p. 29.

12. Graham Allison and Peter Szanton, *Remaking Foreign Policy: The Organizational Connection* (Basic Books, 1976), p. 84. Similar proposals appear in Robert H. Johnson, "Managing Interdependence: Restructuring the U.S. Government," Overseas Development Council Development Paper 23 (Washington, D.C.: ODC, 1977), pp. 16–19; and Stephen Hess, *Organizing the Presidency* (Brookings Institution, 1976), pp. 214–15. The Hess and Allison/Szanton proposals would have the staff serve an active, collegial cabinet as well as the president.

equal assistants to the president and have continuing access to him. But then there are several de facto staff channels to the president, particularly if the aides continue—as generally proposed—to have foreign, economic, and domestic policy portfolios. Then how integrated the staff proves in practice will depend upon how collegially its members behave (which will in turn be affected by whether cabinet or subcabinet cooperation can be established across these foreign–economic–domestic lines). And the senior foreign economic aide's problem of attaching himself to a major stream of presidential business remains. He still probably needs to be placed under either the foreign or the economic policy assistant, rather than being made their coequal.

So whether or not a unified EOP staff is established, the question remains whether the international economic group should be linked to *foreign* or to *economic* policy. A cogent argument suggesting the former was presented several years ago to the House Foreign Affairs Committee by Richard N. Cooper, who later became under secretary of state for economic affairs. Because of the "continuing erosion of the framework laid down in the 1940s," he argued, "much of the energy in the area of international economic policy during the next few years" must be toward creating a "substantially altered" if not "radically new" institutional framework.[13] Since this requires nothing less than asking "how we would like the world to evolve over the last quarter of this century," he concluded that "a much greater role in the framing of foreign economic policy must be accorded to the State Department and to the National Security Council than would normally be the case." Moreover, as noted in the opening chapter, some of the most egregious foreign economic policy mistakes of recent years have been caused, at least in part, by the weakness of foreign policy voices in the decision process—the soybean embargo comes again to mind. Placing foreign economic coordinating responsibility on the national security staff might render imbalanced staffing and advice less likely.

The counterargument is that leverage on most foreign economic issues comes more from domestic economic interests and institutions. Much of the strain on the "framework laid down in the 1940s" has resulted from economic trends and pressures within the major capitalist countries, and no new framework could survive without accommodating these forces. The particular experience analyzed in this study, moreover, suggests that policy coordination needs strong domestic roots. In the process

13. *U.S. Foreign Economic Policy*, Hearings, p. 123.

of protecting the international trade system, STR has moved increasingly into the role of balancer of domestic interests. Conversely, State was powerless to put across a strong proposal for an international system of food reserves because it could not win the support of either the farm or domestic economic policy communities.

Food and trade are, of course, no more representative of international economic policy experience on this question than on others. But what issue areas would yield a better practical case for linking coordination *primarily* to *foreign* policy institutions? Energy? Money? Coordination of national macroeconomic policies? Not likely. Development assistance and policies toward pricing of Third World commodities? Perhaps, but the more that commodities produced or processed importantly within the United States are specifically affected, the more important domestic economic and political concerns become.

The substance and politics of current foreign economic issues, therefore, encourage the conclusion that it is more realistic to build their coordination around economic policy officials and institutions. This conclusion is reinforced by recent practice: foreign economic policy leadership did in fact come primarily from this side of the government in 1971–76. How effective were the policymaking systems of this period in protecting international as well as domestic concerns? And what lessons do they offer for current and future practice?

When dominated by John B. Connally, foreign economic policy was domestically driven and at times chauvinistic. But since it reflected so much Connally's particular personality and style, broader lessons are hard to draw—except that personalities do frequently preempt organizational arrangements, and that when an aggressive individual with strong policy views becomes dominant, the nation gets action at the price of imbalance, as policy concerns not congenial to these views get short shrift. His successor at Treasury, George Shultz, was much more inclined to weigh competing interests and arguments, the soybean fiasco notwithstanding. Shultz also established a more formal set of arrangements—his "second hat," as presidential assistant; the cabinet-level Council on Economic Policy (CEP), which he chaired; a small White House-based supporting staff—though his main procedural vehicle was daily, 8 A.M. meetings of senior presidential economic advisers.[14] But

14. See George P. Shultz and Kenneth W. Dam, *Economic Policy Beyond the Headlines* (Stanford Alumni Association, 1977, and W. W. Norton, 1978), pp. 176–77.

while his approach might conceivably be replicated by a future treasury secretary with comparable style and substantive competence, he operated in a very unusual period, one in which a Watergate-enveloped president increasingly opted out of policy decisions, making Shultz a sort of deputy president for economic affairs.

In some respects, the Economic Policy Board created by President Ford in September 1974 was similar to the Shultz system; in other respects it was a departure. Shultz's roles were split between Treasury Secretary William E. Simon, who was named EPB chairman, and Seidman, an old Ford associate, whom the president named assistant to the president for economic affairs. Unlike almost all previous formal, general-purpose committees at the cabinet level, the EPB executive committee actually met frequently, in fact daily, on weekday mornings in the Roosevelt Room of the White House.[15] And the president met with it about once a week. Its staff met many of the criteria emphasized earlier in this chapter: it was small, totaling around four professionals, and it saw its role primarily as managing the policy process rather than putting across a particular view. It did not have a deputy dealing only with international economics, though it drew on the competence of the CIEP staff. But such a deputy role could clearly be accommodated within an EPB-type system.

The EPB system had problems. It tended to pull more issues up to the cabinet level than really needed to be resolved there. It had considerable difficulty on those international issues in which Henry Kissinger was taking initiatives, because he preferred to operate alone after checking directly with the president and because he and his subordinates viewed the Ford economic policy advisers, not without cause, as substantively hostile on Third World issues. Yet the EPB was, on balance, a successful coordinating institution and a possible future model. It had strong links to the president. Its staff did in fact develop a reputation for communicating competing views fairly and objectively and engaging the participation of officials with stakes in the issue at hand. An interesting indicator of its success is the testimony of a veteran State Department

15. The full board included almost the entire cabinet. The executive committee initially included, in addition to Simon and Seidman, the director of OMB, the CEA chairman, and the executive director of CIEP (a position that was in fact vacant for most of the board's existence). In June 1975 the secretaries of state, commerce, and labor were added to the executive committee. See Roger B. Porter, "Presidential Decisionmaking: The Economic Policy Board" (Ph.D. dissertation, Harvard University, 1978).

economic official interviewed in late November 1976: "I never thought I'd say it at the outset, but I came to believe it is a quite useful instrument."

When the Carter administration came to power, it quickly established the Economic Policy *Group*.[16] This had a number of attributes similar to the EPB's, though initial public descriptions, naturally enough, stressed the differences.[17] The EPG was chaired by Michael Blumenthal, secretary of the treasury (though cochaired by CEA chairman Charles Schultze until March 1977). It sought to coordinate foreign economic issues from an economic policy base; its executive committee met regularly at the cabinet level in the Roosevelt Room (although weekly rather than daily, usually on Monday afternoon). It had a small professional staff whose members conceived of themselves as brokers, not independent policy advisers. Moreover, because its core members and their subordinates were more sensitive to the international economic environment and less ideologically determined to reiterate capitalist doctrine, the EPG did not have the EPB's problems in handling Third World issues. Yet the fledgling EPG system did not survive the administration's first summer. The Carter administration's reorganization study of the EOP found the EPG only intermittently effective and its July 1977 report proposed major reforms in the group's structure and staffing arrangement. Subsequent discussions among the core EPG members, and between them and the president, led to changes that went even further, eliminating the EPG staff and the role of the group as a formal presidential decision channel.

Why didn't the EPG of early 1977 prove more effective? One reason was the size of the forum. Ford's EPB executive committee had started out small—five members including the assistant—and it began by limiting meetings to the principals. Blumenthal and Schultze had similarly wanted a small, relatively informal group: the traditional troika (themselves and the OMB director) plus a State Department representative (formally the secretary, in practice the under secretary of state, Cooper) to facilitate coverage of international issues. But under various pres-

16. The following discussion of the EPG draws upon the author's service, in the spring of 1977, as consultant to the president's EOP reorganization project, with particular responsibility for analyzing economic policy institutions.

17. Drawing on a briefing by CEA chairman-designate Charles Schultze, Hobart Rowen reported in the *Washington Post* on January 14, 1977: "The Carter administration intends to shift the center of its decision-making process from a formal White House organization to an informal Cabinet-level group."

sures, the executive committee quickly expanded to include the national security assistant and the secretaries of commerce, labor, and housing and urban development, plus three ex officio participants: the vice president, the assistant for domestic affairs and policy (Stuart Eizenstat) and the cabinet secretary (Jack Watson). Others besides these eleven would be invited to particular meetings, each would bring one or more aides, and members of various White House and EOP staffs would walk in through the side door. Thus attendance would often approach and sometimes exceed thirty; once, when the vice president arrived late, he found every chair in the room already taken. The size of the meetings made serious, well-focused discussion of real issues and interagency differences hard to maintain.[18] And while the staff sought to combat this problem by enforcing attendance rules stringent enough to generate substantial resentment among those excluded, there were limits to what this could achieve as long as the eleven-person executive committee was the base.

Even more debilitating than the cumbersomeness of the forum was the weakness of its links to the president. Unlike the EPB, its staff was headed not by a major presidential assistant but by an executive director who reported to the chairman and was housed not in the White House but in the Old Executive Office Building across the street. The reason, apparently, was that none of the senior economic officials wanted there to be a presidential economic assistant, and one of them—Charles Schultze—had accepted appointment on the condition that there would be no separate economic adviser on the White House staff.[19] This de-

18. Bator described the problems of this type of forum as follows: "serious work just does not happen in a crowd, blue chips are not played if marginal people are present, records kept and the like. Also they do not get played for subordinates representing their superiors. Anyone who has served time in the inner circles of Government is familiar with what happens to the quality of discussion when participants are wrapped in their institutional roles and surrounded by a bevy of committed and watchful retainers. The poor Secretary of Agriculture or of Commerce, if he is to survive, will tend to argue his bureaucratic brief. He knows that a report of his performance will filter back to his department and then out to his constituency. Even the Secretary of Defense will keep in mind the many fronts on which he is engaged with the Chiefs and the Armed Services Committees." U.S. Foreign Economic Policy, Hearings, p. 115.

19. Carter said at his press conference announcing the appointment: "I will not have a separate economic adviser in the White House other than Mr. Schultze." New York Times, December 17, 1976. He reiterated this pledge in a memo to EPG members the following March, at the time Schultze withdrew from cochairmanship. However, while Schultze was a major substantive adviser, he did not play the policy coordination role that Seidman had played for Ford.

prived the group of the link to the president that a personal aide handling his overall economic policy business would have supplied, and it deprived group members of a senior assistant they could count on to be sure their views were correctly represented. The EPG was of course linked to Carter through Blumenthal, an important senior adviser. But unlike George Shultz in 1973, Blumenthal did not have an overall presidential mandate for economic policy coordination.

Finally, while Ford apparently liked the EPB, Carter did not take to the EPG as an institution. As a sympathetic official put it in an internal EOP memorandum in mid-June, "The most telling criticism of the EPG until now is that there is little direct linkage between EPG activities and President Carter's heavy participation in economic matters." The president attended, apparently, only one formal EPG meeting in 1977. And while he had signed a memo declaring EPG to be "the body I shall look to for coordinating government-wide economic plans and policies and bringing me recommendations for action," he showed, in practice, the normal presidential preference for staff channels managed by his close personal policy staff aides—national security adviser Zbigniew Brzezinski and domestic adviser Eizenstat. He liked to have *them* organizing the papers from which he made decisions. So sometimes an EPG memo setting forth options developed at a group meeting would be sent to the president under Blumenthal's signature, only to be "covered" by a memo written by another staff before going on to the president. This happened predominantly on domestic issues, though there were intermittent problems on trade. But the effect was to undermine the credibility of the EPG and its staff across the board. It could not establish itself as the primary decision channel and broker for economic policy, one that cabinet and subcabinet officials could depend on to get their views to the president.

To link the group more effectively to the president's preferred decision channels, the EOP reorganization study proposed in July that its staff be merged with Eizenstat's domestic policy staff but that the group retain jurisdiction for international as well as domestic economic issues. It also proposed that the problem of the oversized executive committee be addressed by creating a steering group limited to the core EPG members originally envisioned by Blumenthal and Schultze: the secretary of the treasury, the CEA chairman, the OMB director, and the under secretary of state for economic affairs. The staff merger proposal was not implemented; instead, the EPG staff was disbanded. Beginning in August, the Carter administration moved to less formal, cabinet-level consultation, what one senior adviser called the "reinvention of the troika." Secretary Blumenthal hosted weekly Thursday morning breakfasts for the steering group—expanded to include Eizenstat. The meetings were for principals only, except for Blumenthal's executive assistant, Curtis Hessler, who served as the group's secretary. The hope was to strengthen working relations at and below this level, and a certain amount of informal coordination was thereby achieved. But there was no clear procedural link between this forum and the stream of presidential business which moved through Carter's two primary staff channels for issues management: the Domestic Policy Staff and the National Security Council.

In the two years that followed, these meetings continued, with minor adjustments in who attended them and in their frequency. But dissatisfaction with economic policy coordination continued also, as evidenced by Carter's granting a stronger mandate to Blumenthal just a few weeks before he was replaced at Treasury, in July 1979, by G. William Miller. Moreover, the EPG steering group dealt overwhelmingly with domestic economic issues, notwithstanding its broader formal mandate.

What broader organizational lessons can be drawn from this experience? One, demonstrated anew in every administration, is that policy coordination arrangements must not only meet general criteria such as those developed here (for example, a small staff which sees its primary role as process management, making a decentralized system work); they must also mesh with the personal relationships and preferred operating styles of the president and his senior aides. The EPG experience also suggests that collegial forums work only when they are small and when there is a strong staff link between them and the president. They probably require some regularized presidential participation in the forum as well. Furthermore, the EPG experience suggests that building foreign economic coordination around economic policy institutions requires either a strong secretary of the treasury with clear economic primacy and a strong international role stretching beyond monetary issues, or a presidential assistant for economic affairs, or both. And the existence of an economic assistant generates tension between his role and that of the chairman of the Council of Economic Advisers.

In basic concept, there is no necessary conflict. The role of CEA is substantive economic analysis and advice based upon professional analytic competence; drawing on such analysis, the chairman presents his views on the economic impact of proposed policy actions. The assistant, on the other hand, has a coordinating, facilitating role—engaging the appropriate senior advisers in an issue after the necessary preparatory staff work; bringing the issue to the president at the proper time; acting as a two-way channel between the president and senior advisers; assuring that the latter will know when the president is considering an issue so that they can present their views, in writing or in person, when he is most receptive. Indeed, having someone who manages the process in this way can help the CEA chairman shape and time his advice for maximum impact.

But there are risks to the CEA chairman (and other senior economic aides) if the economic assistant does not hold to a procedural role. He is physically in the White House, close to the president, and learning through daily contact with him and other White House aides what is on the president's mind, what his priorities are, and how he operates. The president will almost certainly seek his personal substantive advice from time to time, and he will almost certainly give it. If his advocacy comes to overwhelm his objectivity—or his reputation for fairness to competing views—he becomes less a facilitator than a competitor. He could even come to dominate economic policy if he were of a mind to and if the president allowed this to happen.

Partly because of such problems, real or potential, the primary Carter administration role for foreign economic policy coordination came to be played by an official attached to foreign policy institutions, Ambassador Henry Owen.

Owen first joined the White House as a temporary consultant coordinating U.S. preparation for the Bonn economic summit of May 1977, and he continued to work on summit follow-up in the fall. This task inevitably overlapped with broader international economic policy coordination: economic summits had become an annual event, their agendas included all issues of prime concern to the advanced capitalist states, and their preparation became a major focal point for government-wide policy planning and for engagement of the president personally. Moreover, Owen had Carter's personal confidence and also extensive government experience, having been an influential State Department staff official in the 1950s and 1960s. In early 1978, Carter appointed him to a White House position created for him, that of special representative of the president for economic summits. As such he became the senior White House international economic policy staff official, and a member of the

EPG steering group. He was associated with the NSC staff but not personally on its payroll; his memos to the president went across Brzezinski's desk but under his own name. As of summer 1979, he had a supporting professional staff of four, most of whom were formally attached to the NSC.

Over time Owen came to play much of the international economic role envisaged for the EPG staff, and more effectively than that staff could play it. His link to Brzezinski gave him access to NSC business, but he also became an independent staff channel and presidential adviser, though his substantive portfolio inevitably meant that the volume of his presidential business was much less than Brzezinski's or Eizenstat's. He worked most closely with senior international economic officials in State and Treasury and maintained a productive relationship with special trade representative Robert Strauss. Owen operated with considerable flexibility in how he spent his time but adhered primarily to a coordinating, facilitating role. On some issues (like foreign assistance) he was known as an advocate, however, and on at least one issue—policy toward Japan in early 1979—he assumed primary operating responsibility for the Carter administration during an important two-month period.

Recommendations

Drawing on all of this foreign economic policymaking experience, this study concludes with strong but—in some cases—conditional recommendations:

1. *Accept the inevitability of decentralized foreign economic policymaking.* Do not look for means to eliminate—or even to substantially reduce—conflicts among policy perspectives. Do seek to maintain a central capacity to assure that competing concerns are explicitly addressed in a timely manner, that all major concerns affected by a particular decision are given a hearing.

2. *Pursue this goal through a small international economic policy staff group (three to five professionals), based in the Executive Office of the President and forming part of a staff with broader policy responsibilities.* Do not make this group too large—it will then try to do much of the work itself rather than influence and orchestrate the work of the established departments and agencies. Do not make it an independent EOP

unit—it will probably then be unable to establish sufficient links to the president to be effective.

3. *If possible, attach this staff to a senior presidential assistant who coordinates overall economic policymaking; the international staff group head would be a deputy assistant to the president with direct access to the Oval Office.* If there exists no such aide, or if one exists but is not playing the role well, the international economic staff should instead be attached to a presidential assistant who is playing a relevant broader coordinating role: the national security assistant or, under certain circumstances (like mid-1977), perhaps the domestic assistant.

4. *Define the primary role of this small staff as brokering, overseeing evolution of policy on particular issues, assuring that important concerns are addressed in timely fashion, and that cabinet members and other key advisers get their opportunities to weigh in.* The president may well want substantive advice from the staff group's head, and he is likely to want to give it, but he must not allow this to compromise his professionalism as a broker communicating all major viewpoints. To the degree possible, the staff should be linked to a formal or informal group within the cabinet and work primarily through interagency groups below cabinet level. It should assume operational leadership neither for specific issues nor for tasks like preparing a trade bill for Congress. Leadership for these matters should come from the appropriate agency according to the subject matter and the strengths of particular officials. But the staff should monitor this leadership and intervene selectively to affect its performance.

These steps will not make policymaking more tidy. Issues involving domestic–international trade-offs are inherently messy. But a lightly staffed, flexible coordinating system can help the entire government confront these trade-offs and resolve them effectively.

Officials Interviewed

THE FOLLOWING OFFICIALS were interviewed for the light they could shed on the policy episodes and broader organizational issues treated in this book, under ground rules that provide for listing their names but no attribution of specific facts and interpretations. The interviews were enormously useful, partly for filling in gaps in the substantial published information available, even more for helping the author understand and interpret that information. The positions listed are those held during the episodes about which they were interviewed.

Richard E. Bell *chief, Grains Division, Foreign Agricultural Service, U.S. Department of Agriculture; deputy assistant secretary for international affairs and commodity programs, USDA; assistant secretary, USDA*

Robert Best *chief economist, Senate Committee on Finance*

John A. Bushnell *National Security Council staff; deputy assistant secretary of the treasury for international affairs*

Robert Cassidy *office of the Senate legislative counsel; Senate Finance Committee staff*

Charles A. Cooper *National Security Council staff; assistant secretary of the treasury for international affairs*

Thomas O. Enders *assistant secretary of state for economic and business affairs*

Lawrence A. Fox *deputy assistant secretary of commerce for international economic policy and research*

Charles R. Frank, Jr. *senior economist, office of the under secretary of state; member, policy planning staff*

Ellen Frost *office of the assistant secretary of the treasury for international affairs*

Curtis Hessler *executive assistant to the secretary of the treasury*

Robert Hormats *National Security Council staff*

Julius L. Katz *deputy assistant secretary of state for international resources and food policy; deputy assistant secretary of state for economic and business affairs; assistant secretary of state for economic and business affairs*

Harry Lamar *staff specialist on trade, House Committee on Ways and Means*

Samuel W. Lewis *deputy director, policy planning staff, Department of State*

Harald B. Malmgren *deputy special representative for trade negotiations*

Edwin M. Martin *coordinator, U.S. participation in the World Food Conference*

John M. Martin, Jr. *chief counsel, House Committee on Ways and Means*

Leo V. Mayer *agricultural economist, Council of Economic Advisers; senior specialist in agriculture, Library of Congress*

William McCamy *office of assistant secretary of the treasury for international affairs*

Arthur Mead *assistant administrator for Public Law 480 programs, Foreign Agricultural Service, Department of Agriculture*

Wilbur D. Mills *chairman, House Committee on Ways and Means*

James Naive *leader for grains, Commodity Economics Division, Economic Research Service, Department of Agriculture*

Henry Owen *White House consultant; special representative of the president for economic summits*

Don Paarlberg *director of agricultural economics, Department of Agriculture*

William R. Pearce *deputy special representative for trade negotiations*

Roger B. Porter *executive secretary, Economic Policy Board*

John E. Ray *director, Office of Trade Policy, Department of the Treasury*

Albert E. Rees *director, Council on Wage and Price Stability*

Richard R. Rivers *Senate Finance Committee staff; general counsel, Office of the Special Representative for Trade Negotiations*

John Schnittker *Schnittker Associates*

Gary L. Seevers *member and staff, Council of Economic Advisers*

Al Ullman *acting chairman and chairman, House Committee on Ways and Means*

Sidney Weintraub *deputy assistant secretary of state for economic and business affairs; assistant administrator for interagency development coordination, Agency for International Development*

Marina von Neumann Whitman *member, Council of Economic Advisers*

Index

Abel, I. W., 152

Abourezk, James, 187

Acreage restrictions, 19, 28, 29, 30, 31, 36; failure to lift following grain sales to Soviet Union, 4, 38, 43–49, 212

Adjustment assistance, 133, 139, 143, 145; and trade reform bill, 158–59, 163, 181, 188, 189

Advisory Council on Executive Organization. *See* President's Advisory Council on Executive Organization

AFL-CIO, 135; and trade reform bill, 151–52, 158–59, 162, 164, 175, 186, 187

Agency for International Development (AID), 1, 9, 215; and development policy, 26–27; and food aid policy, 125, 211

Agricultural Act of 1970, 32, 34; 1973 amendments to, 17n

Agricultural Adjustment Act, 177n, 193

Agricultural policy, 21–23; and commodity programs, 28–29; and economic policy, 46–48; and food aid policy, 29–31; and food policy, 20, 27–35, 107, 108, 122; and 1973 soybean embargo, 50, 52, 59. *See also* Agricultural policy community; Agriculture, U.S. Department of

Agricultural Policy Committee, 116

Agricultural policy community, 36; as Agriculture Department's main constituency, 45, 124, 125; decline in strength and unity of, 32–33; dissatisfaction with moratorium on Soviet purchases, 107, 113, 115, 117, 118, 120; goals of, 21–22; instruments and institutions, 22–23; and international grain reserves proposal, 91–92, 97, 102; and trade reform bill, 177–79,

181–82; and U.S. food policy, 31, 33. *See also* Agriculture, U.S. Department of

Agriculture and Consumer Protection Act of 1973, 33, 56, 108

Agriculture, U.S. Department of, 12, 23, 26, 73, 176; and acreage restrictions, 4, 38, 43–49; and development policy, 26, 28–29; distrust of, 118; and Economic Policy Board, 108; and export controls, 55–56, 58, 105, 108, 109–10, 117; and export monitoring, 39–41, 53–55, 108, 110–11; and export subsidies, 41; and food aid policy, 68, 70, 71, 72, 74, 75, 76, 78, 80, 81, 87, 211, 215, 216; and food policy, 20, 21–23, 27–35, 107, 108, 115, 117, 118, 122; and food price inflation, miscalculation of, 56; and foreign economic policy, 212, 216; free trade orientation of, 140; and grain sales to the Soviet Union, 38, 40–41, 42, 44–45, 46, 47, 103–05, 108, 110–12, 113, 119. *See also* Bergland, Bob; Butz, Earl; Freeman, Orville

AID. *See* Agency for International Development

Aid policy. *See* Development policy

Albert, Carl, 166

Albright, Joseph, 47n

Alliance for Progress, 1

Allison, Graham, 4, 14n, 15n, 218n

American Agriculture Movement, 127

American Farm Bureau Federation, 21, 32, 116n; and mandatory acreage limitations, 28n; and trade reform bill, 177, 178, 182n

American Federation of Labor. *See* AFL-CIO

231

Watergate scandal, 52, 58, 93, 150, 182

Nontariff barriers, 130, 137, 170; and multilateral trade negotiations, 193; and 1979 Trade Agreements Act, 201–02, 207, 209n; and trade reform bill, 144, 156–57, 163, 176–78, 184, 188

Novak, Jeremiah, 196n

Novotny, Don, 119

Nuts and bolts industry, import relief for, 205

Nye, Joseph S., Jr., 6n, 14n, 31n, 121n

Odell, John S., 14n

Office of Import Programs, 141

Office of Management and Budget (OMB), 23, 24, 68, 105, 123, 203, 221n, 224; and Economic Policy Board, 108; and food aid policy, 71, 211; and food policy, 73, 74, 80; and food reserves policy, 91, 98, 102; and 1972 grain sales to Soviet Union, 42; and International Food Review Group, 97; and President's Committee on Food, 93; and trade reform bill, 146. *See also* Bureau of the Budget

Office of Price Administration, 57

Office of the Special Representative for Trade Negotiations (STR). *See* Special representative for trade negotiations

Office of the United States Trade Representative (USTR), creation of, 208. *See also* Special representative for trade negotiations

Oil imports, 3, 6; OPEC embargo, 168, 182–83; price increases, 5, 66, 71, 79, 168, 194; suspension of quotas, 15

OPEC. *See* Organization of Petroleum Exporting Countries

Orderly marketing agreements (OMAs), 158, 198, 203–04, 205

Organisation for Economic Co-operation and Development (OECD), 137, 156; Kissinger speech to, 101; trade pledge, 171; and unilateral import restrictions, 193

Organization of Petroleum Exporting Countries (OPEC), 106; oil embargo, 168, 182–83; oil price increases, 5, 66, 71, 79, 168, 194; and trade reform bill, 183; and U.S. food aid policy, 71–72

Overseas Private Investment Corporation, 207

Owen, Henry, 226–27, 230

Paarlberg, Don, 92n, 126n, 230

Paarlberg, Robert L., 25n

Pakistan, and U.S. food aid policy, 78, 80n, 81, 85

Parsky, Gerald L., 196n

Pastor, Robert A., 14n, 144n, 151, 156n, 159n, 182n, 184n

Pastore, John O., 187

Patrick, Hugh, 130n

Pearce, William R., 131n, 137n, 138, 139, 141, 142, 148, 149, 151, 152, 154, 155, 156, 157, 159, 161, 162, 164, 165, 166, 169, 170, 171, 209, 230

Penn, J. B., 126n

Peru, 1, 3

Peterson, Peter G., 10, 138, 139, 214, 215n, 217

Pettis, Jerry L., 162n

Poland, 1975 grain sales to, 106

Pool, Ithiel de Sola, 13

Porter, Roger B., 75n, 114n, 197n, 221n, 230

Preeg, Ernest H., 133, 134

Preferences to developing countries, 143, 147–49, 192; and trade reform bill, 147–48, 161, 163, 182–83, 184, 189

President's Advisory Council on Executive Organization (the Ash council), 12, 154n

President's Committee on Food, 73, 93–94, 108

Price Commission, 46

Price controls, 52, 57, 58, 59

Price support programs, 28, 29, 91, 92, 127, 193

Protectionist trade policies, vs. free trade, 133, 135, 136, 138, 141, 142, 154, 164, 192–93, 197, 199–200, 204

Public Law 480, 22, 25, 26, 29, 31, 39; 1966 amendments to, 68; and 1974–75 food aid crisis, 65, 66, 68–69, 72, 73, 76, 78, 79, 85, 87; title 1, 77, 78, 80n, 81, 82, 83, 84, 85, 86; title 2, 77, 78

Puerto Rico, economic summit meeting at, 194

Rambouillet, economic summit meeting at, 194

Rangan, Kasturi, 77n

Ray, John E., 230

Reciprocity, principle of, 133, 134n, 139

Rees, Albert E., 230

Reference prices, for steel imports, 199

Republican party, 131

Reston, James, 195n

Rey, Jean, 138

Ribicoff, Abraham, 196n, 205, 207; proposal for department of international